*this book belongs to*

_____

*date I started this study*

_____

**Divine Encounters**
in the Old Testament

*Yahweh*

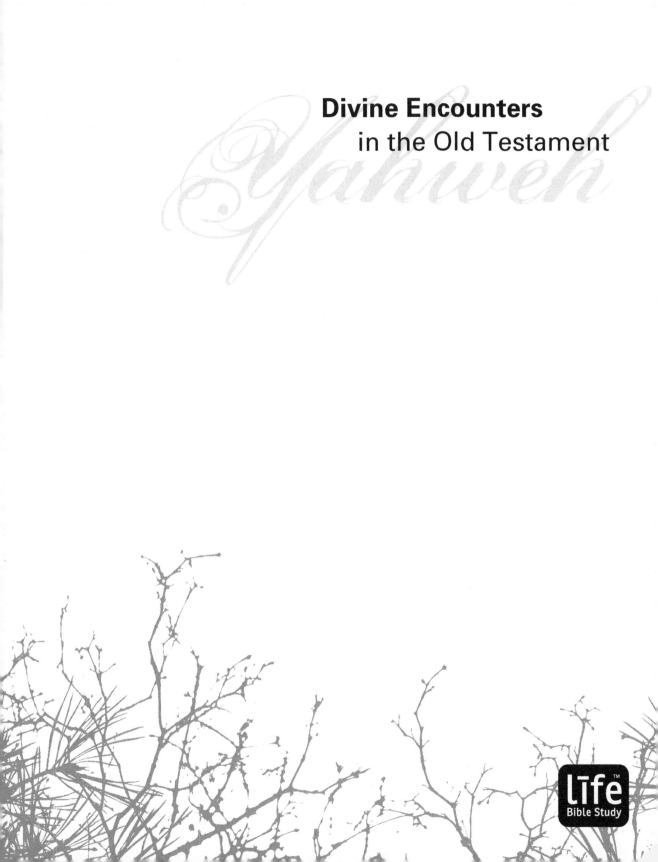

# Divine Encounters
## in the Old Testament

Yahweh

# FOREWORD

Gene Wilkes has been my friend for 20 years. In those wonderful decades he has always blessed me with his books and sermons. But I have great interest in this particular study. I have always had a spiritual hunger for encounter. This book, *Divine Encounters in the Old Testament*, sets the mood and tone of God's one-on-one relational style with all the heroes of the Old Testament. And it provides new insight about God's self-revelation. Gene has brought two very distant planets into a common orbit. The first is God's huge desire to talk with us, His children. The second is our hunger to encounter Him.

I am drawn to people who have a hunger for God. Their altars of worship may not rise high, inflated by egotism. But altars are always frequent. Altars are, after all, places of encounter. This book is a story of altars. The grand hope of Dr. Wilkes is that in reading about all of these altars, you will begin to build your own. Stacking up uncut, desert rocks upon which your make your sacrifice. Your sacrifices—as sacrifices have always been—offer the vestiges of your self-denial. And of course, the most significant sacrifice you can make is your own Galatians 2:20 moments in time. It is daily that you must carry your cross. It is daily that you must die to self. It is daily that you must call upon Christ, your crucified Brother. It is daily that your altar must rise and beg your encounter. That's what this book is about.

Scared to read? Don't be. When you have given up your selfish ambitions and began the good-Friday life you will know at last why encounter is the only hope for real life. Gene Wilkes believes this and has written his book to encourage you to live in the glory of your encounters with God.

Dr. Calvin Miller
Beeson Divinity School

## Editorial and Design Staff

**Executive Editor**
Ty Gulick

**General Editor**
Jill Puckett Aldridge

**Copy Editor**
Kaci Lane Hindman

**Graphic Design**
Brandi K. Etheredge

**Vice President, Ministry Resources**
Paul Kelly

**Author**–C. Gene Wilkes

**C. Gene Wilkes**—Gene is the Pastor of Legacy Church, Plano, Texas, where he has served since 1987. The church has transitioned during Gene's ministry to more effectively carry out its mission "to help people trust Jesus," and to live out its vision as "a mission outpost where every member is a missionary in his or her mission field."

Gene is the author of several books including *Jesus on Leadership: Discovering the Secrets of Servant Leadership from the life of Christ, Paul on Leadership: Servant Leadership in a Ministry of Transition* (a journey with Paul through the pages of Acts as he followed Jesus' call to take the gospel to all ethnic groups), *My Identity in Christ*, and *With All My Soul: God's Design for Spiritual Wellness*. Gene has also written for Student Life, an online Bible study for students.

Gene speaks at national conferences on the topics of spiritual gifts, lay mobilization, making disciples, and servant leadership. He has also led conferences and taught in Canada, China, Albania, Russia, and Cuba.

Gene's hobbies include writing and running. Since 1999, Gene has completed 10 marathons, several sprint triathlons, cycling races, and several ultra marathons.

Gene received his bachelor's degree (1975) from Baylor University and his M.Div. (1979) and Ph.D. in New Testament Studies (1985) from Southwestern Baptist Theological Seminary in Fort Worth, Texas.

Gene and his wife Kim have two daughters, Storey Cook (Graham) and Summer.

# Defining Moments With God:
# Introduction to the Book

As I sat in a hotel room in California 17 years ago, I knew God had called me to change how I did church. I was filled with excitement. I had seen glimpses of what a church with a heart to help people trust Jesus looked like, but I was also filled with fear knowing we would have to change how we carried out God's call on our lives. I got on my knees beside the bed and prayed like I had never prayed before. The mission call of God on my life was clear, the path was not. I knew God had a role for me to play, but I was young, afraid, and unskilled. *That was a defining moment with God for me.* My ministry as a church leader was never the same.

That encounter with God set me on an adventure I never would have imagined on my own. Joy, pain, sadness, mystery, and changed lives fill the story that God has been writing since then. I have had other defining moments since then but that one outlined a plot for my life I would have not chosen for myself, and it has made all the difference in my life and ministry.

*Divine Encounters in the Old Testament* focuses on the defining moments in the lives of the people of old. Their encounters with God defined them. You will read and observe people just like you and me whom God chose to play important roles in the story of God's rescue mission to save all people through His Son. This story happed in history. And history is really the record of God's actions in seeking to restore us to Himself. History is His-Story. You will read, study, and apply God's Story to your own life and experience *your own defining moments with God.*

You will participate in 48 different *defining moments with God* on the journey. We have divided each chapter into five shorter encounters with God and the people He invited into the primary storyline of His rescue mission. You will study the details while taking time to find meaning for your life and relationship with God in His-story as God writes it today.

In order to get the full benefit of the study you will need to gather a few items before you begin:

• A pencil, pen, and highlighter. You will be asked to highlight, underline, and circle words and phrases to help identify important aspects of the story you study.

• A copy of the Bible you feel comfortable marking in. The New International Version is the primary text for this study. However, any translation will work.

• A journal or notebook to record your reflections and thoughts.

• A Bible handbook, dictionary, or commentary to help identify names, places, and cultural details.

My prayer is that as you spend time with God through this study of His-story in the Old Testament you will experience your own *defining moments with God* and that you will soon discover your roll in God's Love Story for all people.

C. Gene Wilkes, Ph.D.
Easter, 2007

# TABLE OF CONTENTS

# STATEMENTS OF FAITH

As Christians, there are some essential truths we believe. We discover these truths in the Bible. At Student Life, we have identified eight truths we believe are essential for every Christian to know and understand. These statements give descriptions of those biblical truths and have been developed to help you talk about your faith. They will help you know what you believe.

## GOD IS

Only one true and living God exists. He is the Creator of the universe, eternally existing in three Persons—the Father, Son, and Holy Spirit—each equally deserving of humanity's worship and obedience. He is infinite and perfect in all His attributes.

## THE BIBLE IS GOD'S WORD

The Bible is God's written revelation to people, divinely given through human authors who were inspired by the Holy Spirit. It is entirely true. The Bible is totally sufficient and completely authoritative for matters of life and faith. The goal of God's Word is the restoration of humanity into His image.

## PEOPLE ARE GOD'S TREASURE

God created people in His image for His glory. They are the crowning work of His creation. Yet every person has willfully disobeyed God—an act known as sin—thus inheriting both physical and spiritual death and the need for salvation. All human beings are born with a sin-nature and into an environment inclined toward sin. Only by the grace of God through Jesus Christ can they experience salvation.

## JESUS IS GOD AND SAVIOR

Jesus is both fully God and fully human. He is Christ, the Son of God. Born of a virgin, He lived a sinless life and performed many miracles. He died on the cross to provide people forgiveness of sin and eternal salvation. Jesus rose from the dead, ascended to the right hand of the Father, and will return in power and glory.

## THE HOLY SPIRIT IS GOD AND EMPOWERER

The Holy Spirit is supernatural and sovereign, baptizing all believers into the Body of Christ. He lives within all Christians beginning at the moment of salvation and then empowers them for bold witness and effective service as they yield to Him. The Holy Spirit convicts individuals of sin, uses God's Word to mature believers into Christ-likeness, and secures them until Christ returns.

## SALVATION IS BY FAITH ALONE

All human beings are born with a sin nature, separated from God, and in need of a Savior. That salvation comes only through a faith relationship with Jesus Christ, the Savior, as a person repents of sin and receives Christ's forgiveness and eternal life. Salvation is instantaneous and accomplished solely by the power of the Holy Spirit through the Word of God. This salvation is wholly of God by grace on the basis of the shed blood of Jesus Christ and not on the basis of human works. All the redeemed are secure in Christ forever.

## THE CHURCH IS GOD'S PLAN

The Holy Spirit immediately places all people who put their faith in Jesus Christ into one united spiritual body, the Church, of which Christ is the head. The primary expression of the Church on earth is in autonomous local congregations of baptized believers. The purpose of the Church is to glorify God by taking the gospel to the entire world and by building its members up in Christlikeness through the instruction of God's Word, fellowship, service, worship, and prayer.

## THE FUTURE IS IN GOD'S HANDS

God will bring the world to its appropriate end in His own time and in His own way. At that time, Jesus Christ will return personally and visibly in glory to the earth. Both the saved and unsaved will be resurrected physically to be judged by Christ. Those who have trusted Christ will receive their reward and dwell forever in heaven with the Lord. Those who have refused Christ will spend eternity in hell, the place of everlasting punishment. The certain return of Christ motivates believers to be faithful in their daily lives.

# 1—Why Study the Whole Bible? (Jesus and the Old Testament)

When you were in the first grade you learned your ABC's. You learned them by singing a song or writing them many times. After you learned the letters you began to put them together to create words, and then sentences, paragraphs, and ultimately stories or essays. Those 26 letters lay the foundation for everything you do with words as a literate person. You will never discard them, and hopefully you will continue to use them in more complex and meaningful ways as you mature.

The Old Testament is like the ABC's. It lays the rudimentary foundation for your faith in God, but it is not complete. The story of Jesus alone reveals the full meaning of your relationship with God. Jesus is the most important person in the Old Testament. While the Old Testament does not mention His name, it gives numerous prophecies about His coming.

To live in the Old Testament alone is to miss why it was preserved and who God wanted you to meet because of it. On the other hand, to read only the New Testament is to miss the work of God in His-story, which His Son, Jesus, came to redeem and fulfill. This week's look into the words of Jesus will answer the question, Why study the whole Bible?

Our Memory Verse for this chapter is Matthew 5:17. Begin your time with God each day by reading this verse. You may want to write it once or twice.

Our question to consider this week is: Are the words of Jesus more important than the rest of the Bible?

## 1.1 Beginning the Journey

What speech or lesson do you find most memorable? One that not only gave you new information, but also inspired you to live differently. Matthew 5–7 records one of Jesus' most famous speeches. In this message Jesus described what a life lived under His leadership would look like. His words help to answer the question, Why study the whole Bible?

Read Matthew 5:1–2. What was the setting of Jesus' message? Who was His audience?

_____

Jesus saw "the crowds" following Him, and He took the opportunity to teach His disciples their first lesson on what it looks like to live with Him as the Leader.

Matthew 5:3–12 is known as "the Beatitudes." Read the passage and highlight the blessing that seems to be Jesus' word for you. Put a star by the phrase that describes your current spiritual or emotional condition.

After Jesus' initial blessings and promises to His followers, He gave them two pictures of how their lives would impact others. Read Matthew 5:13–16 and circle the two word pictures Jesus used to describe His followers.

Read Matthew 5:17–20 slowly without making any marks in order to grow familiar with Jesus' words. Read the passage a second time. On this reading underline the words or phrases that relate to the Old Testament. For example, words like "Law," "Prophets,"

and "commandments." On a third reading, circle the phrases that introduce what Jesus said He came to do. For example, "I have come" and "I tell you." These phrases point to Jesus' intentions for His ministry and His instructions about His relationship to the Old Testament.

In the space below, write your first impression of what Jesus taught about His relationship to the Old Testament and its importance in following Him.

_____

_____

To know the Old Testament from Jesus' perspective is to have the kind of journey God desires for you as you experience Him every day on the pages of His written Word. The journey is similar to climbing a mountain. Climbing a mountain requires effort. The climb begins in the ranger's station by learning from the park ranger, who has climbed the mountain 50 times before. His experience, knowledge, and skill will help you to make the trip safely and you will experience all of the beauty God's creation has to offer. In this journey Jesus is our Leader and Guide. Jesus created the mountain you are about to climb! You begin the journey here with Jesus.

## 1.2 Does the Old Testament Matter?

The difference between a rebel and a revolutionary is that a rebel tears down things without an alternative way to live. A revolutionary confronts a current reality in order to instill a new way of life. Both create conflict, but only the revolutionary brings new options.

Jesus lived as a revolutionary. He brought a new way of life to those who put their trust in Him. Jesus' disciples and a crowd of mostly Jewish people made up the audience at The Sermon on the Mount (Matt. 5:1). When Jesus turned His message from the pictures of salt and light (Matt. 5:13–16), He addressed a major concern of those who listened to Him that day.

Read Matthew 5:17. Underline the object of Jesus' revolutionary statement.

Jesus said He did not come to abolish "the Law and the Prophets." These two things made up the core message of God to the Jewish people. "The Law" referred to the first five books of the Old Testament, known among the Jews as the Torah. Write the names of these five books.

_____

_____

_____

Read Psalm 119:105–109. Circle the word "law" where it occurs in the passage. This entire psalm celebrates the importance of the Law among God's people. The Law was the Jewish way of life. To abolish it would mean to destroy how God had commanded them to live.

"The Prophets" include the books of the Old Testament that record God's message to Israel through His chosen messengers. Isaiah, for example, is known as a "major prophet," and Amos, a "minor prophet." Both the Law and the Prophets gave God's message to His people. Jesus said He did not come to abolish the Law and

the Prophets. He came to _____ them. (Fill in the blank.) Jesus said His purpose was to complete and embody all God revealed of His coming and His intentions for the Law and the Prophets. Jesus went so far as to say that neither "the smallest letter" (the *iota* in the Greek alphabet, which was the smallest letter in that language) nor the "least stroke of the pen," (the part of a Hebrew letter that protruded from it, like crossing a "t" in English) would not pass away "until everything is accomplished" (Matt. 5:18). Both marks represented what may seem like an insignificant part of the Law. But Jesus made clear none of that will "disappear" until "everything is accomplished."

Jesus validated the Old Testament. He affirmed its importance and its purpose. As you go through your day, consider the value Jesus placed on the Old Testament and ask God to create a desire in you to know Him more.

## 1.3 The Seed of Greatness

We all know of people we would call great. We also know of people that some would consider the "least." Jesus told us not to judge others as a way of making ourselves feel superior to them (Matt. 7:1) because He judges every area of our lives.

Read Matthew 5:19. Underline what Jesus said about those who break the "least of these commandments." Go back to the beginning of the verse and underline what He said about those who practice and teach "these commands." Summarize your own interpretation of verse 19.

_____

_____

_____

_____

Jesus said that whoever breaks, literally, destroys, the smallest commandment would be called least in the Kingdom of Heaven. He taught that whoever practiced the Law would be known as great in the Kingdom of Heaven. The word for "least" means "insignificant." Jesus used it in His Parable of the Sheep and the Goats to describe the "least of" in society (Matt. 25:40). Our English prefix *mega* comes from the Greek word translated "great" here. Abolish the Law, and you will be known as the least of His followers, Jesus said. Observe and teach it, and you will be a mega-disciple in His eyes.

Take a moment to evaluate Jesus' words for your life. Which of the two terms, "great" or "least," would you call yourself based on your respect and practice of God's commands in the Old Testament? Why?

_____

_____

Read the second part of verse 19 again. Highlight the two verbs that form the basis of greatness in Jesus' Kingdom. To practice and teach, or to lead others to do the same, equals greatness in the Kingdom of God.

Read Matthew 4:17. What was Jesus' central message as He began His public ministry? Jesus insisted people change the way they live because the Kingdom of Heaven was near. This concept carries both present and future implications.

Jesus warned against discarding the Old Testament, and He called those great who respected and kept its teachings. Every follower of Jesus desires to please his or her Leader; to be called great and to live out His wishes. Write one thing you can do today to exhibit your respect for "the Law and the Prophets." For example, you may keep the Ten Commandments (Ex. 20:1–17) for a day or do something for the poor around you to follow the command in Leviticus 19:10. Write your action below and pray that will God open the door for your action today.

_____

_____

## 1.4 Getting God's Righteousness

How do you know if you have done something well? For example, how do you know if you have run a race well? How do you measure your performance at work? What are the standards for good parenting? Read the list below. Match the measurement with the act(ivity) that helps you know how well you have done in that area.

| | |
|---|---|
| sports | number of sick days from work |
| school | performance review |
| job | grades |
| friendship | authenticity level of conversations |
| health | number of points scored in a game |

Consider this topic: How do you measure your relationship with God and how well you are doing?

_____

_____

_____

Some people use the number of good acts they do to measure whether or not they are doing well with God. Others feel that learning more information about God or figuring out some of the mysteries about God means they are doing OK. Others accept the grace God has shown them in Jesus as their spiritual measurement.

The Bible teaches that the benchmark for our relationship with God is righteousness. The concept means being considered righteous before God.

Read Matthew 5:20. Highlight those to whom Jesus compared righteousness. Why do you think He chose those two groups?

Return to Matthew 5:20 and underline the word that describes the level of righteousness Jesus said we must have. "Surpass" in the verse means to "have more than enough" and to "excel, or exceed" (Newman). This set a high standard, given that the Pharisees and teachers of the Law were considered the most righteous among the Jewish people. What could Jesus have meant by such a statement? Write your thoughts here:

_____

_____

_____

Taking the message at face value without hearing what Jesus said before or after would mean one must know and keep the rules of the Old Testament Law better than the religious leaders of the day!

The third part of verse 20 gives the consequence of not having a righteousness that surpassed the religious leaders'. What is that consequence?

_____

_____

Jesus said that not to surpass the righteousness of these religious leaders meant a person would not enter the Kingdom of Heaven. So, there had to be a way that surpassed the religious leaders' interpretation of how to gain righteousness in order to stand in right relationship with God. That way is Jesus (John 14:6; Rom. 3:21–24). He is the righteousness from God. Jesus' message at the beginning of His ministry showed His relationship to the old covenant. It also played an important part in knowing Him as the Way. Through Jesus, God declares people right before Him.

Jesus introduced a new kind of righteousness. This righteousness would come through Him in a new covenant. We need to read the Old Testament with this reality in mind and seek to know the heart of God. Jesus came to earth to fulfill every requirement for righteousness so we can have an eternal relationship with Him.

## 1.5 Stating Your Faith

Our question to consider this week was: Are the words of Jesus more important than the rest of the Bible? After looking at Jesus' teaching about the Law and the Prophets in Matthew 5:17–20, how do you answer this question? Explain your yes or no response.

_____

_____

Regardless of how you answered this question, Jesus affirmed the importance of the Old Testament Scripture. We cannot ignore the Old Testament if we truly commit to following Christ.

Read 2 Timothy 3:16. Circle the word that describes the nature of Scripture. Then, underline the word that tells what part of Scripture that word describes. Put a square around each of the uses of Scripture.

The Old and New Testaments are God-breathed. God inspired all of Scripture to reveal His righteousness in Jesus. All of Scripture is necessary for people to know the heart and purposes of God. An important part of your relationship with God is your trust in Scripture as God's revelation of Himself and His purposes. Based on this week's study, write a brief personal statement of faith about the Bible. (Share it with one person today and get his or her response.)

_____

_____

_____

You are about to embark on a journey through the Old Testament. As you do so, keep Jesus' teachings in mind. God has inspired everything you are about to read and study so that you can know Him and His ways and so that you can have eternal life through His Son, Jesus. Let the journey begin.

**For further study:**
- **Psalm 19:7–14; 119:1–176**
- **Hebrews 4:12–13; James 1:19–25**

## 2—Does It Matter Where We Came From? (God, the Perfect Creator)

The biblical story of God's relationship with people begins with Genesis, the beginning. Somewhere along the journey with God someone among the children of Israel asked, "Where did all this get started?" God showed Moses the beginning of history. This is really His-story with His people. Moses, a shepherd/leader, wrote down what God revealed to him.

Genesis reveals to us God's great design in the creation of the world. God created the world with purpose and order. He made the world from nothing and set everything in place. We also learn that people are God's treasure, then and today.

Our question to consider this week is: Can evolution and creationism both be true? This chapter will introduce you to the biblical beginnings of your epic adventure with God. You will stand at the portal to the universe and see God create something from nothing and how your place on this planet plays a part in God's intentions for His creation.

The purpose here is not to refute current scientific theories of origins. Our purpose is to expose you to the biblical explanation of creation and allow you to compare that to theories and faith positions you encounter in life.

Our Memory Verse for this chapter is Genesis 1:27. Begin each day's defining moment with God by reading this verse. You may want to write it out once or twice if you learn best that way.

## 2.1 The Genesis of Genesis

What is your favorite beginning to a story?

"Once upon a time . . ."

"It was the best of times. It was the worst of times . . ."

"In a hole in the ground there lived a hobbit . . ."

"There was a man who had two sons . . ."

Write your favorite opening line here:

_____

Write the opening sentence to the Bible's story,
Genesis 1:1, here:

_____

_____

Underline the first three words to the story. Highlight
the One who acted, and circle the action. Underline
what He created.

This first sentence of the Bible lays the foundation of a
biblical worldview for origins of the universe. Genesis
1:1 gives us the starting point of all things, the One who
started it all, and what He started.

"In the beginning . . ." refers to the beginning of time
and space, the origin of all things. The phrase assumes
nothing existed before God moved to create the heavens
and the earth. People can make something from
something, a pot from clay or electricity from solar energy; but people cannot create from nothing. Only God
can do that.

The One who created in the beginning is God, the One
who stands outside time and space to act as He chooses.
The name for God, Elohim, is the most familiar name
for God in the Bible. God did not give His personal
name, YHWH, to Moses until later in the story. (See
Exodus 3; also see John 1:1–14.)

Read Revelation 4:8. Circle the three verb forms for "is"
in the verse. What does that tell you about the existence
of God?

Genesis 1:1 does not talk about the beginning of God,
but what God began. The Bible teaches that God "was,
and is, and is to come." God is eternal. Time, space, and
matter are finite.

Read Genesis 1:2. How does the writer describe the
earth? How does he describe "the deep"?

Before God spoke light into existence (v. 3), the earth
remained a formless void and darkness covered the deep,
but the Spirit of God hovered over it all.

Read Isaiah 40:28. In this verse, the prophet confesses
God as Creator. Write in your own words your
confession of God, the Creator of the universe.

_____

_____

_____

_____

## 2.2 Know Thyself

Have you ever considered the implications of the Big Bang Theory? Not the physical implications but the practical ones? For example, consider a group of sixth or seventh graders hearing about the Big Bang Theory for the first time. Let's imagine that their teacher presents this as a scientific reality by explaining that time and chance somehow resulted in an unintentional bang. This bang resulted in the first simple form of life. What stands out in many of the students' minds is the unintentional bang. This would mean human beings resulted from a mere cosmic accident.

The biblical record of where we came from offers something much different. Scripture outlines our origin as having purpose. We were intentionally created by a loving and powerful God.

Read Genesis 1:3–25. In the space below, list the things God created in the order He created them.

_____

_____

God, who is light (1 John 1:5), first spoke light into existence. He then added elements of form and life that depended upon the previously created ingredient.

Read Genesis 1:26. What did God create last in the biblical list?

_____

Humans are not simply the last thing on God's list to create. People hold the highest place in creation because God gave them the responsibility to rule over all the creatures previously brought into being by God. Human beings are so important to God, that all three persons of the Trinity were involved in creating us.

Read John 1:1–3. Highlight the Person of the Trinity who is connected to creation in this verse.

Read Psalm 104:27–30. Highlight the Person of the Trinity who is associated with creation here. The full witness of Scripture teaches that God is Creator as God (The Father), Son, and Spirit and supports the plural nature of God in Genesis 1:26. An essential truth about God is that He is "three in one."

The Triune God intentionally created people as the crowning work of creation. How does this fact impact your image of who you are? Record your thoughts in your journal.

## 2.3 In the Image of God

Men and women are different. From boyhood males build structures and organizations, start fights and go to war, and turn anything they do into a competition. They are the more aggressive gender. Females, on the other hand, tend to build homes and relationships and nurture children and friendships more naturally than men, and they tend not to compete so much with those with whom they work and play. Why are men and women different? Today's lesson will answer this question.

Read Genesis 1:27. This verse, written in poetic form, tells us two aspects of how God created people. Underline those two things.

God created human beings, "in the image of God" and "male and female." Both of these realities have a part in God's intention for His created order.

The phrases "the image of God" and "in our likeness" (v. 26) have caused speculation throughout the ages. Some have taken "the image of God" as the human mind and "our likeness" of God as having a spirit. Others have suggested people's ability to have moral relationships or our ability to reason and to reflect on our lives as the meaning of these phrases.

Regardless of what else it means, this passage clearly teaches each person carries a divine "image" or "likeness" that sets him or her apart from the rest of creation. People have a special place in the created order because God placed in them something of His likeness. (See Genesis 9:6; James 3:9; and Colossians 3:9–10 for other passages related to this topic.)

What is the second aspect of God's creation of people in verse 27? Write it here:

_____

_____

God created humans as male and female. Gender has a place and purpose in God's created order. This designation has physical, emotional, and relational implications in the lives of men and women. Jesus affirmed that God created people as male and female and made that reality a foundation for biblical marriage (Matt. 19:4–5). Being a male or a female matters to God. Each gender has a unique contribution to make to the creation.

Take a moment to write a phrase or two that describes you as a man or a woman. When you have finished, turn what you have written into a prayer of thanksgiving to God who created you.

_____

_____

_____

_____

## 2.4 Assignments from God

God created you in His image and as either male or female. You have a special place in creation above all other created beings. God gave you the privilege to have the capacity for a relationship with both God and others. You are blessed by God.

Read Genesis 1:28. God blessed the first man and woman and then God told them to do four things. Underline those four things.

God first instructed the couple to "be fruitful and increase in number." God intended for men and women in a marriage relationship to have children. A child born in marriage is as natural as fruit from a tree. God blessed the sexuality of the male and female, and He blessed the children that would come from joining them together.

Second, God told the first couple to "fill the earth" with offspring. What implications does this biblical teaching have on how you view your sexuality, sex within marriage, and the children who are born into that marriage? Write your impressions here:

_____

_____

What was the third command of God found in verse 28? (See also verse 26.)

God told humans to "subdue" the earth. Along with your privileged status in creation, God has given you

responsibility for His creation. Like Adam who named the animals and oversaw the garden, you stand as God's representative in His creation. To subdue the earth does not imply the misuse of its resources. What is an example of subduing the earth without misusing it? Write your answer here:

_____

_____

Finally, God said for people to "rule over" every living creature in the sea, the air, and on the earth. To rule over something does not imply abuse or irresponsibility. Like a king who rules over his subjects and cares for their well-being so they can serve him, we should rule over every living thing so they can serve our needs.

Read verses 29–30. What does God give as provisions for people? What does this say about your stewardship of all living things that you can eat as food?

End today's moment with God by writing a prayer to thank God for who He made you. Also, write a prayer asking God to guide you and your community in the stewardship of resources for which you are responsible.

## 2.5 Divine Art

What was the last project you finished? You may have made or helped produce something. Describe your project here:

_____

How did you feel about the project? Did you feel pleased with the finished product? What could you have done better to improve the end result? Write some of your feelings here:

_____

_____

_____

Read Genesis 1:31. Circle the words that describe God's impression of His work.

Verse 31 says that God looked over all He had made and declared it "very good." God affirmed previous portions of creation as "good" (vv. 10, 12, 18, 21), but when God viewed all He had made, He deemed it all "very good." How does His proclamation about creation impact your view of it? Write your first impressions.

_____

_____

God declared that all He made was good and as He designed it. In the beginning, His-story existed as pure, whole, and in harmony with the Creator's intentions. Humans lived in a perfectly balanced environment with plenty of food and surrounded by beauty. God's creation started out as good. This truth proves foundational to a biblical view of the origin of creation. We will learn later how evil and sin corrupted this goodness, but from the start everything functioned as whole and at peace with its Creator.

Read verse 31 again. Highlight the time references in the verse.

The order of "evening . . . and . . . morning" signaled the Jewish designation of the start of a day at sunset. Verse 31 explains this as the sixth of these time spans, or days. The word for day, *yom*, is a common word for the 24-hour period between the settings of the sun. This language brings us back to our question to consider this week: Can evolution and creationism both be true?

Read Hebrews 11:3. Underline what the verse says about what faith helps us to understand.

By faith we come to trust that God formed the universe from nothing. Whatever method you choose to explain how life developed, the Bible teaches who began life and that it came from nothing when God spoke. Your choice comes down to whether you view the universe as Creator-started and centered or as chance-beginnings and creature-centered. Both positions require faith. But only one fits a biblical worldview.

**For further study:**
- **Psalm 19:1–6; 139:1–24**
- **Colossians 1:15–23; Hebrews 1:1–4**

# 3—Getting Wise on Evil (Adam and Eve)

In the beginning God created a perfect world. All creatures lived in harmony with one another and with God. We know that things do not work that way now. What happened? Where did the the road start to turn? How did evil enter the hearts of people?

Chapter 2 of Genesis tells about God's Sabbath rest after creation and the details of how God formed the first man, Adam. It also tells how God gave man the responsibility of naming and caring for the animals. God saw that it was not good for Adam to live alone, so He took a rib from the man's side and formed a woman, Eve. Creation was complete and in agreement with God's intentions.

Free to work in and roam through that pristine environment, Adam and Eve enjoyed fellowship with God and the freedom to live the life He designed for them. But freedom has a dark side. When tempted to live outside the boundaries God gave them, the first couple exercised their God-given freedom to cross the line of God's provision. Their decision had cosmic consequences that you live with today.

This chapter of His-story introduces us to the reality that even if given ideal circumstances, people will choose sin over God's design for life. We know the act as the Fall, and theologically we describe it as original sin.

Our Memory Verse for this chapter is Romans 16:20. It tells of the fulfillment of the promise in Genesis 3:15.

Our question to consider this week is: Are people born basically good?

## 3.1 Distortion 101

Being prudent, cunning, and shrewd can be desirable traits. The Bible says the prudent acts with knowledge, but the fool shows his ignorance (Prov. 13:16). Clever people do well in tough situations because they have the ability to respond to multiple options. But cleverness can do more than solve problems. It can create them.

Read Genesis 3:1. Highlight how the Bible describes the serpent.

The serpent had a part in the created order just like Adam and Eve. The Bible describes him as "more crafty" or "more cunning" (NKJV) than any of the animals. The creature's gift of cunning, like the humans' freedom, could work to deepen a relationship with God and others. It could also make the creature the center of creation. The serpent chose the latter. (Jesus told His followers to act "as shrewd as snakes"—Matt. 10:16.)

Read the second part of Genesis 3:1. Underline what the serpent asked the woman. How would you describe how he handled God's command? How was he crafty in his question to Eve? Write your answer below:

_____

_____

The serpent did not compel Eve to rebel against God. It simply invited her to reconsider God's commands and played on her pride to become like God. Look up 2 Corinthians 11:3. How did Paul compare the serpent's temptation of Eve to his readers' lives?

The Bible describes Satan as a serpent (Rev. 12:9). Scripture reveals Satan as the Tempter. Satan tempted Jesus (Luke 4:1–13). Satan inflicted Job (Job 1:6–12; 2:1–7). Jesus called him "a liar and the father of lies" (John 8:44). The serpent in the garden represents the evil that seeks to draw people away from God.

Read Genesis 3:2–3. Underline what Eve said God had told them about the tree in the middle of the garden.

Eve quoted what God had told Adam and her about the "tree of the knowledge of good and evil" in the center of Eden (Gen. 2:16–17). They could eat from all but this one tree. This tree, however, was off limits.

Read Genesis 3:4–5. Reword the serpent's lie to Eve.

_____

_____

The serpent first denied Eve would face any judgment for her disobedience. It said she would not die or suffer the consequences of her actions. This was the first lie. God's character requires a response to behavior contrary to His commands. The second lie promised that if Eve ate of the tree she would be like God. No creature can be like the Creator, but many have believed this lie.

In what areas of your life do you allow temptation to overcome you? Is it a result of pride, being your own god, or do you feel pressured by others to live differently than God intends? Confess these temptations to God and ask Him to forgive you and give you guidance as you face them in the future.

## 3.2 End of the Innocence

What are your greatest sources of temptation? You do not have to say them out loud or write them down. You know them. Begin this day's time with God by agreeing with Him that those realities draw you away from the good relationship He desires for you. You can write your prayer in the space below or in your journal.

_____

_____

_____

Eve's response to the serpent's temptation is typical for all people. Subtle tugs at our pride draw us beyond the boundaries of wisdom and God's design for our lives.

Read Genesis 3:6. Underline the three phrases that explain why Eve made the choice she did.

Now, read 1 John 2:16. Underline the three phrases the Letter of First John says come "from the world" and "not from the Father."

The left column contains below the phrases that give the reasons Eve tasted the fruit. The right column contains phrases that describe realities that come "from the world." Draw a line from the phrase in the left column to the similar phrase on the right.

| | |
|---|---|
| good for food | boasting of what he has |
| pleasing to the eye | cravings |
| desirable for gaining wisdom | lust of the eyes |

Eve saw the fruit as a good source for food, a natural craving of the flesh. It was pleasing to the eye, which turns to lust when we desire to get what we see. Eve saw the fruit as desirable for gaining wisdom, which feeds the boasting that comes from what we have obtained for ourselves.

Reflect on which of these desires that come "from the world" you wrestle with the most. (Read 1 Corinthians 10:13 to see God's promise to you concerning the temptations you face.)

Read Genesis 3:7. Highlight the consequences of Adam and Eve's actions.

To sin is to cross the line of God's boundaries. Adam and Eve's sin destroyed their innocence. They did not physically die, but their innocent, pure relationship with

God suffered a quiet death. Because of their sin they covered themselves to hide their exposed disobedience. They experienced spiritual death immediately, and then a physical death years later.

As you end this moment with God, take time to rest in His forgiveness and His desire to have a complete relationship with you (1 John 1:8–2:2). Thank God for His love and patience with you.

## 3.3 Who, Me?

Children have a hard time taking responsibility for their actions. I grew up with four sisters and no brothers. I was the only boy in the house, and that gave me four easy targets I could blame for my mistakes. Whenever I could, I blamed one of my sisters for a mess that I made or a dish that I broke. Of course, after a short period of time, my parents saw through my blame-throwing and held me accountable for my actions. They gave me the gift of integrity by making me confess my mistakes and take responsibility for my actions. It is human to blame others for our shortcomings. It is divine to hold others accountable for what they do.

Read Genesis 3:8. Circle what Adam and Eve did when they heard God moving through the garden.

Like a child who hides in his or her room when a parent discovers colored writing on the living room wall, Adam and Eve hid when they heard God moving through the garden. God did not make them feel guilty. They did that on their own because they knew in their hearts they had done what God had told them not to do.

Read Genesis 3:9–10. Highlight God's question and underline Adam's answer.

God knew where Adam hid, but repentance and restoration begin with confession. Adam's answer revealed his sin. The man now considered his nakedness as something to hide, and he feared the One with whom he had shared a friendship. God continued on like a patient parent toward a guilty child and asked Adam what He already knew (v. 11).

Read verses 12–13. Paraphrase the man and woman's answers to God here:

_____

_____

Adam blamed Eve, and Eve blamed the serpent. Neither took responsibility for what they did. This natural tendency to blame others for our actions has served as an explanation for our misuse of the freedom God gave us from the beginning.

God gave Adam and Eve an opportunity to confess their sin so He could show them His mercy, but they chose to protect themselves rather than to humble themselves.

Read 1 John 1:9. Underline the first five words. Highlight what the Bible promises in response to our action.

The word for confess literally means "to say the same thing." Confession is not telling God what He does not know. It is agreeing to accept His view of your actions. God promises to forgive. What can you confess today?

## 3.4 Consequences and Mercy

Our actions have consequences. Freedom's choices impact both our present and our future. Our sinful actions not only affect others; we will also face eternal consequences for our sinful acts.

Read Genesis 3:14. How did God respond to the serpent's actions? Write His response here:

_____

_____

Read verses 15–16. Underline what God put between the serpent and the woman. What does that word mean? Write your definition here:

_____

_____

Highlight what the serpent will do to the woman's offspring and circle what the woman's offspring will do to the serpent's descendants.

Genesis 3:15 prophesies of Jesus' death on the cross and His victorious triumph over Satan. Jesus, born a descendant of Eve (Luke 3:38), would crush the serpent's head at the final judgment (Rev. 20). The serpent's strike on the heel of Eve's offspring signifies His crucifixion (Mark 15:33–39).

Underline the physical consequences God put in the woman's life.

Read verses 17–19. Summarize in the space below God's judgment on Adam for his decision to go against God's rules.

_____

_____

God made the land, once a flourishing garden at creation, difficult to work in response to Adam's sin. Man would labor for the food it produced. God brought death into His relationship with His creature, "for dust you are and to dust you will return" (v. 19). There is no indication of an end to human life before Adam's sin. God intended to enjoy an eternal relationship with His creation, but the man and woman's choices shortened that intention. Romans 6:23 affirms death as the consequence of sin, not of God's desire. (See also Ephesians 2:1–3.)

Read verse 20. Highlight what Adam named the woman and underline what her name meant.

After God sentenced the man and woman to death, Adam named his partner Eve, which may mean "living," and trusted that she will become the mother of "all the living." In light of our place in biblical revelation, we can see how living can have both a physical and spiritual meaning. From Eve would come living people as in her sons, Cain and Abel, but ultimately, the life of the Son (v. 15) would come from her.

The self-centered choice of the man and woman destroyed the relationship between Creator and creature, but God provided restoration in His coming Son. What are some evident consequences of choices you have made contrary to God's design for life? Taking responsibility for your choices—unlike Adam and Eve—will result in restoration by God, not rejection.

## 3.5 Glimpse of Grace

To punish the child you love is difficult, but it is necessary to build moral and godly character in him or her. Proper parenting insists balancing any punishment with love and support. I dreaded punishing my daughters, but I knew I had to do it. As soon as they recieved the proper amount of discipline I showered them with love and affection. God punished Adam and Eve for their disobedience, but God also showed His love for them.

Read Genesis 3:21. Highlight the two things God did for His children. God did not stop providing for those He created. God made clothing to replace the plant coverings that they had made and He dressed them.

God showed His mercy by giving Adam and Eve clothes to cover them. This paints a prophetic picture of God's cover of sin through the sacrifice of animals and ultimately of His Son, Jesus. (See Hebrews 9:11–14 for the impact of Jesus' sacrifice on the cross.)

Read Genesis 3:22–24. What did God do to protect Adam and Eve from living in eternal separation from God? Write your summary here:

_____

_____

It is possible that God's guarding of the tree of life by placing an angel there was to protect Adam and Eve so they could not eat from it and live forever in their separated condition from their Creator. If Adam or Eve had eaten of that tree, they would live forever in a broken relationship with God. People are God's treasure, and from the beginning God has worked to keep a vital relationship open to them.

That same tree will be in heaven and made accessible to those who believe (Rev. 2:7; 22:2, 14).

Our question to consider this week was: Are people born basically good? After walking through Adam and Eve's choice to disobey God (known as "the Fall") how do you answer that question? Write your answer in the space below. If you answer no, what provisions has God given to cover that condition? If you answer yes, on what do you base your position?

_____

_____

This week's moments with God may have seemed difficult for you. The hard truth of all people's tendency to disobey God creates a stumbling block to faith for many. But God who created you loves you and has made it possible through His Son's final sacrifice for you to find restoration for a right relationship with Him.

**For further study:**
- **Romans 5:12–21; Ephesians 6:10–18**
- **1 Corinthians 15:20–23, 45–49**

# 4—Worshiping Completely (Cain and Abel)

Worship. We all do it. Whether it is to give worth-ship to God or to our favorite activity, we worship—place ultimate value on—people and things.

Part of the image of God placed in us at creation longs to connect us to our Creator. You and I were created for worship, but lesser gods too easily replace the God of Creation in our worship.

Pause for a moment and make a short list of those things and people who draw your attention, time, and resources.

One way to identify what you worship is to consider what or whom you give your time and money to. We will see in this chapter that what Cain and Abel brought to God in worship was not the issue. Rather it was what they had in their hearts that mattered.

The Memory Verse for this chapter is Genesis 4:7. It describes how our heart-driven actions have a part in our worship of God.

Our question to consider this week is: What is worship? As you walk through the birth and struggles of the first brothers, you will begin to understand God's intentions for worship and how you can express your honor of God according to His expectations.

## 4.1 The First Family

Children are a gift from God (Ps. 127:3–5). God promised Eve that although she disobeyed Him she would bear children. Genesis 4 begins with the fulfillment of that promise and the continued consequence of the parents' sin in the hearts of their children.

Read Genesis 4:1. Underline the actions in the sentence. Adam "lay with" Eve, and she became pregnant. To "lay with" literally means "to know." This concept of sex as intimate knowledge of another person signifies the value of the act and God's desire to protect its sanctity. Eve became pregnant and confessed that she received her son "with the help of the LORD."

Read verse 2. Highlight each brother's lifestyle. Abel followed Cain in the birth order. He "kept flocks" while his brother farmed like their father.

The story of beginnings continued with the birth of two boys to the first couple. This was the first family, the core social unit of society. Cain and Abel were brothers, God's blessing to the family and the first generation of people who worshiped God. They grew up together and learned the importance of being part of a family and how to worship God.

What practices of worship did you learn growing up? If your family did not go to worship, what were your earliest experiences of worship?

_____

_____

The sons' two lifestyles were basic to life in an agrarian culture. While they had different roles to provide for living, one role was not superior to the other. The events that follow do not suggest one is more significant than the other for us today. The story focuses on the condition of one's heart, not what one brings to worship.

Pause and reflect on your family of origin. List the names of the family members. Write a brief prayer of concern you have for them today.

_____

_____

_____

_____

You had no choice of the family into which you were born, but God can use every person and event in that family to demonstrate His love and care for you. Take some time now to pray for specific members of your family.

## 4.2 A Heart Problem

Worship not only has to do with what we bring to God, but also with what we have in our hearts when we bring it. Worship is our heart-felt response to God for who He is and what He has done for us. It implies offering something to God. The heart, not the gift, however, signifies our true worship of God.

Read Genesis 4:3 and the first sentence in verse 4. Underline Cain and Abel's respective offerings to God.

Each man brought something from what he cared for as an offering to God. Cain brought "some of the fruits of the soil" while Abel brought "fat portions" from "the firstborn of his flock." While the phrases are not technical terms for worship offerings, we can see that Abel brought more valuable parts from his work than did Cain. The younger brother brought prized portions from "the firstborn of his flock" while Cain brought "some of the fruits" from his fields.

Read the second part of Genesis 4:4 and verse 5. Highlight God's response to the siblings' offerings.

Cain sensed God's disfavor with his gift. He grew angry and "his face was downcast." He looked dejected (NLT). Why did Cain react this way to God's lack of approval of his gift? Write your response here:

_____

_____

Like a lazy, spoiled child, Cain felt he had brought a sufficient offering and he did not want to accept God's value of his gift. His attitude signaled his prideful heart.

Read verse 7. What was God's warning to Cain if he did not change his heart?

God warned Cain that sin, like a crouching tiger, waited at his heart's door to devour him. God told Cain to master his sin and not allow it to drag him away.

Read James 1:13–15. How does the Bible describe the process from desire to death? How does this apply to Cain's situation with Abel? How can you apply this spiritual truth to prideful sin in your life?

_____

_____

_____

_____

## 4.3 Unresolved Anger

Anger is a natural emotion that often arises from our wounded pride. I can respond either in anger or humility when someone points out a mistake I made or a flaw in my character. Anger is natural, but like sin, we must master it. Anger can run as the emotional engine for revenge to those who we feel have hurt us. Cain's anger over God's appraisal of his offering drove him to harm his brother rather than humble himself before God and change his heart. It seemed easier to kill his rival than submit to his God.

Read Proverbs 15:1 and 22:24. What does wisdom teach you about anger? Also, read Jesus' teaching about anger in Matthew 5:21–22. How do Jesus' words apply to our Scripture passage today?

_____

_____

Cain turned his anger toward his brother. The sin of pride turned brothers into competitors for favor. The older brother invited Abel into one of his fields and then killed him there. Cain committed the first murder—a premeditated act intended to take the life of another, the first act of fratricide.

Read Genesis 4:9. Highlight God's question to Cain and underline Cain's response.

As in the encounter with Cain's parents (Gen. 3:9), God asked what He already knew in order to give the sinner a chance to confess his sin. But like his father, Cain proudly snapped back at God with the now famous question, "Am I my brother's keeper?" Why do you believe Cain was able to answer God in this manner? Write your impressions here:

_____

_____

_____

Read Genesis 4:11–12. On the lines below, list God's response to Cain's refusal to live up to his crime:

_____

_____

Read Genesis 4:10. Underline how God knows what happened to Cain's brother. Read Hebrews 12:24. Underline how the Scriptures compare Jesus' blood to Abel's offering.

The blood of Abel cried out from the ground Cain's guilt. However, Jesus' blood shouts the grace of the new covenant between God and those who trust Him. The redemption story has begun to unfold. Here we see the need for someone to save humankind from continual sinful actions.

Because Cain refused to repent, God again had to enforce discipline on His creature for what he had done. Sin has consequences, not only on others but also in our relationship with God.

Who has recently wounded your pride or wronged you? If you still feel angry, begin to pray that God will change your heart and that He will show you a time to seek forgiveness for holding on to anger.

## 4.4 Justice and Grace

Punishment in the Bible has a redemptive purpose. God finds a way even in His righteous judgment to make it possible for the offender to experience His mercy. For example, God graciously made clothes for Adam and Eve in order to cover their shame. Ultimately, God gave His Son, Jesus, to die as a sacrifice for our sin. In today's moment with God, God punished Cain for the murder of his brother, but He also protected him from the vengeance of others. Love and grace always flow from the heart of God.

Read Genesis 4:13–14. Summarize Cain's response to God's curse on his life:

_____

_____

Cain whined that God punished him too harshly for the murder of his brother. He knew that others had the right to take his life for that of his brother's life. Cain should have felt pleased God did not impose the rule He would later give his people, "you are to take life for life, eye for eye, tooth for tooth . . ." (Ex. 21:23–25). God invested His relationship with people for eternity, and even the moaning of a guilty man would not deter His desire to have fellowship with them.

Read Genesis 4:15. Underline the two provisions God made for Cain.

God graciously protected Cain from the revenge of anyone else. "Anyone" can mean people on earth other than the first four or that as others came on the scene they could not seek revenge. God also placed a "mark" on Cain that would prevent his own murder. This does not imply a physical mark on Cain, but may mean that God marked Cain for His purposes and, thus, God protected him.

Cain left the presence of God to live in Nod, which means "wandering." Cain's unrepentant heart prevented God from showing him grace and mercy. What might have happened if he had opened his heart like one of the thieves crucified with Jesus?

Read Luke 23:39–43. Circle the three people in this event. Which of the three had an attitude most like Cain's attitude toward God? Underline the words of the thief who opened his heart to Christ's sacrifice. What did Jesus promise to him that day? (v. 43)

_____

_____

## 4.5 Authentic Worship

Our question to consider this week was: What is worship? Based on your time with the story of Cain and Abel, write your answer to that question here:

_____

_____

_____

Worship is our heart-response to God for who He is and what He has done for us. (See John 4:23–24 for Jesus' description of worship.)

Cain and Abel portray examples of evil and righteousness for those who looked back to the story of beginnings for how to worship God. Clearly, worship was not simply what each man offered. Worship involved the act of offering and their respect of God and each other after the offerings.

Read 1 John 3:11. Underline John's instruction to his readers. Read verse 12. Highlight why John told his readers not to be like Cain.

John echoed Jesus' words for His disciples to love one another (John 13:34–35). The negative example he gave spoke of Cain who acted out of evil desires rather than in righteousness like his brother. Worship includes how we treat those God has put in our lives and that affects our worship of God (Matt. 5:22–24).

Read Hebrews 11:4. Circle the phrase that made Abel's sacrifice "better" and why God "commended" him a righteous man.

Faith is the altar of worship. By faith we "please God, because anyone who comes to him must believe that he exists and that he rewards those who earnestly seek him" (Heb. 11:6). Abel's sacrifice was better because he trusted God deserved his best, and by his faith he still serves as an example of genuine worship today.

Read Romans 12:1. Underline what we should offer to God as a sacrifice of worship.

If faith is the altar of worship, our lives are the offering. God cares more about the worshiper than the worshiper's offering. This verse teaches that our best act of worship is to give ourselves wholly to God. God desires our love for Him and others more than religious acts of sacrifice (Mark 12:33).

Worship God through your heart-felt acts of love. Keep notes of what that looks like and invite others to experience worship with you in the days ahead.

**For further study:**
- **Hebrews 11:1–6; 1 John 3:11–24**
- **Romans 12:1–21; Matthew 5:21–26**

## 5—Obeying God When It Doesn't Make Sense (Noah)

Obedience is a core practice in our relationship with God. We find it difficult enough to obey when we know all the whys and how to's of God's commands, but to obey without any data other than "because God said" is as hard for us as for a four-year-old who argues with his father about playing in the street. The tough part of faith comes in trusting God to the point that when He speaks we act—even if we have no frame of reference or experience to make what He said to do a good idea.

In our age of enlightenment we have been trained to gather all possible information on a topic. From traffic reports before we head to work to business plans before we seek venture capital, we seldom do anything decisive without gathering all the data to support our move.

To trust God, however, sometimes means obeying Him without any supporting data. God instructed Noah to build something he had never seen in order to survive an experience he had never known. God had reasons for choosing Noah to build a boat, but Noah had no frame of reference for either the ark or for rain.

This chapter in the Story of God with His creation tells of God's judgment, salvation, and how God calls people as part of His plans to win back the hearts of people.

The Memory Verse for this chapter is Hebrews 11:7. Read it to see how God valued what Noah did and how his actions provide an example of faith for you today.

Our question to consider this week is: Do you think the ark still exists on the earth somewhere?

## 5.1 The Ascent of Evil

Mystery and chaos filled the early ages of history. "Sons of God" wed "daughters of men." Giants, also known as Nephilim, roamed the earth and along with the women they chose gave birth to the "heroes of old." But the world was not right. The lines between the spiritual and the natural had crossed, and people had begun to desire immortality. In response, God limited their years (Gen. 6:3), but bigger problems persisted in creation.

Read Genesis 6:5. Underline the two conditions of people's hearts that caused God to grieve.

Wickedness and evil ruled the day. The sin of Adam and Eve's pride-filled rebellion had become pervasive in all of society, and God could tolerate it no longer. What God had seen as good in chapter 1, He now saw as evil. We do not see the anger of God but the grief in God's heart in response to the wickedness of people (v. 6). Grief born out of love, not the whim of a capricious deity, moved God to do what He did next.

Read Genesis 6:7. Summarize God's decision in the space below. How do you feel about God's conclusion based on what He saw on earth?

_____

_____

God decided to destroy what He had created. Like a child who turns over and shakes his or her Etch A Sketch™ to start a new drawing, God was ready to start over with His design. Every creature He had delighted in

forming was now subject to His judgment—all but one. A man named Noah found favor with God (v. 8). In the middle of evil God saw one as righteous. In the middle of declared judgment God showed His favor.

Creation had fallen to a state of no return. God decided to start over by destroying His own good work. Have you ever found it easier to just end a project or endeavor and start all over? Describe the situation and why you chose to start over here:

_____

_____

_____

Read Romans 8:19–21. What did Paul reflect about creation and its need for restoration?

_____

_____

With God's judgment came grace. The next verses tell of God's provision for salvation in the middle of His judgment.

## 5.2 One Who Walked with God

Within every good story when danger threatens the main character there appears a way out, a path through the dark forest, someone to rescue those about to perish. The story of creation went bad with people's desire to live like gods. Like climbers who had moved beyond their skill and found themselves trapped on the side of a cliff, the first generations of people had climbed beyond God's intention for their lives. Something had to change or their wicked ways would destroy them. They needed a way out, a rescuer, someone who could guide them from danger into safety.

Genesis 6:9 begins a new era in the story of creation. "Account" can also be translated "genealogy" (NKJV). The phrase signals a turn in the story in which God provided salvation in the middle of His judgment, and verse 10 lists the names of Noah's sons. (See also Genesis 5:32.)

Read the second sentence of Genesis 6:9. Highlight the three words used to describe Noah.

Noah was a righteous man, blameless, and he walked with God. Righteous is usually attributed only to God. (For examples, see Psalm 7:9; 11:7.) But God declared Noah righteous among the wickedness of his day.

God also saw Noah as blameless; especially in light of all the wickedness going on at the time. He could not take the blame for wickedness like those living around him.

Read Genesis 17:1 and Job 1:1. Who are other biblical characters the Bible describes as "blameless"? (See also Deuteronomy 18:13.) We will look at both of these men in later moments with God.

The Bible said Noah walked with God. Read Genesis 5:22 and 24. The Bible describes only Enoch and Noah as men who walked with God. Even Adam and Eve

while in the garden were not described in that way. What do you believe such a description meant in practical terms? Write your answer here:

_____

_____

_____

All we know at the start of this new epoch of history is there was a righteous man with three sons. Evil had corrupted creation. People acted in wickedness and longed to be like gods. God decided to destroy what He had started. The scene looks bleak, and we wait for the next sentence to know how this one man can provide the answer to the problem of evil in the world.

As you close your moment with God today, reflect on the importance of one righteous person in a wicked world. What is your world like today? What role can you play in bringing God's love into it?

_____

_____

## 5.3 The Disease of Corruption

Have you ever had a virus enter your computer or had a hard drive die? What did you have to do to get your computer back to running the way it should? Have you ever had an unwanted plant begin to grow in a garden or flowerbed? What did you do to restore your garden?

Read Genesis 6:11–12. Underline the two descriptions of the earth as God saw it. Write synonyms for each of the words here:

_____

_____

The earth had become corrupt like computer software corrupted by a virus. It no longer worked like its Designer had written it. Violence filled the earth. The "heroes of old" and "men of renown" had become known for their violence instead of for their heroism.

Read Genesis 6:13. Highlight what God told Noah He would destroy and then highlight why He said He would do that.

Like a new code that replaces corrupted computer software, God decided to erase creation in order to re-build it to work like He designed it. We also see in this verse what it looked like for Noah to have "walked with God" (v. 9). God shared His heart and plans with this man who was righteous and blameless. (Jesus called His disciples "friends" because He made known to them everything the Father had revealed—John 15:15.)

Corruption requires restoration, and to restore something often necessitates destroying all or part of the original in order to provide something new or workable in its place. God based His judgment of the condition of people on His original design for them to have fellowship with Him and one another. They, however, had turned to violence and evil and so turned against God. The first family's sins now permeated all of society.

Read Romans 6:23. Underline the wage or payment of sin. Underline the gift of God. Who made that gift possible? Write your answer here:

_____

_____

Sin corrupts our relationship with God and it results in death. The gift that comes through Christ is eternal life or a new code that reconnects us with God and allows us to live as God designed us to live from creation. God's judgment of creation and resulting rescue of Noah lead up to His judgment and rescue of all creation through Christ Jesus.

## 5.4 The Flood and the Covenant

If you grew up going to church, you know the story of Noah and the ark. If you did not go to church in your younger years, you may have heard about the Flood and Noah's boat as one of the many myths of the Bible—if you heard of it at all. Whatever your knowledge or opinion of this story, this ancient episode in history reveals how God provided salvation for those faithful to Him, even while He judged the rest of creation.

Read Genesis 6:14–16. God described in detail the floating zoo Noah would build. The Bible calls it an "ark," not a ship. Note God's specific measurements and design. No one had even imagined the need for such a vessel, much less its design! This four-story tall, rectangular box needed space for animals and buoyancy to float on top of the water.

Read Exodus 2:3. What is the context for this verse? For whom was the pitch-coated vessel made? What are the similarities between Noah and the ark and Moses and the basket?

_____

_____

_____

Read Genesis 6:17. Highlight what God said He would bring to the earth to destroy it.

The word "floodwaters" translates a Hebrew word that uniquely refers to what God did here. (For one possible exception, see Psalm 29:10.) This flood produced more than too much rain for a riverbed. This deluge would destroy all living things except those God preserved. Some believe it was the first rain that fell on the earth. Up until that time, the atmosphere had dense moisture that fully supplied what the earth needed for optimum growth.

Read Genesis 6:18–21. Highlight what God said He would do. What agreement did God make with Noah?

_____

_____

_____

The first use of the word "covenant" in the Story of God is found in verse 18. As we continue to read the bigger Story of God, we will see how this word denotes a special agreement initiated by God through which He chose a person to represent His work to redeem people back to Himself. Other covenants would come in the story, but a "new" covenant would finally come later in Jesus Christ (1 Cor. 11:25).

God provided a way for Noah, his family, and selected creatures to survive His judgment by water. Through a covenant with Noah, God preserved a remnant of His creation in order to restore it to its original design. God always floats grace on the flood of His judgment.

In what ways have you experienced God's grace in the middle of a flood in your life?

## 5.5 Trust and Obey

Faith means obeying God when it does not make sense. The essence of faith is trust. A child trusts a parent's warning not to stick a paperclip into a wall socket because he or she trusts Mom's no, not because Mom explained what 110 volts does to a child's body. Sometimes the difference between a person who follows Jesus and a person who does not follow Him is that the follower actually does what the Trusted One said.

Read Genesis 6:22. This simple statement tells us all about Noah's trust in God. Write some reasons why this verse describes anyone who trusts God.

_____

_____

Noah built a floating zoo for a flood he could not see. He convinced his family to join him in an ark that had never floated. He herded animals and birds into a three-tiered barn with only windows on the top floor. He did "everything" God told him to do—and unlike Moses with God at the burning bush (Ex. 3), we never hear a question or comment from Noah about God's instructions.

Read Hebrews 11:1. Write your own definition of faith from that verse in the space provided.

_____

_____

Faith—always better translated as "trust"—is both the certainty of things we hope for and the evidence of things we do not yet see. This is not based on belief in information or knowledge, but on a person in whom we put our trust. Jesus is the Person in whom we place our ultimate trust.

Read Hebrews 11:7. Highlight why the writer of Hebrews honored Noah.

Noah's trust in God's warning of things he had never seen and his obedient acting out of God's instructions serve as examples for others to trust God. The Bible honored Noah because he acted even when it seemed to make no sense. He obeyed and trusted God with all his life.

What are some things in your life that you have sensed God told you to do when it did not seem logical? When have you obeyed even though you did not fully understand why God wanted you to do something?

_____

_____

_____

**For further study:**
- **Genesis 7:1–9:17; Proverbs 1:7**
- **Romans 2:1–5; 6:23; 2 Peter 2:4–11**

# 6—When Life Falls Apart (Job)

Life is hard. Evil is real. God is love and in control.

The first two realities challenge the truth of the confession about God. People ask, "How can a loving God allow pain and suffering in people He loves?" Some conclude, "God is either not love or not in control because evil and suffering seem to happen everywhere."

In the Story of God people suffer. In the earliest stories God brought pain and death to people because their actions warranted it and went against His purposes. They deserved what they got because either they were wicked or God disciplined them for their ways. But when we observe life, we see that bad things happen to good people. We wonder about the person who loves God, cares for his or her family, and helps others, but loses everything or becomes seriously ill. Why would God allow that person to suffer or die prematurely?

A defining moment with God occurs when you experience pain and suffering and realize God is everything He says He is—loving and in control—and rather than cursing God you find that you love and appreciate Him more than you did before the suffering. Life will fall apart. Who God is and your relationship with Him when that happens will make the difference.

The Memory Verse for this chapter is Job 1:21. It shares the confession of a man who had just lost his family and possessions. Become familiar with it and test your trust in God against its honest faith.

Our question to consider this week is: Where are the devil and his demons? The answer to this comes secondary to the primary lessons in this chapter, but is important to understanding the Adversary.

## 6.1 Upright but not Trouble Free

You have a picture in your mind of people who have made it or who exemplify a model life. As the cliché goes they are "healthy, wealthy, and wise." They have cute children, a big house, and popularity with others.

Read Job 1:1–5. Describe the main character of the story, Job, in the space below. What were the characteristics of his life? Would you like to have everything Job had?

_____

_____

_____

While we do not know who wrote the Book of Job or when it was written, this story addresses one of the biggest problems of faith: Why does God allow or seemingly cause good people to suffer? Job's story gives an answer, and it is worthy of consideration because Job had the kind of life most people want to have, yet God allowed him to suffer greatly.

The story begins like any good story, "In the land of Uz there lived a man whose name was Job." We immediately learn that our main character is "blameless and upright; he feared God and shunned evil" (v. 1).

Who else lived blameless? Look up Genesis 6:9, and write your answer here:_____
Who was considered "upright in heart?" Look up 1 Kings 3:6, and write his name here:_____

Job was in good biblical company. We read Job also feared God. What does Psalm 111:10 and Proverbs 1:7 say about the fear of the LORD? Write the two words in the blanks. The fear of the Lord is the beginning of . . .

_____ and _____.

Job refused to do evil. He was very wealthy and considered "the greatest man among all the people of the East" (v. 3). Job was also a religious man. He had so much concern for his faith that he covered for his children by offering sacrifices after their feasts just to make sure they were seen as right before God (v. 5). Job had it all and respected God and His ways. We tend to equate all of that with God's favor, and while the Bible teaches God blesses those who serve Him God's favor does not necessarily guarantee our comfort.

What or who in your life points to God's blessings toward you? Write a brief prayer of praise to God for these things and people.

_____

_____

_____

## 6.2 Upright and Tested

Who is greater, God or Satan? Can Satan do things God does not allow him to do? The next scene in the opening pages of Job may cause someone to ask these questions and others. In this story, God and Satan discuss whether or not Job would curse God if Satan took everything from him. It seems odd for God to make such a deal with the one who from the beginning of time has tried to keep God's creation from loving Him.

Read Job 1:6–12. What are some initial questions raised by this passage? Write those questions here:

_____

_____

The scene changed from earth (Job's situation) to a heavenly location where "the angels came to present themselves before the Lord" (v. 6). Satan was among the created order of angels. Satan is neither above the angels nor equal with God. Satan, like Adam, chose to rebel against God rather than submit to Him. Note that Satan did not speak until God addressed him.

What does verse 7 say about Satan's activities?

_____

Read verse 8. Highlight God's question to Satan.

God was in control. God knew Satan's heart distrusted not only God but also God's creatures' love for Him. God brought up Job, not Satan. Why? Satan perceived that those who love God did so only because God was good to them. God's motive may have focused more on seeking to redeem Satan by showing him a love without props than to test Job.

It is possible that God sought to show Satan a kind of love in Job that resembled the love He felt toward people who would kill His Son. Yes, the story answers the question of suffering in our lives, but it also demonstrates God's love toward all His creatures. Jesus washed Judas' feet and died for those who hung Him on the cross. God echoed the opening description of Job when He spoke to Satan.

Read Job 1:9–11. What was Satan's challenge to God?

_____

_____

Satan was cynical and did not believe anyone could love without props. Satan accused Job of having artificial faith because he had everything anyone would want. Satan challenged that no one can love God when things go bad.

Read verse 12. Underline what God gave Satan permission to do. Note that Satan can do only what God gives him permission to do. The Evil One does not have the freedom to inflict trouble on whomever he desires, but when allowed, he hurries to the opportunity. God limited Satan's infliction to Job's possesions, not Job.

## 6.3 Job's 9–11

I remember my youngest daughter calling to me from our living room, "Daddy, come here. They think a plane has flown into the World Trade Center." We had stood at the top of the Twin Towers the summer before on family vacation, so this caught her attention. As we watched, a second plane plowed into the second building. You know the rest of the story.

That morning as I drove my daughter to school she asked if we were safe. The words that blurted out of my mouth were, "We live in the strongest nation on earth, and our God is bigger than any enemy. We'll be OK." Without saying a word, she opened the door and went into the school building and into an uncertain future. How did you answer the questions others asked you on that day? Where is God when the unexpected happens? Write some of your thoughts here:

_____

_____

_____

Job found himself in a personal 9–11 day when four different servants crashed into his life with terrible news about his family and property.

Read Job 1:13–19. Highlight the losses he experienced that day.

Job suffered devastating loss that day. He not only lost his children, he lost all that produced wealth in his life. Foreigners cleaned him out of animals and workers. That day, Job essentially experienced what someone would have felt to have had his or her entire family in the Twin Towers on September 11, 2001. How does someone respond to such a reality?

Read Job 1:20. Underline the three things Job did in response to the news of his loss.

Job acted out the cultural signs of mourning—he tore his robe and shaved his head—and then he fell to the ground and worshiped God (v. 20). We would expect the first two, but the third comes only from those who trust God completely no matter what happens.

Read verse 21. Summarize Job's prayer in the space below. What does his prayer say about his faith? Write your answer after you summarize the prayer.

_____

_____

_____

_____

Verse 22 brings an end to the first episode between Satan and Job. The writer said that Job did not sin because he did not blame God or curse God for what had happened.

On a scale of one to 10, one being the most likely to blame and curse God and 10 being the least likely to blame and curse God, how would you grade yourself?

## 6.4 What Do You Value Most?

What are the four most valuable things in your life that you least want to lose? Rank them in order of value, with four being the least and one being the most valuable. Write your list here:

1._____

2._____

3._____

4._____

Imagine a friend had the same list and lost everything on it in an unpredictable tragedy. What would you tell him or her? What Scriptures or prayers would you offer to console and give meaning to what had happened?

_____

Read Job 2:1–3. This scene resembles the one in Job 1:1–2. Highlight what God said differently about Job in this dialogue.

God honored Job by saying he had kept his integrity although God had allowed Satan to ruin him without cause. Note again that Satan did only what God allowed, not anything he wanted to do.

Read Job 2:4–6. Underline what Satan said Job would do if he took away his health. Underline God's response.

Before we observe Job's response to Satan's inflictions, we have to ask why would God let Satan do this? God may have allowed Job's suffering to demonstrate selfless love for another person—in this case Job's love for God. Job's love toward God modeled God's love for His creation. Satan had refused such a love.

Read Job 2:7–9. Underline his wife's response to all of this. Grief and despair had taken over her heart. She felt Job had every right to curse God now. Have you come to that place before?

Read verse 10. How did Job respond? What does this tell you about his trust in God? Have you ever faced such dire conditions and said the same?

## 6.5 Hard Questions

Hard times can drive even the most faithful person to question God. Pain, without times of relief, can weaken one's resolve to continue. Job's three friends feebly tried to console him by offering explanations for his troubles. While Job defended himself, he never questioned God. Finally, when God had enough of their weak explanations for what happened, He revealed Himself to Job.

Read Job 38:1–11. What was the point in God asking Job such questions?

_____

_____

_____

God asked unanswerable questions to establish that while He may have not looked in control, He was. God guides all that happens in creation. Chapters 38–41 record God's words. Spend some time this week reading and reviewing God's extended challenge to Job.

When God completed His soliloquy, Job responded. Read Job's words in Job 42:1–6. Summarize his reply.

_____

_____

After hearing God, Job could do nothing but submit. Read Isaiah 6:5. This verse records Isaiah's response upon seeing the presence of God in the Temple. Hearing about God is one thing. Experiencing His presence is another. When God reveals Himself, people can only respond with submission. Job marveled at the greatness of God and spoke praise to God like all who claim to know His ways do.

God scolded Job's three friends for their poor answers to Job. God required them to sacrifice a burnt offering and then He would accept Job's prayer for them (Job 42:7–9).

Read Job 42:10–17. How did Job's suffering end? God blessed "the latter part of Job's life more than the first" (v. 12), and Job died "old and full of years" (v. 17).

Although the story of Job ends seemingly with "and they all lived happily ever after," the point is not that God will always turn bad situations into good ones, but that God always accomplishes His purposes. God chose to restore Job just as God allowed Satan to afflict him.

God is sovereign. God is ultimately in control of all that happens, and His will is mysterious . . . yet purposeful. Those who view life from this side of heaven can only trust Sovereign God. Any speculation of ultimate cause will fall short.

How has your perspective changed after observing Job's encounter with God and suffering? Write your faith statements here:

_____

_____

_____

**For further study:**
- **James 1:2–4; Job 42:1–10**
- **Romans 5:1–11; 1 Peter 5:8–9**

## 7—Following God's Call (Abraham, Part 1 of 3)

Trust is following someone to a place you would not go to on your own. If you are married, you may have had to trust your spouse's desire to move believing that the move was best for your family. You may have never moved before, but your loving trust for your spouse gave you the courage to take the family to another place. This ended up opening avenues of growth for all of you.

One way God accomplishes His purposes is by calling people. His-story consists of many episodes of God invading peoples' lives in the form of a call that disrupted their status quo but opened up an adventure never dreamed of by those called. God broke into Abraham's life to invite him to go to a land and to form a people God would make His own. One day, Abraham had to trust God enough to load up his family and belongings. He left for the land of promise in order to learn what God had in store for him.

Abram, later called Abraham, came onto the biblical stage at a difficult time in human history (Gen. 11). Like today, it was a time when people cared for themselves over God, but God would not give up on those He loved. This is where our faith hero's story begins.

The Memory Verse for this chapter is Hebrews 11:8. Abraham was the Father of Faith because when God called he went, "even though he did not know where he was going."

Our question to consider this week is: How would you respond if you knew God wanted you to move to a foreign land to serve Him? While God's call on a person's life does not always include this, it could. How you respond gives evidence of your trust in God as your Leader.

## 7.1 Who Do You Trust?

One summer I worked at a conference center in New Mexico located near a national forest. Within the forest stood a cave that other staffers had explored. Some of them invited me to join them on their next excursion. I had no experience spelunking because there was no such thing as a cave on the coast of Texas where I lived. As I got on my stomach to follow a fellow staffer through a tunnel not much wider than my body I wondered if my trust in him was well founded. I did make it through the passage and soon stood in a cavern. It was like nothing I had ever seen. My trust in my guide yielded an underground memory I still enjoy today.

When was the last time you trusted someone to take you somewhere you would not have gone on you own?

_____

_____

Read Genesis 12:1. Highlight the verbs that describe what God wanted Abram to do. The words "leave" and "go" challenge any of us who feels comfortable.

Write in the space below your initial response if God told you to do the same thing as He told Abram.

_____

_____

_____

Along with calling Abram to leave his home and go to a land God would show him, God made several promises to Abram. Read verses 2–3. List the seven promises here:

_____

_____

_____

God did not invite Abram into the saga of salvation without revealing to him the ways God would bless him. God showed Abram how He would use him to bless all the nations of the earth. Abram would step into a story bigger than he could have imagined. He would become a great nation. Those who blessed him would be blessed and those who cursed him would be cursed. The call included purpose and promise, but Abram had a choice to make. This divine invitation would test how much he trusted and loved God.

End this moment with God by praying about some of your hesitations about what God may call you to do. There is only one Abram, but God still calls us to trust Him with all we have and do. To state your reservations up front may allow God to provide answers before He calls you to trust Him more than ever before.

## 7.2 Faith Exhibited

When I was a boy we lived in Pensacola, Florida. The house sat off from a bayou and trees filled the lot from the house to the water. I remember watching a home movie later. I would climb onto a lower limb of one of the trees and jump into the arms of my father. He would catch me, set me on the ground, and I would climb back up the tree and repeat the process. I realized how much I trusted my father to jump into his arms without flinching, and I saw how much he loved me.

Much later as an adult I learned from that picture the difference between belief and trust. I could have sat on that limb and believed my father would catch me. However, I did not trust my father until I pushed off the limb and let gravity hurl me to the earth. The difference between belief and trust is action. You cannot say you believe in God without eventually doing something to demonstrate your trust in Him.

In the space below, describe an incident when you experienced an act of trust in someone. What lessons did you learn about trusting God?

_____

_____

Read Genesis 12:4 and underline the first three words of the verse. Those three words describe faith in action. One day Abram had to demonstrate his trust in God's word by packing up his family and moving to the land God promised. "So Abram left . . ." are words of faith.

Abram was 75 years old when he left. Abram took his family and all his possessions to Canaan, the land God promised him. Like Noah, who had to convince his family that getting into the ark was the sane thing to do, Abram had to gather his family and lead them to a place where only God knew the location. They arrived with

everyone and everything intact, but the story had only just begun. Abram trusted God and left home. Now he would learn what being blessed was all about.

Read Hebrews 11:8. Underline the three verbs of the sentence. Abram when "called," "obeyed" and "went." This is the pattern of faith: a call, obedience (doing what called to do), and action. Not until you do something have you answered God's call. Highlight the last phrase of the verse. How does this phrase add to your understanding of faith as demonstrated by Abram?

_____

_____

## 7.3 Blessings with Problems

Famine results from overcrowding in some countries today. Too many people trying to live off limited resources reduces the potential for food and housing.
In order to protect what little they have available, groups

join together to keep others from taking their resources. Wars often start this way. What countries come to mind when you read of "famine and wars"? What is being done to help?

Today's moment with God focuses on conflict brought on by God's blessings and people's natural tendency to protect and care for their own at the expense of others.

Read Genesis 13:1–2. Genesis 12:10–20 gives the background for how Abram and his family came to Egypt. To avoid potential conflict Abram lied and told the Egyptians that Sarai was his sister instead of his wife. The scheme worked and after some years he arrived in the desert of the Negev as a wealthy man. God chose a person with weak character but a trusting heart to lead His covenant people. Compare Abram's character with that of Noah in Genesis 6:9. What are the differences between the two chosen men? What does this say about God's choice of those He called to lead?

Read Genesis 13:3. If you have access to a Bible dictionary or maps in the back of your Bible, trace Abram's trek from Egypt to Bethel.

This was no short trip. Abram had exchanged his sedentary life in Ur for the life of a wandering herdsman. Famine drove him past Canaan to Egypt, but after conditions changed, he moved his entire estate back to where God had first sent him. The background for what happened (v. 4) is found in Genesis 12:8–9. How did Abram respond when he returned to the place God had given him?

Genesis 13:5–7 describes the problems between Abram

and Lot's tribes caused by overcrowding. "The land could not support them" (v. 6) and "quarreling arose" between the two groups (v. 7). The Bible also mentions two other groups that lived in the area. Who were they?

_____ and _____

The conditions caused by overcrowding plague many countries today and have led to famine and wars. This was the downside of God's blessing on Abram and Lot.

What have you done to participate in meeting the needs of poorer nations around the world? What organizations do you know of whose goal is to stand on the front lines of these problems? Other than prayer, what can you do to involve others in meeting these needs?

## 7.4 Resolving Conflict

There are two simple ways to end a quarrel. One way is to fight until the stronger party gets his or her way. (The strong prefer this way.) The other is for one of the parties to give up his or her claim of ownership and allow the other party to make the choice that will end the conflict. This is the way of a Christ follower (John 10:11–18) and becomes an option only when you trust God to work out His purposes no matter what the other person chooses.

Remember the last quarrel you had with someone. How did it end? What did you do personally to resolve it? Do you still need to reconcile that relationship?

Read Genesis 13:8–9. Summarize Abram's offer to Lot

to end the quarrel between them in the space below.

_____

_____

Abram had confidence in the covenant call of God on his life and offered Lot any of the promised land he chose. Abram would accept what was left and trust God to do the rest. Abram called Lot his "brother" although they were not literally brothers but related (Gen. 11:27–31). The sense of family extended to all relatives, not just immediate family. We begin to see an understanding of tribe and nation in God's Story.

Read Genesis 13:10–12. Why did Lot chose the land he did? Like Eve who saw the fruit as "pleasing to the eye" (Gen. 3:6), Lot saw the beauty of the "plain of the Jordan" River region and chose to live there. The writer also gave two clues of inherent dangers in Lot's choice.

Read verses 10 and 13. What cities were in the region where Lot settled and what was the moral condition of those who lived in Sodom?

_____

_____

Abram and Lot parted ways. Lot chose what looked like the best choice and Abram took what remained. Abram trusted God's promise above what he saw as the best place to live. We will soon see how Lot's choice turned out to be the less profitable of the two.
Read verses 14–17. Highlight the words God used

to affirm His promise to Abram.

Read verse 18. Underline Abram's response to God's words. He moved his tents to the place God had given. He built an altar of worship when he arrived. Obedience followed by worship is the lifestyle of a person of faith.

Abram trusted God's promise and allowed Lot to choose wherever he would like to live in order to resolve the conflict between their families. God affirmed His promise to Abram, and Abram moved his family and set up an altar of worship to the God who called him and continued to guide him. Abram built altars on his journey for God to mark those times when God affirmed His call on his life (Gen. 12:7–8).

Reflect on a time you felt a sense of worship because God affirmed His call and provided for you. What were the circumstances? How did God speak to you? How did you respond?

## 7.5 Go Where?

One Christmas vacation my family traveled to see Colonial Williamsburg in Virginia. The living history of the community posed the question, "What would I have done if I lived back then?" Since only two percent of the population as landed gentry could vote and make laws, I would most likely not have had a choice. I tried to put myself in their places and wonder if I would join the revolution against England as a patriot or remain loyal to the king. If I were the governor's rector of the parish church, for example, I know I would have had a moral dilemma on my hands. What would you have done if you had to choose between loyalty to the king and war that would ultimately bring freedom?

_____

_____

Abram's decision to remain in Ur or to follow God into the land of Canaan had similar implications for him and his family. He, like the first revolutionaries, had to choose between what he had always known and a place he had never gone before.

Our question to consider this week was: How would you respond if you knew God wanted you to move to a foreign land to serve Him? Write your answer here:

_____

_____

_____

When the writer of the Book of Hebrews looked back to describe the heroes of the faith, he chose Abraham as an example of one who trusted God wholly. Look again at Hebrews 11:8. What were the three verbs of that verse that described Abraham's faith? What phrase described his complete trust in God?

Read Hebrews 11:9. How is Abraham described? Isaac and Jacob are two of his descendants. Highlight how the Bible describes them.

When you live in faith like Abraham you may feel like

"aliens and strangers" (Heb. 11:13; 1 Pet. 2:11). This brings uncertainty and feelings of unacceptance among your neighbors. Your family feels the same way because they do not belong in local society. But, you tolerate this because you know you are doing what God wants.

Read Hebrews 11:10. Underline what Abraham looked forward to while living in the land of promise.

Remember that faith is "being sure of what we hope for and certain of what we do not see" (Heb. 11:1).

Abraham never actually saw "the city with foundations," the physical completion of God's call, but he lived with the assurance of God's call and the conviction that what was not yet present would become a reality.

Why was he able to do that? Underline the reason for Abraham's faith. God was the "architect and builder" of this "city," or reality. Abraham lived like an alien in a foreign land without seeing what God had promised, but he did this because he trusted God who was the designer and builder of the promise He had made.

Return to the question we considered for this week and write or say a prayer to God, verbalizing the possibility of going to another place based on Abraham's example of faith.

**For further study:**
- **Psalm 16; 56:3–3**
- **John 14**

## 8—Trust God or Trust Yourself (Abraham, Part 2 of 3)

The danger in trying too hard at something is to push beyond what is effective to do what you want to do. For example, you cannot float on water without remaining still. A golfer performs a swing best at rest rather than powering through the ball. You cannot hurry T'ai Chi, yoga, or bread rising for Thanksgiving dinner. The story of God unfolds according to the Author's timing, not when or how we want the plot to turn. You and I have been taught to create our own realities and to make things happen. We live in a self-empowered world, which insists that we solve problems and create solutions. To trust God to direct our part in His-story requires patience and willingness to wait on our Director to call the shots.

Abraham and Sarah tried to force the timing of God's script for their lives, and they created a mess for generations to come. Yet, God stayed true to His-storyline and gave them the child necessary to fulfill His promise to them. In this defining moment with God, watch out for your own impatience and desire to help God.

The Memory Verse for this chapter is Genesis 15:6. Abraham trusted God, and God considered him "righteous." A person can receive no greater accolade than for the Author of the Great Story to declare him or her "righteous." This verse echoes throughout the Bible's revelation of God's Story as the foundation for our relationship with God.

Our question to consider this week is: Can a person who trusts God daily still make big mistakes? God's choice of those He invites into His-story remains a mystery. One aspect of that mystery is that the majority of those He chooses to play a major role have a character flaw of some kind. They are like us! We will reconsider this question after we observe Abraham's trust-filled journey with God.

## 8.1 The Function of Doubt

Doubt keeps faith hopping. Doubt can drive you back to the one who made the promise, or it can cause you to check yourself to see if you are up to the task. Doubt is not the opposite of faith; like a new operating system it can serve as the platform for deeper faith. Yes, it can force you to trust another. But if allowed to work in the context of relationship, distrust can give the one you trust opportunities to prove worthy for trust.

Read Genesis 15:1. Summarize God's word to Abram in the vision. (See also Psalms 18:2, 20, 24, and 30.) If you have time, read Genesis 14 to understand the context of this verse.

_____

_____

_____

Read Genesis 15:2–3. Summarize Abram's response to God's promise. What had God not done that Abram knew was essential for God's words to come about?

_____

_____

_____

Highlight the name of the person Abram thought would be his heir. What attitude did Abram seem to have as he spoke to God? Have you ever felt that way toward God?

Genesis 15:4–5 records God's response to Abram. Read Genesis 12:1–3 to recall God's first promise to Abram. What did God tell Abram this time about the size of His promise? What did God say concerning Abram's heir?

_____

_____

God came to Abram after he had rescued Lot (Gen. 14:11–16) and encountered the King of Salem, Melchizedek (Gen. 14:18–20). (See also Psalms 110 and Hebrews 5 for how later writers understood this priest and Christ's connection to him.) God declared He was Abram's Protector and Reward. Abram responded with, "Yes, I know, but there's still one part of this deal I don't get. Right now, my slave from Damascus will get all my stuff and Your promise. So, am I right in assuming a servant and not a son will get my inheritance?" Abram doubted God's promise based on what he could see and what he knew. God, however, had a different perspective. The Author and Director of the story answered Abram's doubt and said that he would have a son and his descendants would be as numerous as the stars in the sky.

Read Genesis 15:6. Underline Abram's response and what God did in light of his action.

Abram trusted God's promise, and God declared him as righteous. Faith (best translated, "trust") and righteousness are core concepts in our relationship with God. Only God can credit our trust in Him as righteousness, and that credit is the only amount that balances our account with God. (See Romans 4 and James 2:23–26 for the New Testament's use of this passage.)

End your moment with God by confessing any doubts you may have toward God's promises to you. Take time to listen to God's response.

## 8.2 Fixing Things?

Sometimes we think our efforts will help when they actually hurt situations, or at best complicate them. Have you ever impatiently stepped into a situation to fix it only to discover you did not have all the information and your help only made things worse? When was the last time you did such a thing? What would you do differently today?

_____

_____

_____

Read Genesis 16:1–2. How did Sarai propose to fix to her childless condition? Underline her proposition.

Sarai offered her maid to her husband. This solution was legal and logical. It was legal because she gave Hagar to be Abram's wife, making any offspring of that union heir to his possessions and promise. It was logical because Sarai was "past the age of childbearing" (Gen. 18:11) and the couple needed a child in order to have descendants that numbered the stars in the sky. Her answer to the problem even fit within God's promise that "a son coming from your own body will be your heir" (Gen. 15:4). You would think a legal and logical solution in line with your interpretation of God's words to solve a problem would be acceptable to God. In matters of faith, however, sometimes

even those do not fit what God had planned. Our impatience complicates rather than serves His will.

Read Genesis 16:3–4a. How did Abram respond to his wife's suggestion? Underline the results of his response.

Abram agreed to the plan. Not only did it make sense to him, but we know from his experience in Egypt that he would rather avoid conflict than face the consequences of doing the right thing. Like Adam who did not question Eve's suggestion to eat the forbidden fruit, Abram did not refuse Sarai's solution to the problem of no heir.

Read Genesis 16:4–6. The couple's idea worked, but their relationships suffered. List each character's response to the situation in the space below.

Sarai_____

Abram _____

Hagar _____

Sarai became jealous when Hagar became pregnant. Sarai began to mistreat her, and she blamed Abram! Then Abram, who accepted Sarai's suggestion and followed through with it, turned the blame back on his wife and said, "Your servant is in your hands. Do with her whatever you think best" (v. 6). Sarai mistreated Hagar more, and Hagar fled the chaos into the desert.

The plan of God now looked more like a Friday episode of a soap opera than a precise strategic plan unfolding before the reader. The fix to the problem resulted in a child but not an heir for God's promise.

Pause and write a lesson you have learned from this incident in God's Story. Who would you be most like in the story? How would you respond differently if you had another chance? What might you be trying to resolve that given time and trust in God could bring about a solution?

_____

_____

## 8.3 What's in a Name

Your name means something. To change your name means even more. I know of a woman who came out of such a horrible family origin that she chose to change her complete identity. After Christ rescued her from her dark past, she changed her given name and secured all new legal documents to reflect her new identity in Christ. Her new name told the story of how Jesus found her, defeated the dark influences in her life, and set her on a new path as His adopted child. What story lies behind your name? It may not be as dramatic as the one told here, but it has meaning for those who gave it to you and for you today.

Thirteen years after Ishmael's birth, God came again to Abram. Read Genesis 17:1–2. God initially made His covenant with Abram when God's chosen one asked how he could know that he would gain possession of God's promise (Gen. 15:8). God made a covenant with Abram.

Read Genesis 15:9–17 and summarize the process here:

_____

God "made a covenant" with Abram, and His binding word was that Abram and his descendants would inhabit the land God showed him (Gen. 15:18–21). This was a grace-filled act toward His chosen servant in order to complete God's Story of redemption for all people. Now with Ishmael on the scene, Abram may have wondered about God's promise to him. God came to Abram again to confirm this covenant with him and to assure him that He is always faithful to complete His promises.

Read Genesis 17:3–5. Abram responded in worship to God upon hearing His voice again and God's confirmation of His covenant with him. Highlight the two things God did for Abram.

First, God reminded Abram he would be the father of many nations, and then God changed his name to Abraham as a reminder of God's promise. Abram means, "exalted father." God renamed him Abraham, which means, "the father of many."

Read Genesis 17:6–8. God expanded His covenant by establishing it as an "everlasting covenant" with Abraham and his descendants (v. 7). God made an everlasting covenant with Noah (Gen. 9:16) and would make a similar one with King David (2 Sam. 23:5). God would complete His-story of rescue for all people through His covenants. Jesus is the "new covenant" through which God fulfilled His promise to rescue us from sin's destruction. God changed Abram's name to Abraham, and He later changed Sarai's name to Sarah (Gen. 17:15). The new names signified the certainty of God's promise.

Read Revelation 2:17. Take time to thank God that He cared enough for you that He already chose a new name for you, which you will receive in heaven.

## 8.4 When God Makes You Laugh

Christians smile because they know the punch line to life. They know that Christ, their King, has already won the war and that Satan, the Enemy, burns in the end. All the evil that rages now is but a series of skirmishes by a desperate army who knows their days are numbered.

Genuine laughter is eternity breaking into the temporal. We laugh because we have an eternal perspective in this life and we own a hope that displaces worry and anxiety about ultimate matters. God continually gives us reason to laugh. We see things happen that should not, given what we know and have seen before. God works in such strange ways we can only laugh and continue to trust Him. Sometimes God works in a miracle. Other times He works in the ordinary forms of life. When was the last time God made you laugh by life's unexpected turn? What were the circumstances? Who was involved? Who did you tell? Read Genesis 21:1–2. Highlight how God was

"gracious" to Sarah.

God completed His promise to Sarah by giving her the son He had promised. Although she had tried to help God out by giving Hagar to Abraham, God looked past her sin of anxiousness. He graced her with a son to be the first descendent of the covenant. God gave him to her "at the very time God had promised him"(v. 2). (See also Genesis 18:10.)

Read Genesis 21:3–4. What two things did Abraham do for his new son? Write your answers here:

_____

_____

Abraham named his son Isaac, which means, "he laughs." Sarah explained why the name was appropriate.

Read 21:6–7 for Sarah's reason behind Isaac's name. The humor of a woman her age and a man 100 years old (v. 5) having a child was absurdly ridiculous. Anyone would laugh if you had told him or her the couple would have a child at their age. But that is exactly what had happened. Genesis 18:1–15 tells the story of Sarah's laughter at the message she would become pregnant. Abraham had laughed earlier at the same news (Gen. 17:17). The entire idea was laughable, but God chose to work that way in order to show everyone it was His doing and not the wishes or work of Abraham and Sarah.

The second thing Abraham did for his son was to circumcise him, the physical sign of God's covenant. God gave Abraham instructions for this process so that the male members of Abraham's descendants would be set apart in the world (Gen. 17:9–14). This mark signified God's grace toward them and their chosen status with God. Sons would carry this mark as evidence of their belonging to the covenant people of God.

Abraham named his son Laughter, or Isaac, because the impossibility of his birth made it funny to think of the possibility. However, God fulfilled His covenant promise to Abraham and Sarah in this absurd way to show His power and the faithfulness of His words to His chosen ones.

## 8.5 Who Will God Use?

Our question to consider for this chapter was: Can a person who trusts God daily still make big mistakes? In the space below, write your response based on the episodes in this part of the Story of God.

_____

_____

The story of Abraham and Sarah and their decision to help God tells us the answer to our question is yes! The couple made a huge mistake by trying to provide an heir for God's blessing promised to them. Ishmael resulted from their mistake of trying by their own effort to solve a problem only God could solve. Their sin was impatience. Their mistake was gaining an heir through their ingenuity rather than through the work of God.

Although Abraham eventually brought Ishmael into his family and circumcised him, Ishmael's descendants "lived in hostility toward all their brothers" (Gen. 25:18). Yes, God responded to Abraham's request that his son by Hagar live under God's blessing by making Ishmael the father of a great nation (Gen. 17:20), but God's covenant resided with Isaac. Ishmael would always live as the step-son to the promises of God.

We will see other characters in the Story of God who will trust God yet make mistakes. You may recall King David's adulterous affair with the wife of one of his generals and his son's mistake of marrying women who brought their religion with them. The cycle of the kings who followed David and Solomon illustrate trust in God in the middle of poor or disobedient decisions. What was the constant in all of this? God's faithfulness to His covenant, not the perfection of His people, allowed the Story of God to continue unhindered. We can all rest in the truth that the completion of the Story has more to do with who God is than what we do.

Take some time to evaluate your trust in God and the mistakes you have made that have caused trouble for others. Thank God for His covenant love He shows you through Christ and seek to trust Him above your solutions to life's problems.

**For further study:**
• **Genesis 14–17; 21:11–21**
• **Galatians 4:21–31; Hebrews 11:11–12**

## 9—Taking Faith to the Altar (Abraham, Part 3 of 3)

Jesus told a story about a man who found a treasure in the field he was plowing (Matt. 13:44). It had so much value that he covered it back up, sold all he had, and bought the field so he could have the treasure. Jesus told the story to show us that when we finally realize what a treasure it is to belong to Him, we would sell everything for it. But what if you already owned the treasure and God told you to sell it? We understand giving something up to get something of greater value. But what if you have what you think is the greatest treasure and God tells you to sell that?

Our defining moment with God will challenge the love of a parent for a child and a saint's trust in God. It will take us to a mountain of sacrifice where God tests the heart of humanity. We continue our reading of God's stories with Abraham, but this episode includes a climactic event that will have ramifications throughout all of His-story. Prepare to answer the question, "Would I give up my most valued possession or relationship in order to do what God has told me to do?" Be careful how you answer. Abraham, our hero of faith, thought he had done everything to gain God's blessing in his life before the events in this chapter unfolded.

The Memory Verse for this chapter is Hebrews 11:17. Abraham exhibited a trust in God few of us will ever be asked to do. For this reason, centuries later the writers of faith included him in their examples of how we all should trust God.

Our question to consider this week is: Do you think God asks us to do things that are just too difficult? You will learn the answer to this question as you walk through these events with God and Abraham.

## 9.1 A Call in the Night

I serve as a volunteer chaplain for our city's police and fire departments. Several times a year my phone rings in the middle of the night. The call startles me from my sleep, and I struggle to become alert enough to answer the phone and write down the information. Phone calls from dispatch in the night never carry good news. These calls mean an officer or firefighter has requested a chaplain to come to the scene of a death, fatal accident, or fire, or to make a death notification, console a grieving family member, or assist an officer with a family situation. Calls in the night usually mean something out of the ordinary has happened.

Abraham was asleep when God called him in the night. Life had begun to play out like he had hoped it would. Isaac had been born and was growing into a strong young man (Gen. 21:1–7). Ishmael and Hagar were gone from the family's camp (Gen. 21:8–21), and Abraham settled into the land he had chosen (Gen. 21:22–34). Everything was in place for God's promises to become a reality, but like a call from dispatch at two o'clock in the morning God's call would change Abraham's expectations for tomorrow.

Read Genesis 22:1–2. Underline God's command to Abraham. Note how God described Isaac to his father.

"Take your son . . . go to the region of Moriah . . . sacrifice him there." These words rang in Abraham's head as God left him. God acknowledged that Isaac was Abraham's only son whom he loved. The Author and Director of the Story asked the main character to sacrifice the one we all know as the next star.

Why would God make such a request? Read the first words of verse 1 again. Fill in the blank:

God _____ Abraham.

God tested Abraham's trust in Him by His command. Abraham had failed to trust God completely three other times: he lied calling Sarah his sister when he went to Egypt (Gen. 12:10–13), he agreed to Sarah's plan to have a son by Hagar (Gen. 16:1–2), and he lied to Abimelech calling Sarah his sister and not his wife (Gen. 20:1–2). Like Jesus who restored Peter by asking him as many times to confess his devotion to Him as Peter denied Jesus, God gave Abraham a test to hone his heart to trust in God completely.

A mystery of our relationship with God is that He orchestrates or allows tests to strengthen our trust in Him (Jas. 1:2–4). These tests like the one for Abraham seem unreasonable and contrary to our understanding of God. (For example, God condemned taking human life from the beginning, but here He asked Abraham to kill his son in order to test him.) But like so much in the Story of God, the importance lies in God's storyline instead of our understanding.

What was the last call in the night for you? Did it become a test of your trust in God? How did the events that followed change your perspective on life and your concept of God?

_____

_____

_____

## 9.2 Difficult Obedience

Obedience is to act without hesitation or excuse. An obedient child freezes in his tracks when his mother cries, "Stop!" in a crowded parking lot. An obedient quarterback runs the coach's call in the last minutes of the game even though he has a better play in mind. In matters of faith, obedience is what turns belief into trust. In the Story of God, obedience separates saints from sinners.

Read Genesis 22:3–5. Highlight the first four words of verse 3. What does this phrase tell you about Abraham's trust in God?

_____

_____

At the break of day Abraham got up and loaded up all he needed to obey God's call in the night. Then for three days he traveled to where God told him to sacrifice his son. Was God punishing him for what he had done wrong? How could God accomplish the covenant if Abraham killed his son? Abraham may have asked along the way, "But I love my son. How could God want to take from me something I love so much?"

Verse 5 gives us a clue to his trust in God. He told his servants "we" will worship and "we" will come back to you. He trusted God would provide in some other way than what he could see at the time. It had happened before. God had Isaac in His plan even as Ishmael grew up in the camp.

Read Genesis 22:6–7. Underline what Abraham took with him to worship. What did Isaac ask his father?

_____

Wood, fire, and a knife were needed to sacrifice an offering. Isaac carried the wood, and Abraham carried the knife to kill and the fire to consume the sacrifice. Isaac was smart enough to know that they needed an animal to worship God, and he had avoided the obvious question until now. "Father" must have made Abraham cringe. He knew his son now knew the dilemma they faced. His son's question, "where is the lamb?" cut to the heart of Abraham. He had to tell his son the truth.

"Where is the lamb for the burnt offering?" offered more than a question for a boy to understand his father's actions. It is the question for the ages. "Where is the lamb?" is the question that sums up the entire Old Testament. "Where is the lamb?" begs the answer, "Jesus, the Christ," of the New Testament. The answer to Isaac's question becomes the song of eternity:

**Yahweh – Divine Encounters** in the Old Testament

"Worthy is the Lamb, who was slain, to receive power and wealth and wisdom and strength and honor and glory and praise!" (Rev. 5:12).

Read verse 8. Summarize Abraham's answer to his son.

_____

_____

Abraham had come to trust that God had a plan and whether or not he could figure out the next step, God would provide whatever he needed to complete that plan. Abraham's confession was the basis of his trust: "God himself will provide the lamb for the burnt offering"—and for the final sacrifice that would make people forever right with their Creator.

## 9.3 Life on the Altar

Altars are platforms for worship. We build them in response to God's call or God's acts that draw us to worship Him. What we put on an altar reveals the depth of our trust and love for God. An empty altar is an oxymoron: it presents an object of worship with nothing to offer God. An altar with our most prized possession gives evidence of our true worship of God. Only when we place on the altar what we love most do we truly worship and trust God.

Read Genesis 22:9. Highlight the four things Abraham did when "they reached the place God had told him about." Each detail was an act of faith that brought Abraham closer to offering his son as a sacrifice to God.

Abraham first built an altar. Abraham built altars of worship throughout his relationship with God. This altar served a different purpose, because in the past Abraham had built altars to worship God for His promises. This time Abraham built an altar to worship God with His promise. Abraham could have stopped here, but he then put the wood on the altar. The next step proved the hardest. He bound his son and placed him on the wood to sacrifice him as an offering to God.

Read verse 10 and circle what Abraham did. His resolve was complete. No voice from God, no lightning from the sky, no one else on the hill but Abraham and his son. This must truly be what God wanted, so Abraham prepared to take his only son's life.

Read verses 11–12. In the space below, describe what happened and what God said to Abraham.

_____

_____

_____

God called Abraham as his hand was midair. Abraham obeyed, and God spared his son. Abraham built an altar and placed upon it his only son whom he loved deeply. God saw his obedience, his willingness to do anything God told him to do. Abraham passed the test.

Have you ever come to the point where you have placed your most loved person or possession on the altar of sacrifice? It still may seem like an absurd request by God, but if you have built that altar and placed your loved one on it, you know the trust in God it takes to place him or her there. This is the ultimate test of your trust in God. Take time to meditate on the biblical story and ask God to put you in Abraham's place to help you know His plans for you. Read John 3:16–18 for God's answer to you.

## 9.4 The God Who Provides

Our church needed the largest amount of money we had ever raised to build a worship center that would hold the growing number of people who gathered to worship and join us on mission. A friend, a development officer for a large non-profit organization, had told me that most campaigns to raise money needed at least one gift for 10 percent of the total needed. If God provided that, he said, the rest usually followed. We were a young church at the time and we had no one I knew of with that kind of money. So, we prayed.

During 100 days of prayer, two things happened. One was that without an obvious donor with that kind of potential, I had to let go of my dream of a new building. God worked on my heart and ego to lead me to that place, but I got there. The second thing that happened was that one of our members called and said he wanted to have coffee with me. As we sat in a local coffee shop he told me how God had grown his company and that he and his wife wanted to make a gift to the church. The amount equaled 10 percent of the money we needed for the worship center. Yes, the rest of the money followed. That coffee shop is one of several places around town I call "The Lord Provided."

Read Genesis 22:13–14. Underline what Abraham found in the thicket when he looked up from his son. Highlight what he called the place after he sacrificed the animal. What confession in verse 14 was still said in the time of the writer/author? Write it here:

_____

_____

Read Genesis 22:15–19. Highlight the two reasons the angel of the LORD said God would bring the covenant promise to pass. (The phrases follow the word "because" in verses 16 and 18.)

God confirmed His covenant with Abraham because 1) Abraham had offered his only son as a sacrifice to God, and 2) he had obeyed God. Abraham offered his son to God, which meant he trusted God above God's provision. He obeyed even when it did not make human sense to do what God told him to do. Sacrifice and obedience brought the blessing of God.

Genesis 22:19 tells us that Abraham took Isaac and his two servants and returned to Beersheba where he stayed. Another chapter in the Story of God had been written and the main character rests until the Author picks up His pen again.

Do you have a place in your journey with God that you have named "The LORD Will Provide"? Where is that place and what events surrounding it would make you relate it to Abraham's situation? Take time to thank God again for His provision.

## 9.5 Faith Then and Now

The stories of the Old Testament point to the Coming One of the New Testament. As God wrote His rescue story with the lives of those He chose, He provided pointers that guided people toward God's final provision in His Son, Jesus. The defining moments of the Old Testament make up the prequel to the Story of Jesus. The Old Testament is not simply an ancient record of the faithful. It records the events and people who prepare the way for the rescue of all through Jesus.

Parallels in the Old and New Testaments show us God's purposeful involvement in His-story to provide for our greatest need, a right relationship with our Creator through His Son. The following present some parallels from this chapter of God's journey with Abraham to the Story of Jesus. (Review the Genesis stories and look up the New Testament references to gain greater appreciation for the connections.)

Isaac's birth a miracle:

    . . . Jesus' birth a miracle (Luke 1:35)

Isaac, Abraham's son:

    . . . Jesus, God's Son (Matt. 3:17)

Mount Moriah:

    . . . Calvary or Golgotha (Mark 15:22)

Isaac carried the wood:

    . . . Jesus carried the cross (Mark 15:20–21)

God provided a ram:

    . . . God provided His Son (Heb. 9:26–28)

God chose Abraham as a major character in this chapter of the redemption epic. Abraham trusted God, and he serves as an example of how we can trust God today.

Read Hebrews 11:17–19. What did the writer of Hebrews remember about Abraham's trust in God? Why did the writer consider him a man of faith?

_____

_____

As we conclude, take time to compare your trust in God with that of Abraham. Remember, Abraham was not perfect and sometimes took matters into his own hands, but he eventually trusted God to the point of sacrificing the one he knew was God's gift to complete His purposes.

Consider the following questions in your time with God today. What is your Isaac? Have you come to the place in trusting God that if He said, "Give that to me," you would? How have you taken matters into your own hands to "help God out"? Where are your "The Lord Will Provide" places in life? Have you come to realize the connection between God's work in the Old Testament with its fulfillment in the New? How would the writer of Hebrews describe your faith today?

_____

_____

_____

**For further study:**
- **Genesis 17:15–22; Romans 4:16–25**
- **Hebrews 6:13–20; James 2:20–24**

# 10—Pursuing God's Will the Right Way (Isaac and Rebekah, Part 1 of 2)

If you trust that God writes His-story and that you play a part in it, how do you know your next step? In what ways do you discern what God desires for you? Knowing and doing the will of God demands faith in a relationship with God and His people.

To know and do what God desires is especially important with decisions that impact your life. "What job do I take?" "Whom should I marry?" "Which ministry should I give to in order to help meet a local or global need?" Christ-followers trust God for the answers to all of these questions and more.

This week we will see how God answered the prayer of faith by Abraham's servant as he sought a bride for Isaac among kinsman many miles from his master.

The Memory Verses for this chapter are Genesis 24:26–27. These verses record the joyful prayer of Abraham's servant who experienced God's direct answer to his prayer of faith. Grow familiar with this prayer. It is a prayer of rejoicing that comes when God has led you directly to know His plans for you.

Our question to consider this week is: Does God always answer our prayers? You will see how God answered Eliezer's prayer in this chapter of the Story of God, but this question remains vital as we live daily in conversation with Him and seek His desires for our lives.

## 10.1 Following Instructions

In twenty-first century America people choose who they marry. But long ago in Canaan parents chose their children's spouses. The father chose his son's wife, and they were to live happily ever after. This practice, still part of many cultures around the world, seems foreign and unfair to a generation who can personalize anything from playlists to preferences on their cell phones.

Read Genesis 24:1. What two things described Abraham's life?

_____

This chapter of God's story with Abraham began by describing him as old (140 to be exact) and blessed by God "in every way." God had kept His promise to bless Abraham and to give him a son. Now Abraham had to find a wife for his son of promise, Isaac, so God's blessing could be passed on.

Read Genesis 24:2–4. Highlight who Abraham called to find a bride for Isaac. (Refer to Genesis 15:2.) Write the two things Abraham told him to swear he would do.

1. _____

2. _____

Abraham called his chief servant, Eliezer, to make an oath that he would not chose a wife for Isaac from among the Canaanites where they currently lived. The Canaanites worshiped gods other than the true God. Abraham desired Isaac's wife to come from people who knew God as he did and who would worship the same God as his family. (See Deuteronomy 7:3–4 and 1 Corinthians 7:39 for God's desire that those who trust Him marry those who also know Him.)

Abraham's second command was that his servant would pick his son's wife from among his relatives who lived in Haran, the place God called him to leave for the promised land. They would know of Abraham's faith and journey with God.

Eliezer played the main character in this chapter. He was called to help his master who sought to fulfill his part of his covenant with God. We will follow him on his journey to carry out his master's mission as our example of how to know God's will in our lives.

Reflect on these facts as we move forward in the story: Eliezer knew his master's will because Abraham told him specifically what he wanted from him. We know the Master's will for our lives through the specifics of His written Word in Scripture. For example, God gave 10 clear commands that all of his people should follow (Ex. 20:1–17), and Jesus gave us the "most important" commands that we should live by (Mark 12:29–31).

What instructions has God given you for your life that are clear for the present? List them here:

_____

_____

_____

## 10.2 Trust and Questions

It is OK to ask God questions while you seek His will. Actors freely seek direction from the director of the play. Good employees ask questions before launching critical projects for their bosses. Followers of Jesus continually seek explanation from the "author and perfecter" of their faith as they live out God's mission (Heb. 12:2). The right way to know God's will is to stay in constant contact with Him. A weekly "How am I doing?" at church will not suffice to feel assured of God's guidance.

Eliezer asked a good question to ensure he knew his master's will before he left to find a wife for Isaac. Read Genesis 24:5. Summarize his "What if . . . shall I then . . . ?" question to Abraham here:

_____

_____

Since Eliezer would be over 400 miles from Abraham when he found a wife for his master's son he wanted to know what to do if she would not come back to Canaan with him. If she would not come back with him, he wanted to know if he should send for Isaac to go there.

Read Genesis 24:6–8 for Abraham's answer. Why was it nonnegotiable that Isaac not go to her? What would happen if she refused to come to Isaac? Why was this so important to Abraham?

_____

Abraham declared that the will of God—"To your *offspring* I will give this land" (italics mine)—held more importance than finding a bride. But since the will of God was sure, Abraham trusted God would "send his angel before" his servant and Eliezer would find a bride among his people. Abraham put so much confidence in God's leadership that he said if she would not return Eliezer would be released from his oath (v. 8). But under no circumstance should Eliezer take Isaac to his bride.

Read Genesis 24:9. Underline what the servant did after having his questions answered.

The oath between Abraham and Eliezer represented a commitment to carry out the will between master and servant. Note that Eliezer made the oath to the LORD, not to Abraham (v. 3). This event expanded beyond finding a wife for a son. This was about the Story of God. When a person commits to following Jesus, he or she enters into a covenant that says he or she will live out God's mission with total commitment.

Asking questions to know the specifics of God's desires is OK. To be a disciple is to be an apprentice who learns the skills and ways of the master. The first disciples asked questions to know Jesus' intentions. (For example, see Matthew 13:10, 36.) The night before His death, Jesus sought clarification of God's will and plan for redeeming the world (Matt. 26:39). Jesus is the model of living life for God. He has experienced all forms of suffering (Heb. 2:18). He faced temptation in every way, just like us, but He did not sin (Heb. 4:14–15). Also, He can provide us with mercy and grace in our greatest times of need (Heb. 4:16).

What are some of your greatest struggles? What questions do you have for God today?

_____

_____

## 10.3 Answered Prayer

Prayer is a conversation with God. To converse with God implies listening as well as talking. This sets you free to make specific requests in order to know God more deeply, and to discern His desires for you daily. Jesus insisted that His followers pray. He taught them how to pray (Matt. 6:5–15) and that they could ask specifically for whatever they needed (Matt. 7:7–11). Eliezer was not afraid to ask a specific prayer in order to know God's choice for the bride of his master's son.

After Abraham made his instructions clear, Eliezer packed up 10 camels and made his way to his master's homeland. He traveled over 450 miles to Mesopotamia, or Aram Naharaim, to the town of Nahor, Abraham's brother (Gen. 11:27). When he arrived he went to the well outside the town with his caravan (Gen. 24:11).

What did Eliezer do after he had made his way to the well? (Gen. 24:12) Read Genesis 24:12–14. Summarize his prayer to God here:

_____

_____

God had led the servant safely to his master's homeland. Now the hard work began. How would he find a bride for Isaac? How would he know who she was? Verse 12 tells us that the first thing Eliezer did when he reached his destination was pray. He prayed to the "Lord, God of my master Abraham." God had led his master and he had gone there under his master's command. He had come to trust God through the faith of Abraham, and he depended upon God as Abraham had taught him.

He prayed specifically for God to show him the right woman: the bride for Isaac would say yes when he asked for a drink and then offer to water all of his camels. Notice his prayer ended with "By this I will know that you have shown kindness to my master," not "you have saved my hide." Eliezer desired to please Abraham and the God of the one who sent him rather than to make himself look good. Selflessly serving God and others is the sign of a godly leader.

Read Genesis 24:15–20. How did God answer His servant's prayer? Highlight Rebekah's response to Eliezer.

She did exactly as he had prayed God's choice of bride for Isaac would do. Verse 21 tells us Eliezer did nothing to manipulate the situation. This way he knew her actions were God-directed. (Keep his hands-off stance in mind as we watch Rebekah and Jacob seek God's blessing in the next chapter of our moments with God.)

God answers specific prayers to accomplish His plan for our lives. What prayers has God answered in your life with as clear an answer as Rebekah's response to Eliezer's prayer? How did those answers grow your trust in God?

## 10.4 God-Guided Events

Like many parents, my wife and I prayed that God would direct our daughters to godly men who would love them and live out God's call on their lives with them. One day I answered an email from a colleague who asked if anyone would open their home to his son while he served an internship for six months. My friend taught at a seminary about two hours away. Both of our girls were at college, so after talking to my wife, I replied that we had a room. My colleague's son moved in and began his internship. We truly began to enjoy spending time with Graham and came to respect him for his desire to serve God.

Six weeks into his stay our oldest daughter came home for the first time that semester with some of her friends from college. While staying at the house Graham had

seen pictures and memorabilia from our daughters' high school years, so they had much to talk about. They hit it off, and their relationship began to deepen. He moved back to his hometown at the end of his internship to finish seminary and to work part time as an engineer. Upon my daughter's graduation from college she moved to the same town Graham lived in, found a job as a nanny, and began working on a master's degree. A year later they married.

We are all still amazed at how God guided their lives together, melted their hearts together, and gave them a great marriage. Sometimes there is no explanation other than the work of God for the answers that come from heart-deep prayers.

What are some God-guided events of your life? Or the lives of your family? Write some of your thoughts here:

_____

_____

_____

Read Genesis 24:22–23. Underline what Eliezer took out. What question did he ask Rebekah?

The nose ring and bracelet, along with the 10 camels, signify the wealth of Abraham and what he entrusted to his servant. These items would represent gifts of gratitude for her help and show honor to her family. Eliezer wanted to meet her family and needed a place for the caravan to sleep for the night.

Read Genesis 24:24–25. Underline the names of Rebekah's relatives. (See Genesis 11:28–32 for her genealogy and how her family came to Haran.) What does her response to the servant's request for shelter tell you about Rebekah and her family?

_____

_____

Not only did God answer Eliezer's prayer when Rebekah agreed to water his camels, but God had also providentially guided him to the granddaughter of Abraham's brother!

As you complete your moment with God, take time to thank Him for answering prayer so exactly. Praise Him for His work in your life. Make any petition you have on your heart today.

## 10.5 Thanking God for Answered Prayer

When you see God answer prayer you respond with praise and worship. The Book of Psalms is a book of songs that praise God for who He is and what He has done for people. Praise is part of the script in the Story of God because when we realize His work around us and in our lives our hearts smile and we cannot help but sing praise to Him. We gratefully respond in worship to who God is and what God does. Worship acknowledges God as the Author of our stories. Worship gives credit where credit is due. Worship reminds us of God's greatness and grace and of our need for Him in our lives.

Read Psalm 103. Highlight the many reasons the writer praised God. If you feel creative and like to try your hand at such things, write your own song of praise to God for what He has done in your life or community.

Read Genesis 24:26–27. Highlight the two reasons Eliezer worshiped God.

Our first response to God's answers to our prayers should be worship. Eliezer bowed down and worshiped when he realized what God had orchestrated. He praised God for His kindness and grace toward Abraham and for the amazing reality that God led him to the daughter of Abraham's relative. Chance would not have come close to explaining how all of this came about.

Our question to consider this week was: Does God always answer our prayers? You have read and studied a specific answer to prayer in this chapter of His-story. Based on your moments with God, how would you answer this question? Widen your perspective to your experience and answer the question.

Someone once said that God answers every prayer. He either answers yes, no, or wait. We often have the most trouble with the last two answers. Jesus called us to prayer, and the rest is left up to God who loves us and gave His Son for us.

**For further study:**
• **Genesis 24:5–9, 42–67**
• **Genesis 2:19–25; Ephesians 5:25–33**

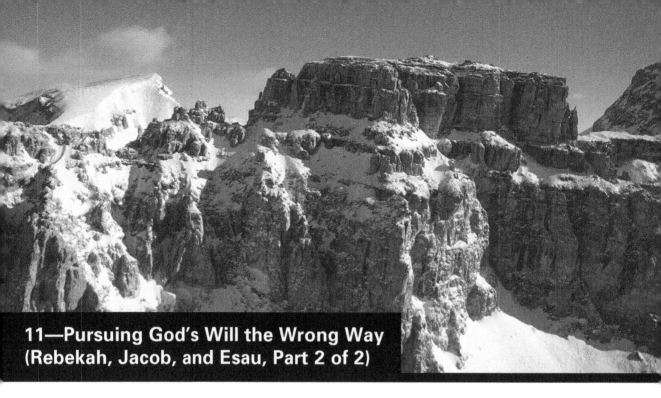

# 11—Pursuing God's Will the Wrong Way (Rebekah, Jacob, and Esau, Part 2 of 2)

Wanting to follow God and do His will is a good thing. For Christ-followers obeying God is normal.

We can pursue God's will the right way. For example, Abraham and Eliezer sought God's will through planning and prayer. Abraham sent his servant to his family's homeland to find a wife for his son. His servant experienced God's choice of a bride for Isaac when he prayed beside a well and waited for God to answer.

As a result of answered prayer, Isaac and Rebekah married and had two boys, Jacob and Esau. When it came time for God to write the next chapter of His-story, rather than allowing the divine plot to unfold, Rebekah and Jacob seized the moment and stole the covenant blessing from Esau, the older son who stood
in line for the blessing. As we open the next chapter in

the Story of God, we will see examples of God's plan pursued in a wrong way. As we will see, the end does not justify the means. This week's study will provide you an opportunity to consider how you pursue not only what you want, but what God wills as well.

The Memory Verse for this chapter is Romans 8:28. God is the Author of His-story. No matter what the characters choose to do—follow the script or improvise—the plot will happen as planned.

Our question to consider this week is: Can the actions of humans hinder God's ultimate will? Outright rebellion, laziness, and self-serving schemes can all hinder God's storyline to rescue people. Can your choices, like Rebekah and Jacob's conniving, really keep God's purposes from happening?

## 11.1 Family Trouble

Sibling rivalry can cause havoc in families—especially when each parent favors a different child. If you had a brother or sister you feel convinced a parent favored, you will identify with the story in this chapter. As we enter the next episode of His-story with God's chosen family, Isaac and Rebekah had twin boys. Isaac favored the oldest, Esau, and Rebekah gave special attention to Jacob (Gen. 25:28).

Jacob was the more cunning of the two sons. He got his older brother to sell his birthright for a bowl of soup—a cheap price for the right to a double portion of his inheritance (Gen. 25:29–34). Isaac had grown old and thought he would soon die. (Genesis 35:28 reveals that he lived another 43 years.) He wanted to show favor to Esau although Jacob owned the family birthright through his wager with his brother.

Read Genesis 27:1–4. Highlight the two players in the story. Underline Isaac's desire for Esau in verse 4.

Isaac was the spiritual heir to the promises of God (Gen. 26:2–5). He also knew that God had chosen Jacob as the son who would bear the blessing of the covenant promise after him (Gen. 25:23). Isaac, however, favored Esau (and loved the taste of wild game) and wanted "Red" to have the patriarchal blessing instead of Rebekah's favored son, "Heel Grabber." Isaac's appetite for Esau's game became the basis for passing on spiritual blessing. Trouble always comes when physical desires govern spiritual realities.

Read Genesis 25:24–27. Compare the boys. Write your descriptions in the space below. Esau means "hairy" or "red," and Jacob means literally, "he grasps the heel," and figuratively, "deceiver."

_____

_____

_____

Jacob and Esau were as different as two boys could be. One loved the outdoors and was covered with red hair. He was the apple of his father's eye. The other boy stayed near the tents and his mother. God had plans for both.

Underline the first phrase in Genesis 27:1. Isaac became physically blind in his old age, but he also grew spiritually blind. His appetite for food and his favoritism for his oldest son prevented him from seeing God's work in progress with Jacob. Isaac conceived a way in which his desires would come about.

What are some similar circumstances you have experienced with your siblings or other family members? Write an example of something your parents did to show favoritism to you or someone else. Write your feelings, too. We will see how God worked through this human rivalry to accomplish His plans.

_____

_____

_____

## 11.2 Deceive to Do God's Will?

In American football there is a popular saying that goes like this: "The best offense is a good defense." Stop the other guy, and you have a better chance to score and win. Keep the other team off the field, and you have longer to run up the score. Some people operate the same way in their relationships. If you can get the jump on your rival, you can get what you want before he or she knows what is happening. For this very reason, people camp out all night for concert tickets or Christmas sales, and the problem of stealing business secrets exists in the marketplace. Deception motivated by greed or self-preservation plays a part in the game of life because people trust their own plans above God's providence.

Read Genesis 27:5–10. Summarize Rebekah's scheme in the space below. What do you think was her motivation behind her plan?

_____

_____

_____

Do not forget what was at stake here. Isaac would soon give Esau the Super Bowl of family blessings. You win this blessing and you are set for life. The patriarchal blessing was similar to the father's last will and testament. It was binding for all involved, and it imparted both material and spiritual benefits. In the instance of Isaac, it also meant the covenant blessing that God gave his father Abraham. The stakes were high for which son received Isaac's blessing.

Read Genesis 27:11–15. Highlight Jacob's reservations about the plan. How did his mother respond to his hesitation?

_____

_____

Jacob knew his father could not see well, but he could still feel, and Jacob was not hairy like his brother. He knew that his soft arms and hands would give him away, and Isaac would curse him instead of bless him. He knew their scheme was wrong. His mother Rebekah, who devised this plan, told him not to worry because she would cover his arms to make them feel like his brother's hairy skin. She also offered to take the curse upon herself.

Deceit is part of a plan that does not trust God to accomplish His purposes in His own way and in His own timing.

**Yahweh—Divine Encounters** in the Old Testament

Read the following verses and see what they say about deception: Proverbs 26:18–19, 24–27. Underline the warnings about those who deceive others.

Read 2 Corinthians 4:1–2. What did Paul confess about his ministry?

_____

_____

_____

If deception runs contrary to God's ways and Isaac's family belongs to God's chosen family, how do you reconcile Isaac and Rebekah's scheming with God's storyline for His covenant people? Write your impressions below. We will return to this question at the end of this chapter.

_____

_____

_____

## 11.3 When Deceit Becomes Strategic

Deceit is like an avalanche. Once snow breaks away from its home and gravity begins to drag it down the mountain, its momentum grows and it soon becomes a danger to everything in its path. One lie piles upon another and the roaring wall of destruction cannot be stopped. It overruns people and things in its path, and their only hope is for a rescue team to find them and dig them out in time. Rebekah put a plan in place that would preempt her husband's arrangements to give their oldest son a blessing. While Esau went hunting to grant his father's wish, Jacob obediently followed his mother's scheme to get what they wanted. Few soap operas are as well scripted as this one.

Read Genesis 27:18–19. Underline Jacob's first lie. Read verse 20. Underline his second lie. Isaac sensed something was wrong even though his son answered his questions well. He asked to touch his son's hands (v. 21).

Read verses 22–23. Notice how Jacob deceived his father. Verse 24 records Jacob's third outright lie. Read verses 25–27 and see Jacob's final deception toward his father.

People usually lie either to get something they want or to protect themselves or their interests. Jacob lied to his father for both reasons. He wanted his father's blessing because he knew its value in property and status. He also knew that he would be in big trouble if his father found him out. So Jacob lied to protect himself as well as to gain something of great value.

Jacob committed to the plan of getting the blessing Isaac wanted to give Esau. Although the blessing belonged to Jacob since he owned his brother's birthright—which he stole from him—Isaac wanted his favorite son to have it. Rebekah thought this was unfair, so she devised a plan for her favorite son to get what she thought rightfully belonged to him. Esau and Jacob went along with each parent's conniving against the other, which resulted in a broken family and generations of strife between the sons' descendants. All of this happened without considering God's plan to continue His covenant with His people.

What have you done—either innocently or intentionally—to get something you felt you deserved that someone else had plans to get? What were your reasons for doing what you did? Did you ever consider stopping what you were doing because it was wrong?

_____

_____

Pray that God would reveal to you His ways and what you can do to trust Him.


## 11.4 The Blessing

A blessing brings hope to the one who gives it and confidence to the one who receives it. A father blesses his son and hopes he will carry on the family's name and traditions to the next generation. The son gains confidence because his father sees in him what it takes to fulfill his father's hopes for generations to come. When Isaac smelled Esau's clothes on Jacob, he felt satisfied this was the son to bless and he rejoiced (v. 27b).

Have you ever "blessed" your child or grandchild? Did you say anything similar to Isaac's words? Write your words and feelings here:

_____

_____

Read Genesis 27:28–29. Underline what Isaac prayed God would give Esau (v. 28). Verse 29 combines God's blessing to Abraham and Isaac's blessing to his son.

The patriarch blessed who he thought was the oldest son so Esau could regain his place as heir to the family inheritance. Isaac's words expressed his heart-felt desires for the one he loved. Isaac's inclusion of some of God's blessing to Abraham signaled he also believed he passed on the covenant blessing of God for his descendants. While Isaac thought he blessed Esau, he actually blessed the son God had chosen to receive His blessing (Gen. 25:23).

The self-seeking schemes of both parents resulted in how God said things would go. God would continue His covenant with Abraham through Jacob. While we can condemn Isaac and Rebekah for their efforts to bless their favored sons, God used their efforts to complete this episode of His-story. Only God can use our sinful maneuvers to make His will happen.

Close your time with God today by reading Jesus' blessings on those who followed Him. Read Matthew 5:1–12. Highlight His blessing that best fits your life today. Allow His words to give you confidence as you follow God's plan for you today.


## 11.5 The Paradox

Our efforts and God's providence combine to create a paradox in our thinking about how life works. We find it hard to understand how we can make choices freely and

God providentially works through them to accomplish His will. Theologians, those who study these aspects full time, have struggled to explain how God can be in control while we make choices every moment. Can God accomplish His will in my life if I choose to disobey Him at every turn? What role do my efforts play in accomplishing God's will in the lives I affect? Write some of your own questions here:

_____

_____

_____

You cannot solve this paradox completely, but you can gain some insight from this defining moment with God. You read in Genesis 27 how Isaac and Rebekah's selfish choices to bless their favorite son actually resulted in fulfilling God's promise that Jacob would lead God's people. This presents a clear example of how God's foreknowledge and people's free choices combine to bring about God's will.

Summarize your understanding of what happened in this chapter of His-story in the space below.

_____

_____

The Apostle Paul struggled with the paradox of God's covenant promise to Abraham's descendants and the new, superior covenant in Christ Jesus.

Read Romans 9:6–13. Paul concluded that the true descendants of Abraham were "children of the promise" (v. 8) and that Jacob became the true heir to the promise "not by works [of the parents] but by him [God] who calls" (v. 12). Just as God chose Abel over Cain, he chose Jacob over Esau (v. 13). The will of God "does not, therefore, depend on man's desire or effort, but on God's mercy" (v. 16). Paul concluded that in the end, the purposes of God come about ultimately by His merciful will to rescue people. We participate, but God completes.

Read Romans 8:28. What you have read in Genesis may shed some light on this verse in Romans. Given the events in Genesis 27 and Paul's explanation in Romans 9, write your application of Romans 8:28 concerning your life today in the space below.

_____

_____

_____

God is the Author and Director of His-story. You are a character in the story, and you have the privilege to choose to act the lines of the Director or to create your own scenes. God's storyline will play out to the final episode. You can feel confident that God can use your choices that line up with the divine script and those you chose to write on your own to complete the lines He wrote before the beginning of time.

**For further study:**
- **Genesis 25–28**
- **Romans 9:10–16; Hebrews 11:20**

# 12—Persevering Through Unmet Expectations (Jacob, Part 1 of 2)

God prepares whom God chooses. However, God's preparation does not always fit in our school of choice or the workload we desire. Scripture teaches that God uses hardship to prepare us (Heb. 12:7–11). We develop endurance and perseverance through difficulty and trials (Rom. 5:3–5).

Jacob had to learn this principle. He also learned that the sins of his past could be used to develop his character. While he traveled to his father's homeland he made a stone for a pillow and dreamed of a stairway to heaven (Gen. 28:10–15). In the night God confirmed His covenant call on Jacob's life and promised Jacob would one day inhabit the land upon which he slept. Jacob named the place Bethel, the House of God, and made a vow to honor God's call on his life (vv. 16–22).

This chapter of His-story tells how God molded Jacob's character through his relative beating him at his own game. Although the deceiver was deceived, he persevered through his circumstances and got both his first love and God's blessing.

The Memory Verses for this chapter are Galatians 6:7–8. A spiritual reality is, "You reap what you sow." This proverb holds true in agriculture and in relationships. In knowing these verses you will learn a secret to how life works.

Our question to consider this week is: Do we always reap what we sow? Our Memory Verses say the answer is yes. But to what extent? Is it like Newton's Third Law of Motion? "For every action there is an equal and opposite reaction." Or is it less mechanical and more chaotic? Gather your thoughts. We will talk later.

**Yahweh—Divine Encounters** in the Old Testament

## 12.1 Motivated Choices

We often do things for our reasons rather than for God's purposes. Jacob journeyed to his distant relatives to escape his brother's wrath and to fulfill his father's wishes, which actually came from his mother (Gen. 27:41–46; 28:1–4). No wonder Jacob was such a conniving person. The dysfunction of his family could support a modern family therapist for a lifetime! But God used them with all their quirks. This should give us hope as we follow God today.

Read Genesis 29:1–5. Notice what Jacob learned when he arrived in "the land of the eastern peoples." Highlight the person Jacob inquired about to the shepherds.

Jacob made his way to the land of his relatives in the east. Jacob followed his parents' wishes—no matter his personal motives—while his brother did not. Esau knew how much Isaac did not want his sons to marry Canaanite women, so Esau rebelliously married one (Gen. 28:6–8). Jacob had his father's blessing and followed his wishes. Along the way, God confirmed His blessing on Jacob's life—an unexpected blessing as he obeyed his parents.

Read Genesis 29:6–8. Highlight the person the shepherds pointed out to Jacob. What excuses did the shepherds give for not watering the sheep?

_____

"We can't" and "until" are excuses of those who had fallen into traditions that ordered their lives but that could prevent them from experiencing God in new ways. Jacob, now confident of God's leadership in his life, broke their habits to meet the woman who caught his eye. Jacob met his future wife at a well, just as Abraham's servant had met Isaac's wife, Rebekah. Both boldly approached those around the gathering place and trusted God to guide them to those He wanted them to meet.

What choices have you made out of rebellion like Esau? What you have done out of respect for God's leadership in your life? These may include anything from big choices such as leaving home to some seemingly small choices such as following this walk through the Bible. Briefly write some consequences of those choices.

_____

_____

_____

## 12.2 Glimpse into the Hand of God

I remember the first time I saw my spouse-to-be. She was walking across our college campus from her karate class to her apartment. Her looks and our unguarded meeting embarrassed her, but her choice of karate as a physical education credit and her spirited, unkempt look attracted me. We had met before, but something about this time tugged at my heart more deeply than just seeing an attractive young woman as I crossed the campus. I somehow understand Jacob's attraction to Rachel as a shepherd. I saw in Kim a strong, yet innocent, woman with whom life would be an adventure.

Read Genesis 29:9–10. Underline how the Scriptures described Rachel. Circle the word describing her vocation.

The Bible said Rachel worked as a "shepherdess." Only boys and men carried out this task, while the women had the chores of cooking and keeping a home for the family. When Jacob saw Rachel he knew he was not far from Laban, his mother's brother. He found out Laban was in good health, and that Rachel was his kin. Upon seeing her approach, Jacob went to the well, removed the rock and began to water her sheep.

Read Genesis 29:11–12. How did Jacob respond to Rachel? Underline how he described himself to her. What did she do in response? Write your answer here:

_____

Jacob was happy he had found his kinsman, and when he was certain of Rachel's identity, he kissed her and wept. Both actions showed his genuine emotions of joy. God had guided him specifically to the place and person of his parents' wishes. Rachel ran home to tell her father Laban about her cousin's trip and possibly his kiss!

This episode gives a brief moment in the bigger Story of God's people, but it shows again how God connected the next two main characters together in what looks like a chance meeting. Yet, from our perspective we watched how God guided each step of Jacob and Rachel to intersect that afternoon at the well.

God got involved not for their happiness, though they were filled with joy, but to insure His promise would come true. What can this meeting add to your understanding of how God works in people's lives to bring about His purposes? If you are married, how did God work in your life for you to meet your spouse? What other "chance" encounters resulted in furthering God's purposes?

_____

_____

## 12.3 What Comes Around, Goes Around

Jesus taught, "All who draw the sword will die by the sword" (Matt. 26:52). He could have also taught, "All who deceive will be deceived." Jacob met his match in his uncle Laban. Jacob had manipulated his brother out of his birthright and deceived his father for the patriarchal blessing, but Jacob was a padawan compared to the jedi Laban when it came to deception. The Force of deceit stood strong in Laban and Rebekah's family of origin. Jacob became blinded by Rachel's beauty and unsuspectingly fell into his uncle's trap.

Read Genesis 29:13–19. How does the storyteller describe Laban's two daughters? What did Jacob offer in verse 18?

_____

_____

Laban invited his nephew to live with him. Laban observed Jacob's attraction to Rachel, and a month into Jacob's stay Laban approached his young guest about what he could pay him for his work (v. 18). Unlike Abraham who sent a slave with much wealth to give a dowry for Isaac a wife, Jacob had nothing to offer Laban for the hand of his daughter. So, Jacob offered to work for seven years to accumulate enough value to marry Rachel. Laban accepted his offer (v. 19). Seven years of free labor and a husband for his daughter sounded like a good deal.

Read verse 20. Underline why the seven years seemed like a few days to Jacob.

Laban had two daughters. Rachel was clearly the more attractive of the two (v. 17). We do not know if Leah's "weak eyes" referred to her sight or how people saw her, but her younger sister got the nod for beauty in shape and sight. Rachel's beauty caused Jacob to loose his sense of time, and the seven years seemed like days to him.

Read Genesis 29:21–28. Summarize Laban's deceit in the space below. Highlight the last question in verse 25.

_____

_____

After completing the seven years, Jacob went to Laban and asked for "my wife" (v. 21). Betrothed couples were seen as legally bound in that culture. Laban threw a wedding feast and in the morning after the marriage ceremony, Jacob found himself in bed with Rachel's older sister, Leah! (vv. 22–25) The irony of the entire event is that Laban deceived the deceiver! Heel Grabber was the one manipulated for the other's benefit and deceived for the other to get a blessing that did not belong to him.

Read Genesis 29:26–27. How did Laban respond to Jacob's outcry? When do you think he came up with that explanation?

In this episode we see that God had plans to change the character of His chosen one. Trumped by his uncle, Jacob spent the next seven years learning the lessons of humility and perseverance to get what God had provided for him.

When have you sensed that God allowed you to get in a situation to mold your character?

_____

_____

_____

## 12.4 When God Has Us Wait

They say, "Absence makes the heart grow fonder." The idiom means that the longer you are away from someone you love, the more your affections will grow for them. Jacob's heart must have felt the most fond of Rachel the day he finally married her. His 14-year engagement had finally ended, and he began to desire children with her. But they did not come. Leah, his first wife and his marriage night surprise, had children easily. Again, God orchestrated a situation in which the man who had gotten everything he wanted by controlling and manipulating others had to learn to wait for God's timing.

When was the last time you desired something very deeply but could do nothing to get it and had to wait for it to happen? Write your situation here:

_____

_____

Read Genesis 29:29–31. Underline the differences between the two women in verse 31.

Laban was now true to his word. He now had a husband for his two daughters and 14 years free labor from his son-in-law. Jacob, too, finally got what he wanted, but the one he loved, Rachel, could not bear him children. Leah, on the other hand, bore him four sons quickly.

You or someone you know may desire children and cannot have them. Take a moment to describe the emotions that people feel in that situation.

Also, if you know someone suffering with this pain write a prayer for him or her.

_____

_____

Read Genesis 29:32–35. Highlight the names of Leah's four sons and underline the meanings of their names.

God would change the name of Jacob to Israel and Leah's sons would become the heads of some of the twelve tribes of Israel. (See Genesis 30:1–24 for more of the names.) God would use these baby boys to form the family out of which the Main Character of His-story would descend: Jesus of Nazareth, Son of God, Son of Abraham. Leah's fourth son, Judah, formed the tribe Jesus' genealogy would follow (Matt. 1:2). The unloved wife bore the son God chose to bring forth His Son. This presents another twist in His-story that causes us to keep our eyes open to the unsuspecting work of God.

God caused Jacob to wait on his first love and gave him children by the wife less loved. God had blessed Jacob (Gen. 28:13) and then placed him in the crucible of circumstances to mold his character.

What were some of the results from this time of waiting in Jacob's life? What are some lessons you have learned while you waited on God?

_____

_____

## 12.5 Sowing and Reaping

Most who read this book live in a city. Farming is as foreign to them as climbing Mount Everest. If the disasters of Y2K had happened, most of us would have had to totally depend—as we still do—on others for food. We have long progressed from the days when each family raised its own food and built its own shelter. So when we come to a biblical truth like our Memory Verses we may understand its simplest meaning, but we have no context to grasp the deeper implications of its concept. But God's truth is timeless and crosses all cultures and periods of history. Even though you may not farm, you can still gain life application from the Bible.

Read Galatians 6:7–8. What is the biblical truth revealed by this passage? Highlight the phrase. Take some time to meditate on the phrase from a farmer's perspective as much as you can. If you grow plants indoors or out, use that frame of reference. Write your initial insights here:

_____

_____

_____

Meditation, like growing your food, is a lost skill for many in developed cultures. Our lives are too busy and noisy to meditate. The spiritual exercise involves simply stopping long enough to ruminate on a passage of Scripture in order to see or sense the meaning God intended. Spend a little more time with the proverb (v. 7) and its application in verse 8. When you have finished, apply the truth of the passage to Jacob's life. How do the events that happened while he lived with Laban reflect the truth of this passage? Is the truth necessarily negative? If so, why? If not, why? Write your thoughts here:

_____

_____

Let's look at it another way. If Jacob were a seed and his 14 years with Laban were the garden, what fruit would he bear—other than sons—at the end of that growing season? Write some ideas here:

_____

_____

Let's add another perspective to our evaluation of Jacob's life. Read Hebrews 12:7–11. Do you believe God disciplined or punished Jacob through Laban? Or do you believe Jacob simply got what was coming to him? Write your answers here:

_____

_____

Each of these questions add insight and perspective to the narrative events in this chapter of the epic of God's love toward all people. Plan times in which you can spend extra moments with God to see all His Word has for you.

**For further study:**

• **Genesis 30**
• **2 Peter 1:3–11**

# 13—Healing Broken Relationships (Jacob, Part 2 of 2)

You have probably experienced a broken relationship. There is a good chance that you currently have an unresolved relationship challenge or will in the future. This problem has existed since the first family. This week's study will give a glimpse into how Jacob dealt with these issues in his own life. You can find inspiration to repair relationships with those who have hurt you and those
you have hurt by studying these events in Jacob's life.

After 20 years of working for his uncle, Jacob had enough and decided to take Leah and Rachel and return to Bethel, the place God promised to him. He left without telling Laban, and his employer/uncle pursued him. A caution from God in a dream may have been all that saved Jacob from his angry father-in-law. Laban and Jacob repaired their relationship, but Jacob had yet to meet Esau, his estranged brother, as he returned

home. He had no idea if his older brother had forgiven him for what he had done or if he planned to kill him on sight. Jacob wrestled with God on the eve of meeting his brother and he walked the rest of his life with a new name and a limp. Esau forgave his younger brother, and Jacob settled at Bethel. There he restored his relationship with God and his relationship with Isaac.

The Memory Verse for this chapter is Genesis 32:30. Sometimes people name places that have a special meaning to them. Jacob named the place of his wrestling match with God Peniel because he had
seen the face of God.

Our question to consider this week is: Are all broken relationships supposed to be healed? We will talk about this question more after we watch Jacob's actions in this chapter.

## 13.1 Seeking to Amend

In college I was afraid to break up with girls. I feared I would have to explain my decision, and they would tell me how crazy it sounded. So I mostly just walked away and quit calling them. When I dated Kim she told me that if I ever broke up with her, she would find me and I would have to explain to her why I broke up with her—and we would remain friends after the breakup. I had never heard of such a thing, and since I could never do that, I married her. Seriously, relationships are hard to repair when either one has decided it is over or if one has abused or hurt the other.

When has someone hurt you by not ending a relationship well? What is the status of that relationship now?

_____

_____

_____

The first 42 verses in Genesis 31 tell of Jacob's stealth departure from Laban. Jacob had worked for his father-in-law for 20 years: 14 years for his two daughters and six years for his flocks, and Laban changed Jacob's wages 10 times (v. 41). Laban pursued Jacob and after seven days caught up with him in the hill country of Gilead (v. 23). Laban was not happy when he overtook Jacob. But the night before God had warned him in a dream not to do anything to Jacob (v. 24). Divine intervention in a dream, not Jacob's wit or power, saved him. Jacob began to see that he could depend only on the power of God for his survival.

Read Genesis 31:43–44. Underline Laban's offer in verse 44. Laban heard the anger in Jacob's voice (v. 42) and moved to make a treaty with him. Laban wanted Jacob to care for his daughters and to ensure Jacob would not return to seek revenge for all the wrong he had dealt him.

Read Genesis 31:46–50. Highlight the names each character named the heap of rocks. Family members brought rocks in order to create a marker for both clans. Laban used the Aramaic name Jegar Sahadutha, and Jacob used his native language of Hebrew to call the stones Galeed. Both names mean "the heap of stones."

Read Genesis 31:51–55. Summarize what the stones meant for both clans in the space below.

_____

_____

The heap of rocks created a boundary of separation between the families. Neither could cross the line to harm the other. Both swore and took an oath before God, and the next morning Laban kissed his kin and returned home. The estranged relationship between father-in-law and son-in-law was reconciled. Jacob forgave Laban's abuse, but he laid a clear boundary between them that protected his family from further abuse. This is an example many families can follow today.

Have you made amends with those who have mistreated you? Have you set up clear boundaries for future relationships? You may want to answer these questions in your prayer time today.

## 13.2 Wrestling with God

A scar is a physical reminder of a previous open wound. I have one from a youth camp where I dragged my knee across the face of a rock on while swinging into a swimming hole. If the scar is visible, people ask, "How'd you get that?" If hidden, you can live the rest of your life with it concealed from all except those who know you best. We all live with physical and emotional scars. The stories behind them serve as backdrops for who we are and how we live.

Describe a scar you live with and the story behind it.

_____

_____

Consider sharing your story the next time someone asks, "How'd you get that?"

After Jacob's treaty with Laban, he headed home to Canaan. There his brother, Esau, waited for him. Twenty years had passed since Jacob fled to Haran to put distance between him and his older brother who wanted to kill him (Gen. 27:41). He did not know whether Esau would still want to kill him or want to embrace him when they met. The night before he met Esau, he divided his family into two groups. If one was attacked, the other could escape (Gen. 32:7–8). Having done all he could do to ease his brother's anger with gifts, he found himself alone beside a riverbed praying for his life.

Read Genesis 32:24–28. Underline the two things that happened to Jacob the night he wrestled with God.

In the night, Jacob wrestled with a man. We thought he had met his match in Laban, but this man of God was greater than anyone he had ever faced. The battle was so violent, the mysterious warrior dislocated Jacob's hip. He then told Jacob to let go of him because it was daybreak. Jacob refused to let go until his attacker blessed him. Instead, the man changed Jacob's name to Israel, which means, "struggles with God," because he wrestled both God and man, and prevailed (v. 28). Heel Grabber was now God Struggler, the father of the twelve tribes of Israel.

Read Genesis 32:29–30. Jacob received a blessing (v. 29). Highlight what Jacob named the place and what it meant.

God Struggler named the place Peniel, which means, "the face of God." He had seen the face of God in the man who broke his hip and gave him a new name, and Jacob had survived. The prophet Hosea said that Jacob wrestled with an angel, whom he overpowered, but he also wept (from the pain of his hip?) and begged the divine being

**Yahweh—Divine Encounters** in the Old Testament

for a blessing (Hos. 12:4).

Jacob saw "God face to face" (v. 30) and got a new name (v. 28) and a limp (v. 31). Jacob walked into a new day broken and blessed. He would never be the same. Pause for a moment and meditate on what each of these results meant for Jacob's life. Record your thoughts and apply what similar events would mean in your story with God.

_____

_____

_____

## 13.3 When God Changes the Way You Walk

Jacob walked away from his night-long wrestling match with a limp. He would never walk the same again because God had broken him in the night. Yes, he got a new name from God but he would bear it with a limp. I heard someone say once that God cannot use greatly those He has not broken deeply. Brokenness is the limp with which God's people bear their new name in Christ. God breaks us so He can use us. God has always done this with those He chooses to lead.

God broke Joseph before he became Number Two in charge of the known world with cisterns and jail cells. God broke Saul of Tarsus with blindness before He sent him on his journey of salvation to the non-Jewish people. God broke Peter through his denial of Jesus before he stood boldly before thousands at Pentecost. God humbles those who exalt themselves and exalts those who humble themselves (Luke 14:11).

Read Psalm 51:17. What is the context of this verse? What does it teach us about our relationship with God? Write your answers here:

_____

_____

Read 1 Peter 5:6. What does Peter call us to do? This may imply that if we do not humble ourselves, God will because He cannot use us any other way.

Have you had an experience in your life in which God allowed you to be broken or humbled? If so, write memories of that experience. If not, reflect on what God did to Jacob and list positive outcomes of experiencing brokenness.

_____

_____

_____

Read Genesis 31:31–32. Underline what the Jews practiced at the time the storyteller wrote this episode in Israel's life. Out of respect for the father of their nation, the Jews would not eat "the tendon attached to the socket of the hip" (v. 32). Like the altars in the sand reminded Abraham of God's promises, so the refusal to eat a portion of meat reminded Israel of Jacob's brokenness and God's blessing.

We are often humbled by humiliation, and we are

usually broken by outside forces. Israel limped. The limp made it possible for the name to become what it has.

## 13.4 Going to Bethel

I experienced the presence of God one day on the side of a mountain in Colorado. I wondered about my future and whether or not what I perceived as God's call on my life was accurate. I felt paralyzed about what to do. I had a great job and felt I was doing meaningful ministry, but I wondered if God had called me and then left me to figure things out for myself. That day God whispered that I could have any job and do what He called me to do. I had put too much value in the job of my calling rather than my calling regardless of the job. I left that hillside encounter confident of God's hand on my life.

Do you remember the place and time you first sensed the real presence of God or when you gave your life to Christ? Have you visited that place since then? Write your memories of the event and your visit here:

_____

_____

God came to Jacob one day after Dinah's debacle (Gen. 34) and told him to return to Bethel, the place God had confirmed His covenant blessing with Jacob (Gen. 28:19).

Read Genesis 35:1–5. Underline the things Jacob told his family to do to prepare for their visit to Bethel. What was the purpose of his request?

_____

Jacob called his relatives to purify themselves and remove all other gods from among them because they were to return to the sacred place of Bethel, the House of God. Verse 5 tells us that the terror of God's presence was so overwhelming that none of those who had a right to revenge dare pursued them.

Read Genesis 35:6–7. Highlight what Jacob did when he arrived at the place where he saw the stairway to heaven. Highlight the expanded name he gave it.

Thirty years had passed since Jacob made a stone for a pillow and saw angels ascending and descending to and from heaven. God promised him then he would bear the covenant blessing of his father, Isaac. Little did Jacob know what that would mean as he ran in fear from his brother into the trap of Laban, his uncle.

Genesis 35:8–15 records God's affirmation of Israel's new name and promised covenant. Israel erected a pillar and poured a drink offering and oil upon it to signify the importance of what had happened there.

By the end of his journey from Paddan Aram to Bethel Jacob had reconciled his relationships with Laban, Esau, and God. He had wrestled against all three and prevailed, but in the end, God broke him and gave him a new name to remind him who was truly in charge.

What is the status of your relationships with your in-laws, siblings, and God? Ask God to guide you in doing what you need to do to make things right.

## 13.5 Seeking Reconciliation

Our question to consider this week was: Are all broken relationships supposed to be healed? Also, when should you make every effort for restitution and when should you walk away?

After your walk with Jacob through the episodes of this chapter, what are some of your answers to these questions?

_____

_____

_____

Read Matthew 18:15–17. Write out the process Jesus said you should follow if someone has offended you. How does Jesus' teaching answer the question for this week?

_____

_____

_____

Read Acts 15:36–41. Describe briefly what happened between Paul and Barnabas, two friends who had traveled and served together in the mission to the Gentiles. How does this incident affect your answer to the question we considered this week? Write your response here:

_____

God expects us to reconcile all broken relationships. To do this we must humble ourselves before God and others. By doing so, we give God a chance to work in our own hearts and the hearts of others.

Paul and Barnabas remind us that sometimes God's people separate, but God will continue His purposes as He did with Barnabas and Mark, and Paul and Silas. His first desire is for us to forgive one another as He forgave us (Col. 3:13).

**For further study:**
- **2 Corinthians 5:18–19**
- **Romans 12:9–21**

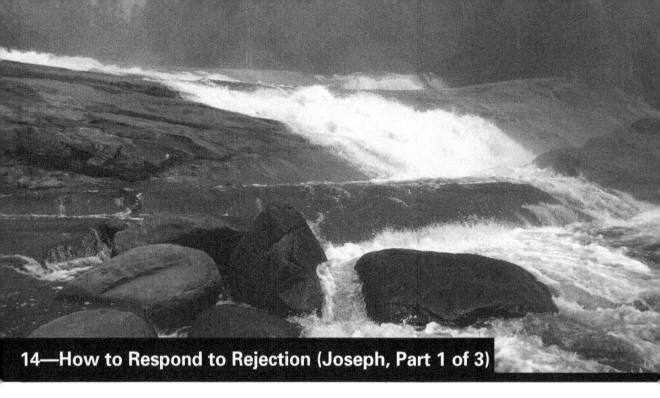

People that are used greatly by God are not immune from pain. They suffer the same hurts as everyone else. The difference is that people whom God uses learn to love God and others deeply through their pain while others become vengeful and bitter. Joseph was a person that God used greatly.

Jacob favored Joseph most out of his 12 sons. Joseph was the oldest of two boys born to Rachel, Jacob's favorite wife. Add dreams of future greatness to his father's favor and you have the formula for a family feud that literally held worldwide implications.

What his brothers did to him was unforgivable, but the work of God in Joseph's life trained him to forgive rather than seek revenge. The main character of this episode in the Story of God found the road to his dreams paved with betrayal, cisterns, and jail cells. God would use that rocky path to prepare him to protect God's covenant people so His blessing to Abraham would continue. God does the same for us. The troubles we face today prepare us for God-given opportunities in the future.

The Memory Verse for this chapter is Genesis 50:20. This verse serves as the cornerstone of the foundation for forgiving others. God's purposes are bigger than our ego. When we learn this, even the hurt of those closest to us become God's way to get us to where He wants us.

Our question to consider this week is: How much do the sins of the family affect us? Jacob learned deceit from his mother. His uncle deceived him. His sons tricked him. Deceit was a family trait for Joseph's family. Would he end or continue the cycle?

## 14.1 Playing Favorites

Parents who play favorites help create sibling rivalry. We observed this between Esau and Jacob. Whether or not it is intentional or subtle, favoritism creates ill feelings between siblings. I am one of five children and the only son. Ask any of my four sisters who is my parents' "favorite," and I get the nod hands down. We can tease about my favored status now, but I have learned that they struggled with my perceived superior status as we grew up. I am grateful everyone in my family trusted Christ at an early age and that my parents instilled biblical values in our behavior. Otherwise, our relationships would be much less than the friendships they are today.

Jacob, now Israel, had 12 sons by Leah, Rachel, and their two maidservants (Gen. 35:23–26). Joseph, the oldest of Rachel's two sons, was Jacob's favorite. (He learned this habit from his parents, Isaac and Rebekah, who favored Esau and Jacob respectively.) These sons would become the twelve tribes of Israel who entered the promised land under Joshua's leadership. They, however, had to work through their jealousy of Joseph before God could use them as His covenant people.

Read Genesis 37:1–11. Highlight the three things our storyteller gives us that set Joseph apart from his brothers. (See verses 3, 5, and 9.)

A multi-jeweled coat from Dad and two dreams in which his family bowed down to worship him set the 17-year-old Joseph apart from everyone in the family. A father's favor and grandiose dreams gave him confidence above the others.

Read Genesis 37:12–17. Underline the names and places in the passage. If you have a Bible atlas or map, locate Shechem. Dothan was about 15 miles north.

Read Genesis 27:18. Interpret the feelings of Joseph's brothers by the description in the verse here:

_____

_____

_____

The scene was set for trouble. Eleven jealous brothers plotted to kill the favored son. Episodes like this one cause us to wonder how the main character can "get out of this one." God's storyline does not always take the turns we want or can foresee. Sometimes the reader can only trust in the Author's sovereignty over the plot.

## 14.2 The Sting of Betrayal

You read in another chapter of this book the idiom, "Absence makes the heart grow fonder." However, in a rivalry, absence can make the heart grow harder. As all 11 of Joseph's brothers tended sheep while he stayed home in the luxury of their parents' place, their hatred of "daddy's boy" grew more sinister. They had lit the fuse to a terrible explosion in his absence. The powder would soon explode as he approached them wearing his famous "coat of many colours" (Gen. 37:23, KJV).

Read Genesis 37:19–20. Highlight what they called Joseph. Underline their plot. If you have access to a Bible dictionary or encyclopedia, look up the word "cistern" to learn about these objects in the Ancient Near East. How did they mock him?

_____

_____

"Here comes that dreamer!" they muttered as he came up on them. They mocked his dreams by saying they would see what would come of his dreams if they killed him.

Every covenant character in God's story has a rescuer. The theme of being rescued out of a hopeless situation carries throughout His-story and culminates in Jesus' rescue of us all (Col. 1:13). Joseph needed a rescuer.

Read Genesis 37:21–22. Highlight the brother's name who sought to rescue his little brother. Where was he in the family's birth order? (Gen. 35:23) What was his plan?

_____

_____

Read Genesis 37:23–24. Underline the verbs that described the brothers' actions toward Joseph. Why is it important that the cistern was empty?

_____

_____

Joseph's brothers violently overpowered him, stripped him of his coat, and threw him in an empty cistern. Although Rueben planned to take him back home, Joseph knew nothing while he sat alone in a hole in the ground beat up by those who according to his dreams would worship him. He had to wonder if his father's favor was such a good thing now. He certainly had to question how the dreams would ever come true.

Quietly recall a time when those you trusted betrayed you. How did you feel? What did you wonder about your future? Associate those feelings and thoughts to those of Joseph in order to empathize with his situation and the affects it must have had on his faith in God's dreams for his life. Write your thoughts here:

_____

_____

## 14.3 The Scourge of Rejection

Crimes of passion happen in the moment. Given some distance from the offense, cooler heads prevail. This is why your father taught you to turn and walk away as soon as tensions ran high, rather than fight. Proverbs teaches that "a gentle answer turns away wrath, but a harsh word stirs up anger" (Prov. 15:1). Joseph's brothers had some time to think about their plan to kill him. Rueben's intervention kept them from destroying his little brother, but Joseph's protector was off doing something else (planning to rescue Joseph while the others ate?) when a caravan moved past the tribe at dinner time.

Read Genesis 37:25–28. Highlight the name of the brother who suggested they sell Joseph rather than kill him. Underline the amount of money they received.

Judah, Leah's fourth son and the tribe from which King David and the Messiah Jesus would come, devised a plan to sell Joseph to passing Ishmaelites, the descendants of Abraham's son by Hagar. The irony is that the one whom God chose to preserve his people rode with those whom He had rejected as His covenant bearers. (See God's promise to Ishmael in Genesis 17:20–21.) God uses both the chosen and the rejected for His purposes.

The brothers agreed to Judah's plan, pulled their little brother out of the cistern, and sold him for the price of a slave (Lev. 27:5).

Read Genesis 37:29–35. Highlight the characters in this scene. Underline the similar responses of Rueben and Jacob when they realized Joseph was gone. Circle the verse number that describes the deceit of the brothers.

Both Rueben and Jacob tore their clothes when they saw Joseph was gone. Rueben grieved because as the oldest son he would be held responsible for his brother's death, and Jacob tore his clothes out of genuine grief for the loss of his favorite son. Verse 31 tells of the brothers' cover-up scheme to make their father believe Joseph was dead rather than on his way to Egypt.

One more irony of this act is Jacob's deceitful ways caught up with him again. His boys learned well how to make a lie look like the truth, and he mourned a living son. Although Jacob emerged from the riverbed with a new name, he still limped from a life he had sown for so

long.

While Jacob wept, what does verse 36 tell us about the next chapter in His-story? If you have time, read on through Genesis 39–49 to see what happened to Joseph in Egypt.

## 14.4 A Dream Come True

How do dreams come true when you feel helpless to do anything about them? How does a boy playing basketball on an inner city outdoor court ever get to the NBA? Or how does a girl kicking a roll of tape in a Central American ghetto ever play in the Olympic soccer finals? As Joseph sat in a jail cell falsely accused of sexual assault, he must have wondered how on earth his youthful dream in which his family bowed down to him would ever happen. Was he just a wishful thinker, or was what he saw in his dreams God's plan for his life? Are dreams just childhood fantasies, or are they pictures of our deepest desires?

What childhood dreams did you have that you have seen come true? What dreams have been just that, a wishful thought of what life could be?

_____

_____

Dreams continued to play a part in Joseph's life, and his gift to interpret them put him in Pharaoh's service. This not only saved Egypt but also Israel's family during a worldwide famine. Genesis 39–49 tell of how God orchestrated events to make Joseph the second most powerful person in the known world. The music of Joseph's circumstances sounded more like Edvard Grieg's In the Hall of the Mountain King than Handel's Water Music Suite. Everything climaxed to his meeting with his brothers after his father's death. What would he do now that it was just he and they? The tables now turned on Joseph's brothers. After their father Jacob died, they stood before their brother who could take their lives just as they had tried to take his.

Read Genesis 50:15–17. Circle the verse number that holds the deception of Joseph's brothers. Underline the last two words in verse 17.

Parents often serve as the safety fence between siblings, and when they are gone trouble can begin. Jacob's death caused his sons to think if Dad was no longer around, their little brother whom they sold into slavery might want to take revenge on them. So they did what their family does to get out of trouble: they lied. This partially answers our question to consider this week: How much do the sins of the family affect us? They had not changed through the years, but God had changed Joseph. When he heard their story, Joseph wept. Joseph cried because his brothers still could not see God's plan in all of this. Jesus wept centuries later. He wept because His friends could not see He was the "resurrection and the life" and that Lazarus' death played a bigger role in God's plans than in their grief (John 11:25, 35).

With whom do you empathize? Jacob, Joseph, or his brothers? Why?

_____

_____

_____

Spend time in prayer asking God to reveal your true emotions toward those who could either rightly judge you or those who lie to you.

## 14.5 Forgiving and Serving

True forgiveness comes when you have the upper hand and the power to destroy but choose to forgive instead. Joseph could have waved his hand and his brothers would have ended up in jail or sold as slaves as they had done to him. What they put him through gave him reason enough to take revenge on them. However, God had worked through all the hardships he experienced in Egypt to change Joseph's youthful pride into a mature love for his brothers. In his brokenness he saw the work of God in their lives.

Read Genesis 50:18–19. Underline the brothers' words and then Joseph's response.

Joseph had become a humble man. How do you know? He held as much power as Pharaoh, yet he knew his role in His-story. He confessed to his groveling brothers, "Am I in the place of God?" No matter the earthly power he bore, Joseph knew by experience that he came to his position by God's grace, not by his efforts. He held no pride in who he was and so had no rivalry or revenge with those who had tried to hurt him. He had gained a different perspective on trials and struggles than they had.

Read and highlight Genesis 50:20. This is the Memory Verse for this chapter and a confession for all who trust God's purposes for their lives. Write how you can apply this truth to your own life in the space below.

_____

_____

Read Genesis 50:21. Write an opposite and more natural response to his brothers than the actual response Joseph gave them.

_____

_____

God taught Joseph to respond to rejection differently than how we respond naturally.

Read Matthew 5:38–48. This passage gives Jesus' advice on how to respond to those who hurt us even when we have the law on our side. List the most notable exceptions to our natural behavior when others have treated us wrongly.

_____

_____

Joseph saw the hurt in his life as the way God prepared him to meet a greater need than his wounded ego. Joseph could not hold a grudge against his brothers who saw life so selfishly. God had shown him the purpose of his hurts, and he humbly forgave and cared for his brothers. Jesus taught and showed us the same truth through His life, death, and Resurrection. A defining moment for Christ-followers is when we forgive rather than hurt those who wound us.

Take time to write how this chapter has impacted your perspective on how to respond to those who have hurt you. Ask God to make you more like Joseph and Jesus in these matters. Ask also for the love it takes to forgive those who have rejected or hurt you.

**For further study:**
- **Genesis 37**
- **Genesis 42–47, 50**

Temptation is part of everyone's life. Even Jesus faced temptation (Matt. 4:1–11). Some people view temptation as sin. But this is not the case, because though Jesus faced temptation, He did not sin (Heb. 4:15). The issue rests on how to handle temptation. This week's study will give you a picture of how to handle temptation the right way by looking even further into Joseph's life.

After his brothers sold him into slavery, Joseph soon found himself in charge of his master's house. He gave direction to everything and everyone except Potiphar's food and, of course, Potiphar's wife. He came a long way from the bottom of a cistern and the scorn of his jealous brothers to the wealth and ease of this important Egyptian. He now enjoyed plush surroundings and the trust of his master. But with every promotion comes a test of character, and Joseph was no exception to the rule.

Potiphar's wife wanted to sleep with her husband's powerful and handsome slave, but he refused. Joseph resisted her offer because he respected his master and feared God. Although he did the right thing, he landed in jail. Joseph was a man of character who made the right choice no matter the consequence—and an example anyone could follow today.

The Memory Verse for this chapter is 1 Corinthians 10:13. It promises that no temptation is unique to you and that God provides a way out for every temptation.

Our question to consider this week is: Can all temptations be refused? If so, why do we still sin? Our Memory Verse says yes to the first question. The second question is harder to answer. But Joseph's resistance of Potiphar's wife can give us hope as we seek to say yes to God's ways and no to those things that seduce us away from Him.

## 15.1 The Seduction of Success

Proud people see advancement as solely the result of their gifts and effort. Humble people do acknowledge their abilities and hard work but ultimately give God credit for the breaks and advancement they receive. Take a moment to describe your philosophy of how success happens in a person's life.

_____

_____

We do not know the exact amount of time from when the Ishmaelites bought Joseph from his brothers until when Potiphar put him in charge of his house, but our storyteller described his advancement as meteoric.

Read Genesis 39:1. Highlight the names in the verse and underline Potiphar's position in Egypt. Joseph found himself in the home of a powerful and wealthy man in a foreign country. How does that sort of thing happen? Joseph's skills? Potiphar's ability to chose good help?

Read Genesis 39:2–5. Highlight every time "the Lord" occurs in these verses. What does this tell you about who the storyteller believes made all of this happen?

_____

_____

The writer of His-story made it clear that "the Lord" was the reason for Joseph's success. Five times in four verses "the Lord" shows up as the subject of success. Even the

pagan Potiphar recognized this (v. 3). The word for "the Lord" was the proper name for God given to Moses at the burning bush (Ex. 3). "Lord" is usually translated in all caps to represent the importance of God's name. You can pronounce it Yahweh or Jehovah.

Read Genesis 39:6a. Notice the extent of Joseph's responsibility here. Underline the only thing Joseph did not direct for Potiphar.

God rocketed Joseph to a place of prominence and power. He could have won the Up and Coming Hebrew Slave of the Year award hands down. Take a step back from this scene and recall the focus of this part of His-story. You must always remember the biblical context of an event to completely understand the event. God made a covenant with Abraham and provided blessings to his descendants so that they would receive the promised land as their inheritance. Given that the preservation and growth of the divine blessing was the storyline of His-story up to this point, how do you describe the work of God in these verses? Explain from the biblical perspective what was going on with Joseph at this time.

_____

_____

God was at work to preserve His people and His covenant with them. However, God gave those same people and those they lived around the choice to stay true to the covenant or not. Joseph would soon go through a test that would prove to whom he pledged his true allegiance.

## 15.2 Plagued with Attractiveness

I have never been accused of being "well-built and handsome." I know people who have, though. You could probably name one or two—even if you are a guy. Every society has a category of "well-built and handsome" for men and "shapely and beautiful" for women. (Remember Rachel? See Genesis 29:17.) We tend to give these people celebrity status if they also happen to act or do something that is broadcast for everyone to see. Write the names of several people whom you would put into the categories of celebrity men and women in the space below.

_____

_____

Joseph, Hebrew son of Israel, slave of the Egyptian Potiphar, would make the list in Egypt about 2,000 years before Christ. The second part of verse 6 in Genesis 39 describes him this way.

Joseph had it all: Power, prestige, looks, and muscle tone. This 20-something Hebrew served his Egyptian master well, and made a good life for himself. But Potiphar's wife was the fly in the ointment that would disrupt his good life.

Read Genesis 39:7. Underline what Potiphar's wife did and said to Joseph.

Joseph became an object of affection for his master's wife. Potiphar most likely stayed away from the house serving Pharaoh and left his wife alone. One day, she gave in to her desires and demanded Joseph come to bed with her

(v. 7). She had the right to do this since the family owned him as a slave. Joseph now had to choose between her demands and his loyalty to his master and his God.

"After a while" means she had time to watch and want this young, handsome slave. Her desire grew over time, and she finally blurted out her lust for him. Push pause on the DVR for a moment. Let's take a look at how this scene developed.

Read James 1:14–15. Notice how this passage explains the progression of a desire that results in sin.

James, the brother of Jesus, taught that natural desires, not God, tempts us. They drag us away and entice us. After a period of conception—mulling possibilities around in our hearts and heads, a desire births an act of sin. When that self-pleasing action is full-grown it births its own offspring—death. Desire conceives action. Sinful actions birth death—death of the soul and relationships.

Potiphar's wife took each of these steps that led to her brazen proposition to Joseph. Her desires drug her away from her husband and enticed her toward his slave. She let her desire incubate until she spoke her demand to her servant. If Joseph said yes to her, that act—fully grown—

would give birth to his literal death. The Bible warns us of how such things work. Now that we know how this works, we must make the right choices.

Write out the process from desire to sin that you experience in your own life. If you do not want to write anything now, no problem. Sit quietly and allow God's Spirit to apply this truth to your life choices. Don't worry. There is hope in the study to come.

_____

_____

## 15.3 Refusing Sexual Sin

Adultery begins with a desire for another person other than your spouse. Adultery consists of more than the temptation to take a drink while 30 days sober or to cheat on a diet. The act ruins families and friendships. It can ruin ministries and bring down businesses. It also violates the ideal sexual union God designed for marriage.

The Apostle Paul taught that "all other sins a man commits are outside his body, but he who sins sexually sins against his own body" (1 Cor. 6:18). Paul's words remain true in every way from sexually transmitted diseases to guilt that can cause psychosomatic illness. Death in many forms comes to this desire-turned-act. Any moral person, especially those committed to following Christ, knows that adultery is wrong. So, why does it happen so often and how can God's people resist its temptation?

Write some of your thoughts about these questions here:

_____

_____

Potiphar's wife was not the last one who would try to seduce God's leader away from his divine mission. (See Judges 16:17–19 and 2 Samuel 11:2–4.)

His-story includes men and women seduced to dishonor their commitment to God and to their spouses. However, not everyone propositioned by another participated in the sin. Character and integrity made the difference.

Read Genesis 39:8–9. Summarize Joseph's reasons for resisting temptation by his boss's wife in the space below.

_____

_____

What about his answer tells you his resistance is more than self-preservation or to keep his plush job?

_____

_____

Joseph did mention the authority Potiphar had given him, but when it came to an explanation for why he said no to his master's wife, he said, "How then could I do such a wicked thing and sin against God?" Joseph was accountable ultimately to God, not Potiphar.

As much as respecting the boss can keep anyone from immoral behavior, commitment to God is greater.

Read verse 10. Describe the nature of Potiphar's wife's persistence. How did Joseph respond?

_____

Joseph did not want to violate either his master or God's trust in him. He not only said no to her constant requests but he wisely refused to be alone with her. An ounce of prevention is worth a pound of cure when it comes to moral purity. What boundaries have you placed in your life to prevent unfaithfulness?

_____

_____

## 15.4 Fury of a Scorned Woman

Unchecked lust can lead to desperate measures. You must discipline the desire so it will go away, redirect it to something more productive, or you must feed it. Both require much energy. So, why not expend it on a positive outcome instead of one that can destroy you? Potiphar's wife chose to feed her lust. She waited until they were alone in the house, and then she sprang her trap for him.

Read Genesis 39:11 and the first part of verse 12. The verses describe a normal work day for Joseph. The difference was that no one was in the house that day but Potiphar's wife and Joseph. She made her move, insisting he lie with her. She would not take no for an answer.

Read the last part of verse 12 in Genesis 39. Highlight Joseph's actions.

Joseph wiggled out of his cloak and ran outside the house. You may think he responded immaturely and that he should have stood up to her instead. However, he ran from sin. In fact running from sin is what many passages in the New Testament indicate as the mature response.

Read 1 Corinthians 6:18 and 2 Timothy 2:22. What is the same action word in both verses?_____

Notice what Joseph did when Potiphar's wife grabbed him. He did all he could do to remain true to his master and God. He fled from temptation and removed himself from the situation. Outside, she had no chance of seduction. Joseph did the right thing, but a wounded ego often seeks to hurt others. Potiphar's wife wanted revenge for Joseph rejecting her.

Read Genesis 39:13–20. What was Joseph's reward for doing the right thing? Underline where Potiphar put Joseph after hearing his wife's story. Joseph fled the scene of a potential moral wreck. He swerved and missed a head-on collision with adultery but got hit by oncoming traffic—his boss. Potiphar's wife would not stand for humiliation, so she lied about the situation. Potiphar had no choice but to trust his wife. He put Joseph in jail.

Joseph could have acted bitter about his ill fate. But rather than whining over receiving punishment even though he did the right thing, Joseph worked to do well with his given circumstance. Soon he was head of the jail where he was housed, "because the LORD was with Joseph and gave him success in whatever he did" (v. 23).

Joseph did the right thing, but he got trapped in the lies of an angry woman. We never hear complaints from Joseph about God abandoning him or how life is unfair. He never gave in to sin because "I deserve something for all my bad luck." Joseph remained true to God no matter the circumstances. Whether in charge of a powerful Egyptian's household or prisoners in the king's jail, Joseph constantly served God. And God blessed him.

Have you ever suffered terrible consequences because someone lied about you? Have you ever been demoted or lost a job? How did you respond? Compare your actions and attitudes to those of Joseph's.

## 15.5 Dealing with Your Own Temptation

Read Hebrews 4:15. We have a high priest who sympathizes with our weaknesses. Jesus is the high priest. We trust He faced temptation but did not sin. That is the basis of our trust in Him as the perfect Son of God. But sometimes we find ourselves seemingly trapped by temptation. God inspired Paul to write to his Christian friends in Corinth who faced temptations like we do today. His instructions to them are valid for us, too.

Read 1 Corinthians 10:13. Write the truths about overcoming temptation in the spaces below.

1. No temptation _____

2. And God is faithful; he _____

3. But when you are tempted, he _____
The promise says that no temptation is unique to you.

Do not try to convince yourself that no one has ever had the same desires that entice you. This is just not true. Second, God promised that no temptation is unbearable. Yes, addictions brought on by physiological and psychological influences do exist, but God is faithful not to allow temptations that we cannot bear. And, third, God will show you a way out of the temptation.

Let's apply these promises to Joseph's situation. Sexual seduction was not unique to him. He was a red-blooded Hebrew male. He was attracted to women like other men his age. The temptation to sleep with his boss's wife was not beyond what he could handle. He resisted every advance Potiphar's wife made toward him, and God provided a way out of the situation: the door!

God's given promises help us to overcome temptation. You may ask, "If so, why do we still sin?" Given what you know about God's promises, why do even godly people do ungodly things? (See Galatians 5:16–18 for an answer.)

Joseph lost his privileged status because he resisted temptation. God put him in the crucible of a jail cell to test his character. He passed the test, but other tests would follow. Each event that seemed like a setback to success actually showed how God molded his character in order to prepare him for the responsibilities he would eventually hold for both Egypt and Israel.

**For further study:**
- **Genesis 39:1–23**
- **James 1:13–17**

I have a picture of Andrés Segovia practicing his guitar in his studio in Madrid, Spain. I cut it out from a issue of National Geographic and put it in one of those acrylic picture frames. Segovia is considered one of the greatest classical guitarists in modern times. He led a renaissance of classical guitar music worldwide. I took classical guitar lessons while in college and learned to appreciate his greatness.

I keep Segovia's picture in my study to remind me that practice in solitude produces greatness on the stage. Great performances are first played in the studio. The time I spend alone in preparation for my messages directly affects how God can use me when I deliver them publicly. Jesus' performance of great acts, for example, resulted from the time He spent alone with the Father in prayer and the solitude He spent in relationship with the One who had sent Him.

Joseph made a great leader for those he served as well as for the millions he led through a worldwide famine. But before he was great on the world stage he practiced greatness in a dungeon.

The Memory Verses for this chapter are 1 Peter 5:6–7. God calls us to humility so He can exalt us in His season for His purposes. Like Joseph, God may put us in humiliating circumstances in order to help us become humble. Live by these verses in private so that God can use you in public.

Our question to consider this week is: How does a person achieve the status of greatness? Begin to form your answer now, and then we will return to it at the end of this chapter. Do not forget greatness defined by your culture is different than a greatness declared by God.

## 16.1 Falsely Imprisoned

Have you ever received an unjust punishment? We read stories of people convicted of a crime who then, through the technology of DNA testing, were proved innocent and released by the courts. I wonder how they felt in prison when all the time they knew they were innocent but sentenced as guilty. Did they become bitter or did they accept the punishment given to them? What did they do after they got out of prison? Write some of your thoughts or experiences here:

_____

_____

Potiphar threw Joseph in jail based on the false testimony of his wife (Gen. 39:19–20). Joseph's brothers unfairly threw him into a cistern and sold him into slavery, but he ended up the servant of a high Egyptian official. He found himself unjustly imprisoned in a hole in the ground again. We, however, never read a negative word from him, and we see him practice his God-given gifts even while in a dark dungeon.

Read Genesis 40:1–13. Summarize the events in the jail in the space below. Highlight the main characters. Use a Bible dictionary or handbook to learn more about the two men in the prison with Joseph.

_____

_____

Although Joseph was in jail, God continued to surround him with important people. The king jailed his chief cupbearer and baker because he became angry with them. The captain of the guard who trusted Joseph placed them in his care. We know that in Joseph's teenage years he had significant dreams that he could interpret (Gen. 37:1–11).

God gave Joseph the gift to interpret the dreams of others in the prison. Joseph gave God all the credit for his ability to interpret others' dreams (Gen. 40:8). His confession proved Joseph's growing humility.

You have observed Joseph as a proud teenager who had no fear in criticizing his brothers and telling them they would one day bow down to him. He is now a young adult who honors God for his gifts. Write your impressions of how those changes occurred in Joseph's life in the space below.

_____

_____

Read Genesis 40:14–15. Underline the two phrases of Joseph's request to the king's chief cupbearer (v. 14). Also, underline the two injustices Joseph mentioned in verse 15.

The cupbearer would return to the service of the king in three days. Joseph wanted out of prison. He asked his fellow prisoner to remember him and to refer him to Pharaoh. Joseph wanted some good will returned for the kindness he showed those he oversaw. Joseph made the case that he was put in prison unfairly. Both his trip to Egypt and prison came about by unjust acts toward him.

Did Joseph show a lack of faith in God's ability to get him out of prison by his request to the king's cupbearer? Was he whining by claiming innocence, or was he simply letting the king's servant know about his circumstances? Write your comments below. What would you have done in that situation?

_____

_____

## 16.2 Prepared to Make a Difference

The saying goes, "It's not what you know but who you know" that brings you success. This adage suggests relationships are more important to your advancement than knowledge and that those who nurture associations and friendships can gain more success than those who spend time with books and spreadsheets.

What about your experiences? Do you agree or disagree with the saying? Write your impressions here:

_____

_____

Genesis 41:1 begins, "When two full years had passed." Joseph remained in prison two more years after God interpreted the cupbearer and baker's dreams. Our storyteller gives us no indication that Joseph doubted God or tried to escape. In God's timing, however, Pharaoh had two dreams that no one could interpret. In

that moment Joseph's launch to success and power fell in place.

Read Genesis 41:9–13. Highlight the main characters. Summarize what the cupbearer related to Pharaoh here:

_____

_____

The chief cupbearer was near Pharaoh many times. His job included tasting drinks before the king to ensure they were safe for the king to drink. The cupbearer overheard the king's request for someone to interpret his dreams. He remembered Joseph had interpreted his dream. He advised the king about Joseph, and since no one in the king's service could explain his dreams the king sent for the Hebrew prisoner. The headlines read the next day: "Great Egyptian King Calls On 20-Something Jailed Hebrew Slave for Help." That's a scoop.

Read Genesis 41:14–16. Observe the speed with which they prepared Joseph to meet Pharaoh. When the slave arrived Pharaoh made his request of Joseph. Underline Joseph's response in verse 16.

"I can't do it" is the confession of a humble person. An egotist would answer, "Yes, I can. How may I help you?" even if he or she knew full well that the ability to do so came solely from God. Joseph had his opportunity to get out of jail, to "make something of himself;" who he knew had gotten him to the place to show what he knew. Any savvy businessman would tell him to seize the moment and to show off what set him apart from the others. But not Joseph. He never wavered from his confession that God gave him the ability to interpret dreams. He never trusted his own ability to get himself out of a tough situation.

Joseph promised, "But God can tell you what it means and set you at ease" (v. 16, NLT). Joseph put his confidence in his relationship with God, not his own abilities. He could promise what he did to Pharaoh because of what he had learned about God in the quiet moments alone in jail. The quality of his public performance was certain because of his private practice with God.

Take some time to observe your life and notice how God used both other people and times out of the spotlight to prepare you for times of service to Him. Write some of your experiences here:

Read Genesis 41:32. Highlight whom Joseph said was behind both the dream and what would happen.

Joseph said God gave Pharaoh his dream in two forms because He wanted Pharaoh to get the message that He would soon do something significant. God, not Pharaoh, was the focus of the dream given to the king.

## 16.3 The Power of Humility

Humility is the assurance that God, not you, makes things happen. However, it does not deny personal skills or talents. Such a denial signifies false humility. True humility involves submitting to God all you have and who you are. You put your confidence in God, but you are aware of how God made and gifted you. Humility is a quiet confidence that God has empowered and placed you where you are for His purposes, not your ego.

Write your own description of humility here:

Read Genesis 41:33–36. Summarize the plan Joseph gave to Pharaoh in the space below.

Joseph was a skilled leader. Potiphar put him in charge of everything he owned. When in jail, the captain of the guard soon placed him in charge of the other prisoners. So when he stood before Pharaoh and knew what the country faced, he naturally began to lead. He offered a plan that would collect and store resources during the productive years and distribute them during the years of famine. His giftedness and experience of leading others rose to the surface as he spoke with the leader of Egypt.

Do you think Joseph was out of place to offer a solution without Pharaoh asking him? Did he act pushy or simply confident? Write your answers below:

_____

_____

Read Matthew 11:29. Highlight how Jesus described Himself. Jesus described Himself as He called people to put on His yoke of discipleship. Given what you know of Jesus from the Gospels describe how Jesus was "gentle and humble" while certainly being confident and bold. How would you compare Joseph to Jesus' humility?

_____

_____

## 16.4 The Danger of Self-Exaltation

Jesus taught His disciples, "For everyone who exalts himself will be humbled, and he who humbles himself will be exalted" (Luke 14:11). Jesus taught this truth to His followers at a banquet while everyone rushed to the head table to sit near the host (Luke 14:1–10). He told them to take a seat in the back of the room and wait for the host to call them forward. In this they would find

great honor. Jesus' lesson presents a spiritual truth for all times and all people. Write how you would apply Jesus' teaching to both Joseph's life and your own life.

_____

_____

Read Genesis 41:38–41. Underline the rhetorical question Pharaoh asked his advisors (v. 38) and the first phrase of verse 39. For what reasons did Pharaoh give Joseph the authority to carry out his plans to lead Egypt through both the prosperous and the lean years?

Based on Joseph's own witness and interpretation of his dreams, Pharaoh credited Joseph's abilities to "the spirit of God" being in him. The king saw more than an intelligent or experienced young man. He saw God's work in Joseph's life. The king also said that "since God" informed him of both the dreams and the plan, no one else had more capability or wisdom to lead than Joseph.

Joseph's humble confession and confident plans combined to make Pharaoh certain he could trust his entire kingdom to a foreigner who was once a slave. God catapulted a member of His covenant family into the second most powerful position in the world. Why?

_____

_____

Read Genesis 41:53–55. When the seven years of prosperity ended and the famine came to whom did Pharaoh direct the people as they looked for food? (v. 55)

Pharaoh observed how Joseph followed his plans during the years of plenty. Now, when famine began to squeeze the people, he guided them to Joseph. His past performance gave his boss confidence of his future success.

Return to Jesus' teaching about those who humble themselves and those who exalt themselves (Luke 14:11). Joseph's life confirmed this truth. Take time to pray about your ability to humble yourself before God. Ask God how you can be humble and confident for His purposes.

## 16.5 Achieving Greatness

Peter, Jesus' lead disciple, knew the principle of humility. He learned to be humble through his denial of Jesus (Luke 22:54–62) and his restoration to ministry by Jesus (John 21:15–19). He boldly spoke before thousands at Pentecost (Acts 2) and became the leader of the first church. When he wrote to Christians in Asia Minor to encourage them in their suffering, he restated Jesus' teaching about humility.

Read 1 Peter 5:6–7. Underline Peter's command and what he wrote would happen when you follow the command.

Peter wrote that we should humble ourselves "under God's mighty hand" because then He would exalt us "in due time." The word for time in this verse also can be translated "season." Paraphrase this principle:

_____

_____

Joseph humbled himself to the events God orchestrated. He never complained or tried to escape the situations he found himself in, although he got there unjustly. Joseph acknowledged God as the source of his interpretations of dreams. He never took credit for God's work. He carried out his duties and spoke boldly because he had confidence in God's leadership in his life. As we have observed, God exalted the Hebrew dreamer in His season to protect His covenant family from the famine. God exalted Joseph not to save the Egyptians but to preserve His covenant. Do not forget this plot throughout the story.

Our question to consider this week was: How does a person achieve the status of greatness? You came up with ideas when you first read this question. Write them here:

_____

_____

Now that you have observed how God made Joseph a great man how would you modify your answer?

_____

_____

Greatness for God's people is faithfulness to God. When you make that your definition of greatness God can use you as His tools in the world.

**For further study:**
- **Genesis 40–41; 45:1–15; 50:15–21**
- **Romans 8:2; James 2:1–8**

# 17—Leading When You Feel Inadequate (Moses, Part 1 of 2)

When we recall defining moments with God in His-story, Moses' encounter with God at the burning bush will make our Top 10 list. Wouldn't you do God's will if He showed up in a miracle of nature like that and told you exactly what He wanted you to do? You might think about how easily you could know your part in the epic of God's redemption story if He made His presence and direction as obvious as He did with Moses.

But as plain as God spoke to Moses he balked at what God called him to do. God seldom shows up so clearly without having something big to say. Most people would rather cherish the miraculous moment in the desert than go into the city and lead a people out of bondage. They long for burning bushes but feel skittish about the call of God that comes with them.

Moses is an example of a reluctant servant-leader who eventually trusted God to fulfill His call on his life although he felt fearful and hesitant.

The Memory Verse for this chapter is 2 Corinthians 12:9. God's equation of power is the inverse of ours. God tells us He perfects His power in our weakness. Become familiar with this verse as you observe God's power in Moses' weak resolve to lead.

Our question to consider this week is: Are leaders born or made? This modern question has sparked many debates in business schools and seminary classrooms. Keep this question in the back of your mind as you review Moses' call to leadership. We will address it at the end of this chapter.

## 17.1 When God Gets Your Attention

How do you know when God wants to say something to you? How do you know God's voice apart from all the chatter in our noisy lives? One of the challenges of playing your part in His-story is to know what your role is. When you look for defining moments with God in the Bible you find seemingly obvious encounters with God and "you can hear a pin drop" receptions of God's voice. Moses saw a burning bush and heard God's voice. Why doesn't that happen with everyone who desires to know God's will?

Write some of your first answers to that question here:

_____

_____

_____

Read Exodus 3:1. Highlight the names of people and places in the verse. Find them in a Bible dictionary or on a map.

We step into Moses' story when he was 80 years old. His parents saved him from certain death as an infant, and he ended up in the arms of Pharaoh's daughter who raised him in the courts of Egypt as her own (Ex. 2:1–10; see Hebrews 11:23 for the recognition of their faithful act). When he was grown and a member of Pharaoh's family, he killed an Egyptian officer who beat an Israelite slave (Ex. 2:11–12). Pharaoh found out about the murder and wanted to kill Moses, so Moses fled to Midian where he kept his father-in-law's sheep for 40 years (Ex. 2:15–22).

God saw the suffering of His covenant people and needed a leader to bring them out of Egypt and into the land He had promised them.

Read Exodus 3:2–3. Highlight the objects and persons in the verses. Underline Moses' response to the phenomenon.

"The angel of the Lord" represented the presence of God. The angel of the Lord had called to Hagar (Gen. 16:7) and Abraham (Gen. 22:11, 15). This same divine being appeared to Moses in the flames of a burning bush. (See Judges 6:11–12 and 13:13–21 for other encounters with this messenger of God.)

God chose an unnatural event in nature to capture Moses' attention. Fire would come to represent the leadership of God as Moses led the Israelites from Egypt (See Exodus 13:21). Fire engulfed the bush but did not consume it. Moses was smart enough to know something out of the ordinary was happening so he turned to observe it (v. 3). When he did God spoke.

How has God gotten your attention before? Did He use nature? Did He use an event in the ordinary work of life or a time and place unique to your lifestyle? In the space below, describe a time when God showed up in an obvious way to get your attention. Pray a prayer of thanks to Him for that experience.

_____

_____

_____

## 17.2 Responding to God's Call

When you sense God has entered your experience, you hold that time and place as sacred or special. Abraham built an altar when God showed up to remind him of God's covenant (Gen. 12:7–8). Peter wanted to build little tabernacles for the saints on the mountain of Jesus' transfiguration (Mark 9:5). Something within you desires to recognize those places where you sense your connection with Holy God.

Read Exodus 3:4. Underline Moses' response to God's call.

How did Samuel answer to God's voice in the night? (Look up 1 Samuel 3:10.)

What did Isaiah say when God asked who would go tell Israel His message? (Look up Isaiah 6:8.)

What did Peter and Andrew, the fishermen brothers, do when Jesus called them to follow Him? (Look up Matthew 4:18–20.)

Your response to God's call should be "Here I am." But as we will see with Moses, when God begins to unveil the details of His call your willingness may sometimes wander.

Read Exodus 3:5–6. Underline why God told Moses to take off his sandals in verse 5. Highlight the names of God in verse 6.

God told Moses to remove his sandals because he stood in a "holy" place. Holy means, "set apart for God." Look up Leviticus 19:2. What command did God give to

Israel? (See also 1 Peter 1:16.) Moses stood in the presence of Holy God. To remove his sandals showed that the ground under his feet was different from the other ground he had walked on that day.

God revealed Himself through names Moses would know. We know the God of Abraham, Isaac, and Jacob through the defining moments of this study. God wanted Moses to know that he would soon play a major part in His-story, and God identified Moses' role with those who had served God before him.

Describe a time when you sensed you stood on "holy ground." Describe the setting and your feelings. Did you feel you needed to hide your face like Moses, or did you sense a closeness to God? Write your answers here:

_____

_____

_____

## 17.3 Why Did God Speak to Moses?

God did not reveal Himself to Moses in order to deepen Moses' spiritual life. Too often Christians seek God for the purpose of "knowing Him more deeply" or to grow "closer" to Him. They look to God to help them with their situation. They desire to experience God rather than to do what they know He wants them to do. The burning bush was not a "spiritual high" for Moses after which he sat down and recorded the event in his journal. The heart-stopping encounter revealed God's call to Moses to step out of his ordinary, guilt-driven life and into His-story to rescue the covenant people of God. Rather than giving Moses hope for retirement God unsettled his entire existence and called him to lead a nation of unarmed, overworked slaves out of the most powerful country on the planet.

Read Exodus 3:7. What three things did God say caused Him to come to Moses?

_____

_____

_____

Read verse 8. Underline the two things God said He would do because He had seen His people suffering.

Read verses 9–10. Underline God's command to Moses. Notice why God sent Moses back into the palace where he was raised.

God said He saw the suffering of His people and that He had "come down" in order to deliver them from the Egyptian oppression. God wanted to bring them into the land He had promised Abraham, Isaac, and Jacob. God would keep His covenant promise (Gen. 15) and rescue His people from slavery and put them in the promised land, "a land flowing with milk and honey."

The exodus or rescue of Israel in Egypt would be the defining moment of Israel's relationship with God. It would signify God's unfailing love for those He had chosen to reveal Himself through to the world.

Read Colossians 1:13. Underline the word similar to God's promise in Exodus 3:8.

God reveals Himself as a rescuing God. In both the Old and New Testaments the primary metaphor of God's work in His-story is that of rescue. The exodus and the cross form the highest peaks in the two mountain ranges of God's covenant love for His people.

God came to rescue Israel from Egypt and He called Moses to represent Him before Pharaoh. God called—actually commanded—Moses to go (v. 10). Moses now had to decide whether or not he would obey God's call. What would you have done? Write your responses here:

_____

_____

_____

## 17.4 The Relatively Reluctant Leader

As you observe God's choice of leaders in the Bible you do not find one who stepped up and said, "Hey, I'll lead!" without first hearing God's call. Yes, Abraham left Ur and Joseph ruled Egypt but those episodes focused more on receiving and keeping the covenant blessing of God than rescuing anyone. God called Moses to go and promised him he would end up in the promised land. But first, he had to return to the scene of his crime and the people he had offended in order to bring an entire nation of people with him out of Egypt. This may be one reason Moses balked at God's command.

Recall the time when you lived a different lifestyle before Jesus rescued you.

Read Exodus 3:11. Moses did not jump at the chance to return to Egypt and lead God's people in the exodus. He had killed an Egyptian there, and he had betrayed Pharaoh's family by doing so and fleeing the country.

Write some of your thoughts as to why Moses would respond that way he did here:

_____

Read Exodus 3:12. Write God's two assurances to Moses in the space below.

_____

_____

God assured Moses He would be with him as He delivered His people. Moses asked, "Who am I?" (v. 11) God answered, "I AM WHO I AM" (v. 14). It does not matter who we are if we allow God to be who He is. The issue rests not on our competence to perform a certain feat, but on our willingness to allow God to be who He is through us.

God also promised that Moses would worship with those he led out of Egypt on the mountain where he stood. Mount Horeb (Ex. 3:1), or Mount Sinai, was where God gave Moses the Ten Commandments (Ex. 19:20). God made good on His promise to Moses.

What has God clearly called you to do? What excuses do you have for not obeying Him? How can you apply God's assurances (His presence and His promises) to your life situation? Write your thoughts in the space below.

_____

_____

## 17.5 The Servant-Leader

Moses became a servant-leader the day he went to Jethro and told him he was leaving to do what God had told him to do (Ex. 4:18). Servant leadership begins when we make ourselves servants to the mission call of God on our lives. Moses lived the rest of his life as a servant-leader to God's call on his life. His life would be dangerous but also an adventure with the One who led him as he led others.

God patiently answered Moses' questions about God's mission for his life as long as He could, then God grew angry. At this, Moses quit asking questions and did what God had commanded him to do. (See Exodus 3:13–4:17 for the biblical background.) He went home, said goodbye to his family, and headed to Egypt. On the way God orchestrated his meeting with Aaron, and the two leaders made their way to the elders of Israel (Ex. 4:18–31). The elders of Israel initially received Moses' message well. He then went to Pharaoh with the words of God. Pharaoh scoffed at Moses' demands and added to the workload of the people.

Read Exodus 5:21. How did the Israelites respond to Moses' message the second time he told them what God would do?

Read Exodus 6:10–12. Underline what God told Moses to do again. Underline Moses' response to God.

Moses now had neither the support of Pharaoh nor the people God sent him to rescue! How do you lead in that situation?

Write your feelings about Moses' response in the space below. Did he respond in a reasonable way? Would you have said the same thing?

_____

_____

_____

Read Exodus 6:13. Describe in your own words what

God did to get Moses and Aaron back on track.

_____

_____

Servant leadership is about remaining faithful to the mission call of God on your life, not about how people respond to you. Both Pharaoh and the Israelites resisted Moses' message from God.

The hard work of servant-leaders is to continue with the mission even when those they try to lead refuse to follow what God has told them to do. God encouraged Moses and Aaron, and they continued to go to Pharaoh until he let God's people go. (Read Hebrews 11:24–29 for how Moses was commended for his leadership.)

Our question to consider this week was: Are leaders born or made? How would you answer this question after seeing God's work in Moses' life?

_____

_____

God called Moses to a place of leadership to complete the next episode of His-story. The reluctant leader soon found himself on the front lines of a battle for the very survival of God's covenant people.

**For further study:**
- **Genesis 15:5–21; Exodus 2:1–6:13**
- **Deuteronomy 34:1–12; Hebrews 11:23–29**

Every follower of Christ is to represent Him. Jesus calls us the salt of the earth and the light of the world (Matt. 5:13–16). You can also describe our role by saying that you should influence others. You are to lead others. Everyone is a leader to some degree and as Christ-followers God has chosen us to fulfill His purposes.

God chose Moses to lead the mission to rescue the people of Israel from Egyptian control and take them into the promised land. Moses made himself a servant to God's mission and served the people by representing them to God and God to them. Moses not only served as a leader of the people but also as a priest for the people. As God's priest he represented the God of Israel before the king of Egypt and the people of Israel before God.

The Memory Verse for this chapter is Exodus 24:3. God used Moses to lead the people out of Egypt and do what God commanded. Moses had remained faithful to God's call, but even better the people agreed to follow what God said through him. A servant-leader rejoices when those he or she leads agrees to join him or her in God's mission call on their lives.

Our question to consider this week is: Can timid people accomplish something great for God? Or is it better to have a strong personality or will? Begin to formulate your answers now. We will return to these questions later.

## 18.1 Speaking for God

When is the best age to do something great with God? Does a 20-something have advantage over an 80-year-old?

Many value youthful passion above seasoned experience when characterizing the kind of leader God would chose to lead His people. Others would rather follow someone who has studied in the school of hard knocks than follow a wide-eyed, hair-on-fire youth. Would you rather lead or follow?

Exodus 7:1 gives God's response to Moses' question at the end of chapter 6. Moses wondered aloud, "Since I speak with faltering lips, why would Pharaoh listen to me?"(Gen. 6:30) Moses continued to ask for assurances that God would not hang him out to dry when he went to see Pharaoh. Moses knew the power of the Egyptian king and his own infamous reputation in the palace. As at the burning bush, God patiently spelled out His plans for Moses and the people of Israel.

Read Exodus 7:1–2. Highlight what God would make Moses and Aaron.

God said He would make Moses like "God" to Pharaoh. The word for god here is not the name of God given to Moses at the burning bush, but the generic word for god. The Lord is God alone. God, however, would make Moses like a god compared to Pharaoh by what God would do through him.

Read Exodus 7:3–5. Underline what God said he would do to Pharaoh and how Pharaoh would respond to Moses. Look up Exodus 10:1, 20, 27, and 11:10. Underline how God fulfilled His words to Moses. God foretold what Pharaoh would do in order to prepare Moses for his response and to give him confidence although Pharaoh resisted God's words through him.

Read Romans 9:14–18. Paul wrote to the Jews in Rome to explain the hope they shared with the Gentiles in Jesus Christ. Summarize Paul's explanation. How does this help you understand the ways of God in His-story?

_____

_____

God raised up leaders in His-story and used them for His purposes. God not only raised up Moses but He put Pharaoh in power to bring His people into the promised land. God empowered one to serve Him. God hardened the other's heart so He could display His power to show His superiority over the beliefs of the Egyptians so they would know that "I am" is the Lord (Ex. 7:5).

Read Exodus 7:6–7. Fill in the following blanks: Moses was _____ years old and Aaron was _____ years old when they stood before Pharaoh. How do these facts affect your answer to the questions at the beginning of this chapter?

God chose particular leaders for particular times and circumstances to display His power so all would know who He was. Faith allows you to embrace this same truth today. How has God surprised you with His choice of leaders in your life?

## 18.2 Doing Our Part

I like to run trails in mountains. This is a rare treat for me because I live in the plains of North Texas. So every chance I get, I run on hiking or bike trails in elevations higher than the elevation of my home—500 feet above sea level. I ran once in Estes Park, Colorado, and found myself on a ridge in the lower range. I stopped when an opening allowed me to see beyond my narrow path. I took in the majestic sight of the far range and spent time in prayer and worship. I sensed God's presence in the beauty and silence of the moment. That spot marks one of the "set apart" places in my life where I know God came near to encourage me as I played my little part in the bigger Story of God's redemption.

Have you ever experienced God in such a way? If so, describe your experience. If not, when have you sensed God's presence in your life?

_____

_____

God did all He promised Moses and Aaron. After plagues that culminated in the Passover caused Pharaoh to let Israel go (Ex. 12), the Israelites crossed the Red Sea (Ex. 14:21–22), and the Egyptian army died while pursuing them into the sea (Ex. 14:26–28), God led Moses and the people to Mount Sinai (Ex. 19:1–2).

If you have a Bible atlas, look up Mount Sinai on a map. This was the mountain also called Mount Horeb in our earlier studies (Ex. 3:1).

A servant-leader performs whatever tasks the One who called him or her requires. Moses had served as leader, prophet, and warrior for the people according to what God had asked him to do.

Read Exodus 19:20–22. Circle the role God now asked His servant-leader Moses to play:

shepherd            priest            king

God called upon Moses to serve as a priest to the people. A priest represented God to the people and the people to God (Heb. 5:1). God gave careful instructions to Moses for how He wanted the priests of Levi consecrated, or set apart, for His purposes (Ex. 29). The tribe of Levi and their ancestors performed the acts of worship and held the feasts that God ordained for His people in order for them to worship and revere Him.

Read Exodus 19:23–25. Moses represented God to the people, yet he also represented the people to God. How did he do this in these verses?

_____

_____

Moses served the people of Israel as God's priest or representative to them. God also guided him to set apart an entire tribe to lead the nation in worship of God. In what ways do you perform the role of priest in people's lives?

_____

## 18.3 Follow the Leader

One way to know if you are a leader is to look behind and see if you have anyone following. Find whom the people follow, and you will find the leader. Those who hold a leadership position may find themselves alone at the front of an organization with the majority following someone else in the group. Simply holding a leadership position does not guarantee people will follow you. A servant-leader serves those he or she leads by giving a clear picture of the future and a path that leads there. People follow the leader who serves them in this way.

Describe a situation either in which you gladly followed the leader in front of you or in which you found it difficult to follow someone placed in the position of leadership. Describe your situation here:

_____

_____

The people followed Moses out of Egypt and across the Red Sea to the foot of Mount Sinai. The question at this juncture was if they would follow the laws God gave Moses to show them how to live as His chosen people.

Read Exodus 24:3. Underline what the people said they would do when Moses told them the "words and laws" of God.

The people agreed to do all that God had told them to do through Moses. They gave the proper response toward God's leadership. James, the brother of Jesus, tells Christ-followers to not just listen to but to do what God says (Jas. 1:22). God gave the Israelites the "words" of the Ten Commandments (Ex. 20:1–17) and the "laws" that governed how they should live together (Ex. 21:1–23:19), and the people committed themselves to living that way.

Read Exodus 24:4–7. Underline what Moses did in response to the people's allegiance to follow God's "words and laws."

Moses paused and took time to write down all he had heard from God while on the mountain (v. 4). He then built an altar and had young men offer animal sacrifices to the LORD (vv. 4–5). When he divided the blood of the sacrifice (v. 6), he read the "Book of the Covenant" to the people (v. 7). The Book of the Covenant contained the "words and laws" he had written down.

Read Exodus 24:7 again. Underline what the people repeated to Moses. Write the last word of the verse here:

_____

The root word for the word "obey" in Hebrew means, "to listen." Obedience begins with listening and is complete when you have done what you have heard. The people would not have had complete commitment if they had said, "We have heard everything you said." They promised to obey, to do what God told them through Moses.

How would you judge your obedience to what you have heard or read about what God has told you to do? Are you simply a listener or a doer? Take time to prayerfully listen to God and write a prayer in response to Him.

_____

_____

## 18.4 Leading Toward the New Covenant

His-story does not consist of merely random events that happened as people woke up in the morning and decided to go to work and have families. The Story of God's redeeming love for all people purposefully placed people in scenes that not only served the needs of the plotline at the time but also pointed to greater scenes and characters later in the storyline. His-story is ultimately about the Story of Jesus, and the Bible records how God prepared the way for His Son to serve as the final sacrifice and High Priest so that everyone can have access to eternal and abundant life.

Read Exodus 24:8. Highlight "the blood of the covenant that the LORD has made with you."

Moses declared that the blood of the bull they sacrificed represented the covenant God made with the people,

which he had read. The blood and the words made up the elements of God's covenant love. (See Genesis 15:9–21 for the sacrificing of animals when God made His covenant with Abraham.) The blood of an animal sacrificed to God served as the basis for Israel's covenant relationship with God. This practice may seem foreign to twenty-first century city dwellers, but in the world of the ancients taking the life of an animal that supplied food and wealth for the clan displayed a significant trust in God.

Blood of the sacrificed bull is a type of the blood of Christ on the cross, the sign of the new covenant. A biblical type is an Old Testament practice that points to a New Testament event, which brings its completion. For example, when Moses sprinkled the blood over the people to symbolize God's covenant with them he also pointed to the new covenant in Jesus. Later, the Day of Atonement for all of Israel (Lev. 16) offered a more complete type of Jesus' sacrifice for the sins of all people.

Read Luke 22:20. Highlight what Jesus said the cup of the Passover meal represented.

Read Hebrews 9:14–15. Highlight "blood of Christ" (v. 14) and "new covenant" (v. 15). What do these verses tell us about the new covenant in Jesus?

_____

Jesus Christ serves as the "mediator" of the new covenant between God and people. His death on the cross offered the final sacrifice that satisfied the requirements of the old covenant and established a new one through

His death, burial, and Resurrection.

As you read His-story recorded in the Bible look for people, roles, and events that God gives as clues to point people to His Son Jesus. Record some of your thoughts on what this aspect of God's Story means to you.

_____

_____

## 18.5 What if I am Timid?

We usually think of leaders as confident, charismatic people. The leaders people want to follow have certain skills and personality traits that make them attractive and that instill confidence in those who follow them. The only problem is that those kinds of leaders are few and far between. We seem to end up with flawed and failed leaders whom we must make ourselves follow rather than follow with excitement and trust. Leaders are people too, and Moses' reluctant agreement with God to lead the tribes of Israel out of Egypt reminds us that even God's leaders are not always the boldest. The difference between effective leaders in God's Story and those who failed does not rely on personality or skills but on a willingness to be used by God.

Our question to consider this week was: Can timid people accomplish something great for God? Now that you have observed God's use of Moses, based on your study write your answer in the space below.

_____

The issue centers not so much on timid or bold people but on broken or proud people. God can no more use a timid person absorbed in his or her personal affairs than He can use a bold person convinced he or she can do great things on his or her own. One's heart, not one's personal disposition, makes the difference.

Read Numbers 12:3. Write out the verse in the space below. (If you have time, read the story around the verse to see why the writer noted Moses' humility.)

_____

_____

The storyteller wrote that Moses was "more humble than anyone else on the face of the earth." The operative word is humble; submitted to God, aware of whom he is before Holy God. God chooses the humble person, who may come across as timid because he or she does not care to be the first to speak or to lead.

Servant leadership begins with brokenness to ensure that we serve God's mission call on our lives rather than our own agendas. Moses was a servant-leader. He looked timid in comparison to Pharaoh's stubborn strength, but he acted humble and God used him.

As you lead today consider your willingness for God to use you for purposes in His-story over your desire to have it your way.

**For further study:**

• **Exodus 6–14; 15:22–20:20**

• **Luke 22:20; Hebrews 9:16–23; 1 Peter 1:2**

# 19—Developing Strong Convictions (Caleb)

Conviction has seemingly opposing meanings. On one hand, it can mean someone receives a penalty for doing something wrong. On the other hand, the word describes a firmly held belief. For those of us who know God as Father, conviction reflects the work of God inside us. Believing God can do something when the majority says otherwise is the mark of God-given conviction.

Joshua and Caleb play heroes in His-story because they trusted God rather than the negative reports of their peers. They stood against the majority's strength and called the people to follow God's leaders, Moses and Aaron, into the promised land.

The land provided everything God had promised. It teemed with abundant resources, but presented a few minor challenges like the strong tribes who would not want a million foreigners moving onto their land. But no matter the obstacle, Caleb would not budge in his confidence in God's ability to complete His promise.

The Memory Verse for this chapter is Numbers 14:24. Caleb had a "different spirit" than those who refused to trust God to bring them into the promised land. Grow familiar with this verse as it describes a person whom God uses for His eternal purposes.

Our question to consider this week is: When people are completely committed to God, what do their lives look like? As you begin to think about your answer to this question have a person's name in mind.

## 19.1 Learning to Trust God

To trust God means to trust Him when the terrain is tough as well as when the trail is smooth and flat. I have mentioned that I like trail running. My place of respite is nature, and the trails help get me away from the city and into God's good creation. I admit that I prefer flat, well-groomed trails. But I also know that the steepest and most rugged trails lead to the most spectacular views. I could not see them without the struggle to the top.

I ran the Ouachita Trail 50 Mile outside of Little Rock, Arkansas in 2006. The run started up Pinnacle Mountain, which consisted of climbing on all fours over boulders to the top. When I arrived at the end of the rockslide, exhausted and wondering if I could complete the remaining 40-plus miles, I saw the most beautiful sunrise I had seen in my life. A fellow runner took a picture of the horizon with his digital camera, and I keep that picture as the desktop background on my computer as I write. The ecstasy of the moment made the pain of the climb worthwhile.

Do you have a memory of where the work you did paid off in a memorable or profitable experience?

_____

_____

God rescued the tribes of Israel from their slavery in Egypt. They finally arrived at the border of the land God had promised in His covenant with them. Moses sent scouts—one from every tribe—into the land to observe the terrain and potential resistance (Num. 13:1–16). He sent them to see what it would be like when they entered, not to see if they should enter. Committees too often forget the reason they came together in the first place.

The spies returned to report that everything God had promised them was true! However, doubt quickly presented itself, "We know God can do it, BUT we have no money in the bank." They reported, "the people who live there are powerful, and the cities are fortified and very large" (Num. 13:28). Joshua and Caleb tried to convince the people to have faith rather than fear. The other 10 won their persuasion and incited the people to rebel against the leaders who trusted God to enter the land (Num. 14:1–9). God had seen enough of their disobedience and resolved to destroy them all. Moses interceded and pleaded with God not to pour out His anger on them (Num. 14:10–19).

Read Numbers 14:20–23. Highlight what God said He did in verse 20. Underline what God said He would do to the generation whom He had rescued from Egypt.

God forgave the people for their lack of trust in Him. This shows the mercy side of God. However, God refused to lead a generation who consistently would not trust His words or His leaders. Therefore, He promised not one of those who disobeyed Him would enter the land of promise. This shows the justice side of God's character.

What does this incident between God and Israel tell you about the Author of His-story?

_____

_____

## 19.2 Wholehearted Devotion

God seldom picks leaders based on what others think of them. God watches for those who trust Him and regardless of their name, stature, or abilities He stands them in front of a crowd to demonstrate His power through them. Caleb was one of these people. Caleb's name means "dog." I need not explain that such a name did not have much nobility as say, Joshua, which means, "the LORD saves." Write a sentence or two about what Caleb might have experienced in life with a name like Dog.

_____

_____

This is pure speculation on my part, but when it came time for the tribe of Judah to pick one person to go spy out Canaan, they either said, "Let Dog go, if he gets knocked off, that won't be such a big loss," or "Send Dog; He's scrappy. If anyone can handle a fight or see a way out, it's Dog."

One other sentiment may relate, "Dog has gotten picked on all of his life, but he has never given up his faith in God. Let's send him. We know he'll come back with an honest report and tell us what God told him." Dog did exactly that (Num. 13:30). Caleb's trust in God outweighed the cries of the majority. Junkyard dogs will more likely do such a thing than groomed palace dogs.

Read Numbers 14:24. Underline the two phrases God used to describe Caleb.

God judged the people for their lack of faith, but He honored Caleb for his resolute trust in Him. God saw Dog had "a different spirit" than that of the other spies and that Caleb followed God "wholeheartedly," or "fully" (NASB). A spirit of trust and a deep loyalty to God caused God to suspend judgment upon Caleb and his family. God promised that because of Caleb's trust he would survive the 40-year wilderness wanderings and enter the promised land. His descendants would inherit the land as their own. (Joshua 14:7–12 tells about Caleb's reward for his faith.)

Read Numbers 14:25. Notice the direction God sent Moses and the Israelites in the next day. Consider why He did this.

God directed Moses for them to return the way they came to begin the purge of the unfaithful generation who refused to trust God and enter the land. "The Amalekites and Canaanites" inhabited the valleys that the spies had entered. They had caused the people to fear, so God sent the people around them since He knew their lack of faith would keep them from going through their land anyway.

Reflect on how God described Caleb's trust in Him. How would God describe your faith? Memorize Numbers 14:24 and use this verse as a benchmark of a faith that stands against the opinions of others and leans entirely on God's words.

## 19.3 No Room for Wishful Thinking

"Be careful what you wish for, you may receive it" is the old adage that warns us we may get our wish but not in the way we had hoped. For example, you wish for wealth. So you get a degree and a good job, and then your bank account grows. However, when you turn 50 you realize you have all you ever wanted but you are also divorced and your children only call on holidays. Or less dreadful, you wish for a parking place and you drive around until you find one close to the store only to discover when you return that it made an ideal spot for theft and your car is no longer there.

Wishful thinking is not faith, but part of our human condition causes us to want things to change. Rather than letting things take their natural course or trusting God's way as the best way, we had rather wish something to happen and let it be.

Have you ever wished for something that you wanted but realized when you got it that your wishes were empty? How do you distinguish between wishing and faith?

_____

_____

When the spies returned from Canaan, they persuaded the people that the odds against them were too great. So, the people shouted aloud their wishes and rebelled against Moses and Aaron.

Read Numbers 14:2–3. Write what the people wished here:

_____

_____

Read Numbers 14:26–32. In the space below, summarize what God said He would do to the people for their lack of trust in Him. Compare God's judgment with the people's wishes in verses 2–3.

_____

_____

God judged the people according to their wishes. He said, "I will do to you the very things I heard you say" (v. 28). God gave the people what they desired: they would die in the desert (v. 2), every one of them 20 years of age and older (v. 29). But rather than their children falling to the Canaanites as plunder (v. 3), their children would receive God's promise and enter the land (v. 31). They would not be the enemy's plunder, but they would suffer the wilderness wandering because of their parent's wishes.

Read Numbers 14:33–35. Underline what the children would do while in the desert and how long the people would wander. What would be the result of their wandering?

God resolved that those who had "banded together against Him" would die in the desert (v. 35). This judgment may seem excessive to you, and yes, God had forgiven and used others who did not trust in Him initially. However, God needed a generation who would trust Him like Caleb and Joshua in order to face and overcome the trials of taking the promised land.

Write what you have learned about the character of God from today's study. Complete your time with a prayer to God, asking Him to give you faith to want things His way rather than to have your wishes fulfilled.

_____

_____

## 19.4 Experiencing God's Discipline

Coaches sit troublemakers on the bench or kick them off the team. Teachers send them to the office, and parents try different ways to discipline them. Troublemakers ruin the spirit of a team, class, or family. While fairness would require you to keep them around and try to train them to contribute to the mission of the group, sometimes you must simply remove them and not let them play again.

The team plays better, the students learn more, and the family . . . that's a hard one. How do you deal with a troublemaker in a family? How far do you let that person push the limits before you have to do something radical to change his or her behavior or let him or her go?

Write some of your thoughts about dealing with troublemakers and the impact they have on the group with which you work or live. Answer the questions given, and if you find yourself in a similar situation pray for God to give you ways to guide those who war against you.

_____

_____

Read Number 14:36–38. Underline what God did to the 10 who incited the people against Moses. Highlight who God spared from the plague.

God made an example of the troublemakers among the people. You may not agree with His tactics but in order for the people to see the seriousness of their lack of trust in God and His leaders, he struck the 10 spies dead with a plague before the rest of them could load their camels and head back out into the desert. This dramatic move signaled God's serious need for His chosen people to obey Him. Like a coach who benches a troublemaker to show the rest of the team he or she will not tolerate such actions or attitudes, God "benched" the 10 spies to demonstrate how their attitudes would harm the entire group and keep God's game plan from being successful. God needed His people to absolutely trust in Him and His plan before they entered the big game and faced their opponents.

Read Hebrews 12:7–12. What does this letter teach about God's discipline?

Just like a parent who disciplines a child so that child will have good character when he or she grows up, God disciplines His children so "we may share in his holiness" (v. 10). It seems painful at the time—for both parent and child—but in the end it produces "a harvest of righteousness and peace for those who have been trained by it" (v. 11). God trains and disciplines those He chooses as His own. Discipline is acting out of love to shape the one loved into the person he or she was made to be. God, the great coach, removed the troublemakers and sent the team back on the field to strengthen their trust in Him and His plan before they played the big game of entering the promised land.

Reflect on a time when someone disciplined you and while painful, it resulted in strengthening your faith or making you a stronger person. Take time to thank God for His loving discipline in your life.

## 19.5 Believing What You Can't See

Caleb refused to allow the reality of the situation to keep him from trusting God's words. Yes, the Canaanites were huge and their cities fortified, but he trusted God knew all that before He sent them in to spy out the land. Nothing surprises God. Caleb trusted that truth when he stood alone with Joshua against the other spies who saw the same things he did.

Read Hebrews 11:1. Notice the definition of faith. Remember, faith in the Bible is more about trusting in God or in a person than about what you believe. Belief is important, but as in Caleb's situation, sometimes you must suspend what you believe—that a rag-tag band of slaves cannot conquer a fortified city—and trust God's promise of victory. Israel learned this when they took

Jericho in an unconventional way.

Our question to consider this week was: When people are completely committed to God, what do their lives look like? What were some of your initial thoughts, and who did you think about when you read the question?

_____

_____

You have observed Caleb's trust in God compared to those of the other 10 spies. Based on this chapter in His-story, write any different perspectives you have gained.

_____

_____

One of the challenges of Bible study is to allow Scriptures to read you rather than for you to read the Scriptures. You have observed several defining moments with God so far in this book. How have these studies changed what you know about God and how God works? How have they confirmed your trust in Him? Take some time today to evaluate the impact of reading God's Word at face value and allowing it to influence the way you see things. Prayerfully listen to God's prompting.

The next chapter tells how God used Joshua, Caleb's faith partner, to lead the people into the promised land after 40 years in the desert.

**For further study:**
- **Numbers 13–14**
- **Joshua 14:1–15; Judges 1:19–20**

# 20—Secrets to Effective Leadership (Joshua, Part 1 of 2)

Moses never saw what God promised to him at the burning bush. This was not God's fault. Sin kept the promise from becoming reality. Moses' sin of anger and the people's lack of faith the first time they came to the borders of the promised land kept them from obtaining God's promise. His-story does not flow evenly like the Mississippi River through St. Louis. It surges and twists more like the Colorado River through the Grand Canyon. God intended for Israel to go directly from Egypt into Canaan, but the people's choice to resist His leadership caused them to wander in the wilderness for 40 years. The whitewater rapids of the exodus slowed to a muddy, meandering flow as the unbelieving generation died in the desert.

This chapter focuses on the second member of the "Let's trust God" duo of Numbers 13. Joshua, Caleb's partner in faith, would lead Israel across the swollen Jordan River to the land that God had promised Abraham centuries before. This crossing marked a defining moment in God's Story with Israel. Spoken promise would become tangible land as the Israelites followed Joshua into the river and onto dry land.

The Memory Verse for this chapter is Joshua 1:8. God does not abandon those He calls. This verse gives a promise to all who risk leadership for God. By knowing this promise, you have God's formula for success in your heart as you lead others in His name.

Our question to consider this week is: What makes someone a great leader? Start your list. We will compare it later with what we observe in Joshua's life.

## 20.1 Mentoring Others

Someone once said, "You are not a success without a successor." Successful servant-leaders mentor a successor to carry on the mission after they are gone. God gave Moses the mission of leading the Israelites out of Egypt. Moses did that, and he had hoped to lead them into the promised land. However, his sin and their lack of faith prevented him from setting foot on the fertile soil of Canaan. Someone else would lead them there.

Read Joshua 1:1. Highlight the names of the two leaders. Underline how the verse described each.

The verse refers to Moses as "the servant of the LORD," and to Joshua as "son of Nun, Moses' aide." Moses' identity had moved from being a child of his earthly family to a servant belonging to YHWH, the God of Israel. Paul, the Apostle, described himself the same way. (See Romans 1:1.) Biblical servant-leaders identify themselves by whose mission they complete rather than whom they have made themselves to be. Moses died in the desert with only a glimpse of the land "flowing with milk and honey" (Deut. 34:1–8). He died a success because he remained faithful to God's mission call on his life and raised up a leader to carry on God's mission for the people.

Look up the following passages to see how Moses mentored Joshua to lead after he was gone. (Do not forget to read the context around the verses.) Write out how Moses mentored Joshua and made him his clear successor.

Exodus 17:8–13_____

Exodus 24:13–14_____
Exodus 32:15–20_____
Exodus 33:11 _____
Deuteronomy 31:1–8_____

Read Joshua 1:2–4. Underline the two words God told Joshua and the people to do. Highlight the boundaries of the promised land. If you have access to a Bible atlas or maps, look up the names on a map. You can find all four of those names on a modern map of the Middle East.

Read Joshua 1:5. Write the verse out in the space below. As you do, insert your name after each "you." Claim this verse as God's blessing to you today.

_____

_____

## 20.2 God Will Be with You

His real name was Joseph, but his nickname was "Barnabas." It means, "Son of Encouragement" in his native language. When you read about him in the New Testament you soon discover why his friends gave him that name. He encouraged the Church through giving (Acts 4:36–37). He encouraged the ethnic groups in Antioch that had begun to trust Jesus (Acts 11:22–24). He also encouraged Saul of Tarsus, later called Paul, to join what God was doing in the church at Antioch (Acts 11:25–26). He played a key role in the emerging movement of Christ-followers among non-Jewish groups around the world.

God called Joshua to complete the mission to lead the

people of Israel into the promised land. Like a good coach who encourages his team captain before the team takes the field, God encouraged Moses' successor before the tribes formed together to cross the Jordan.

Read Joshua 1:6–9. Highlight every time God said "Be strong and courageous." Underline the direct instructions God gave Joshua, and circle what God promised to him if he would do those things (vv. 7–8).

Three times God called Joshua to "Be strong and courageous" (vv. 6, 7, 9). God told him to obey and do everything in the Law God had given him through Moses. If he would do that, God promised he would have success in everything that he did (vv. 7–8).

WARNING: Success in these verses relates to the purposes of God, not necessarily to our happiness and wealth. God promised Joshua success and prosperity as he completed the mission God called him to do. Be careful not to take the verse out of its context in His-story and interpret it by our culture's definition of success.

Take some time to interact with the above warning. Do you agree or disagree with the caution? Why?

_____

_____

_____

_____

The Memory Verse for this chapter is Joshua 1:8. Write it out in the space below and allow God to write it on your heart as His promise for you as you obey Him.

_____

_____

God promised Joshua He would be with him wherever he went (v. 9). God would not send His servant-leader on a mission in which He would not be present the entire time.

Read John 14:15–20. Underline verse 18. Summarize Jesus' words to His followers here:

_____

_____

No servant-leader launches on a mission with God without God's presence. Write a prayer to God thanking Him for His presence as you seek to obey what He has clearly called you to do.

## 20.3 Let's Roll

"Get up; it's time to get ready!" It was 4:30 on the morning of my first attempt at a 100-mile run. Get ready? I had been doing that for the last eight months, but I knew what my friend meant. Get ready for the actual event. Get ready for the run of your life. Make sure all your drop bags have enough supplies for the potential 30-hour experience. The training had ended. It was time to step up to the starting line and see if I had what it takes to complete 100 miles of Arkansas forest trails. I only made it 73.2 miles on that attempt, but I will never forget the experience or the call to get ready that morning!

Write about one of the most memorable times you woke up to someone calling for you to "Get ready!" You may remember getting ready for a special trip you were about to take or a holiday you anticipated for many weeks.

_____

_____

_____

Read Joshua 1:10–11. Underline what Joshua commanded the people to do.

They had traveled here before—40 years earlier. This time, the people were ready to follow God's leader. With the people's trust and God's encouragement, Joshua went to his officers and told them: "Get ready! In three days we're going in." They would cross the Jordan and take possession of the land. These two acts will outline the next episodes of His-story. Joshua 2–5 will tell of the events when they crossed the Jordan, and chapters 6 and following tell how they took possession of the land.

Read Joshua 1:12–15. Highlight the three tribes mentioned in these verses. Notice what Joshua said to them. (Read Numbers 32:1–27 about the deal the tribes of Gad and Reuben and the half-tribe of Manasseh struck with Moses before Joshua became the leader.)

To get ready to cross the Jordan Joshua told the people to get their supplies together (v. 11), and he confirmed a

previous agreement Moses had made in order to have the full support of all the tribes (vv. 12–15). Once he stepped into the river there was no turning back to get what they needed or to stop and negotiate with anyone. Adequate supplies and settled promises play a crucial part in any campaign. Servant-leaders know to prepare people for what lies ahead by giving them time to do these things.

Let crossing the Jordan serve as a metaphor for the next big thing God has asked you to do. If God said "get ready" today, would you have adequate supplies (emotional, spiritual, and physical), and have you settled agreements you have made with people that could slow you down once you "crossed over"? Prayerfully consider those things and write your situation in the space below.

_____

_____

## 20.4 Divine Boldness

Servant-leaders need the trust of the people, and the people need to trust their leader. Nothing in the mission gets done if the leader cannot gain the trust of the people or the people do not trust their leader. Sometimes, since God does not always choose those whom we would naturally follow, He has to help create trust among the people—thus, the 40 years of follow-ship training in the desert for the Israelites. On the other hand, people cannot trust or follow a leader who sounds the call to action and then hesitates at the first hint of resistance. Leaders gripe about people who won't follow, and followers gripe about leaders who won't lead.

Whether in a marriage, family, church, or business, you most likely can relate to the above description about leaders and followers. Take time to describe a situation in which you as the leader have received criticism for wavering too much or in which you as a follower have not given the leader the trust required to accomplish the mission. Write some of your thoughts here:

_____

_____

Read Joshua 1:16–18. Underline what the people said they would do for Joshua. Highlight what they requested of Joshua. Hint: "Only may . . ." (vv. 17–18).

The people pledged they would obey Joshua as they had Moses. Remember, this happened after 40 years in the desert where God allowed an unbelieving generation to die off and trained those who remained alive to trust Him regardless of His requests. God, through Moses, had also prepared Joshua to lead the next stage of the mission. The training camp in the desert made them strong and trusting of their leaders for when the season of conquest began. The people spoke true words.

Return to the phrases you highlighted in verses 17–18. Summarize the requests of the people to Joshua.

_____

_____

The people asked that "the LORD your God" be with Joshua as He was with Moses. This held Joshua responsible to the people in making sure he spent time hearing and obeying the words of God himself. Servant-leaders cannot stay on mission without a consistent relationship with the One who sent them. Secondly, the people asked that Joshua "be strong and courageous." Followers need to trust that their leader will prevail and stand bold when resistance comes—either from external enemies or internal dissension. Joshua would stand strong because God had promised His presence.

You are a leader if you influence a group of people's lives. Based on the interaction between Joshua and the people in this scene, what leadership lessons have you gleaned from this passage?

_____

_____

## 20.5 Seeking Greatness

We all have our idea about what makes someone great. Begin today's defining moment by writing the name of someone you consider great and then write a description as to why you consider him or her "great."

_____

_____

Our question to consider this week was: What makes someone a great leader? Take your impressions from above and review Joshua's leadership. Describe why you consider him a great leader. Add to your ideas what you have learned about him in the Bible.

_____

_____

Read Mark 10:42–44. How did Jesus describe someone who would be "great" among His followers? How did He describe one who would be "first?"

_____

_____

How do you reconcile "great" equated with being a servant and "first," or the leader, as being like a slave? Write your thoughts here:

_____

Read Mark 10:45. Jesus reminded His followers that even

He, the Son of Man, did not come to be served, but like a servant He came to serve and to lay down His life as a ransom for many. Jesus lived out the example for His own description of a great leader. He modeled great leadership in the Kingdom of God as a servant who gives up his or her life so that many can experience God's purposes in their lives. Joshua fit Jesus' description because, he too, was a servant to the mission call of God on his life and to the people so they could have what God wanted for them. Jesus and Joshua were servant-leaders because they gave their lives so others could receive God's promises to them.

God continually calls out servant-leaders to help Him write an episode of His-story. Joshua was one of those leaders. He was a servant of God and served the people by being and doing what they needed him to be and do. You can have confidence that if God has called you to join Him on the pages of His-story He will not abandon you. He will empower you to "be strong and courageous" no matter the circumstances.

Write a prayer to God that speaks of your willingness to be a servant-leader in the circle of influence in which He has placed you. Also, check your lifestyle to see if you fulfill the needs of those who follow you: Have you made time so "the LORD your God" is "with you," and have you been "strong and courageous" for those who trust you enough to follow you?

**For further study:**
• **Numbers 13:8, 16; 14:6–30**
• **Numbers 27:18–23**

## 21—Risking Everything for God (Rahab)

Risk is something that likely repels you or compels you, depending on your personality. Regardless, few people will risk their lives unless they have a good reason. For the people of God, risk is part of life. God has called us to obey Him and trust that the future is in His hands.

Israel stood ready to cross the Jordan River and enter the promised land. Joshua had ordered the people to get their provisions ready because in three days they would pick up and move into the land of Canaan. While the people prepared, Joshua sent spies into the closest major city to scope out potential resistance. (Does this sound reminiscent of another group of spies some 40 years earlier?) For cover, the spies entered the house of a prostitute in the busy city of Jericho. And so began an episode in His-story where a woman of ill repute turned into a hero of faith whom the ancients would honor for centuries to come. Rahab, the prostitute, shows up in

two New Testament lists of people God used because of their trust in Him. While the faithful should not emulate this woman's lifestyle, she models a trust in God that all should embrace.

The Memory Verse for this chapter is Hebrews 11:31. Faith is trust in action. Rahab got inducted into the "Hall of Faith" because she protected the spies from her king. Memorize this verse as a reminder that no matter our background, God honors those who honor Him.

Our question to consider this week is: Does God really want us to take serious risks? Rahab risked her life to protect the spies of Israel. She endangered not only her life but that of her family. Should we jeopardize the lives of others even when the risk has to do with our trust in God? Begin to formulate your answer and then observe Rahab's experience.

# 21.1 Who Can God Use?

Prostitution and lying easily make the Top 10 of any "do not do" list for moral people. No one would quarrel over whether or not these acts were wrong. They break two of the Ten Commandments (Ex. 20:14, 16). Most religious people would hesitate to accept a person who did these things, and they most likely would choose anyone else on a list of people whom God would use in His-story to accomplish the plan. God, however, will use someone who trusts Him over one who simply keeps His rules. Every character's storyline matters in His-story because God's plan stands superior to our judgments of people.

Be honest and write some biases you hold against a person who commits sexual immorality and who lies. What is the likelihood of God using this person in His-story according to your perceptions?

_____

_____

Read Joshua 2:1. Highlight the city they went to spy out, and underline where they stayed in the city. If you have a Bible atlas or maps, look up Jericho's location. You can also find it on a modern map of the region.

Joshua remembered his spying experience from earlier and followed his mentor's practice; he sent two men in to scope out the land. In order to get inside the city gates, they entered the house of a prostitute named Rahab and stayed there. Foreigners could remain less conspicuous staying in a brothel instead of staying in an inn or asking around for a place to stay.

Rahab was a prostitute. No word study can get around it. She sold her body for money, and her home was on the network of where to go when men came to the city looking for sex. Women in those days often got forced into prostitution when their husband died or the family could not support them. Rahab's name meant "broad" and may have influenced the negative use of the term for a woman today.

Read Joshua 2:2–7. Word of foreign men inside the city gates made it quickly to the king. He sent a message to Rahab to bring the travelers to him (vv. 2–3). Underline what she did with the men (vv. 4, 6). What did she tell the messengers of the king? (v. 5)

Rahab lied to the king. She hid them on her flat roof under stalks of flax, which she stored until making them into linen. Nothing would look out of place while the spies hid under the stalks. Rahab's lie worked, and the king's men left her house to pursue the phantom spies into the night (v. 7).

One way to enter the story of the Bible is to put yourself into the life of a character. Take time today to imagine how Rahab got to this place in her life, how she may have felt about her reputation in town, and why she hid the foreigners. Read about Rahab in a commentary or Bible dictionary to get more background on her life.

## 21.2 Prudent Actions

When you meet a person, you do not know what God has already done to reveal Himself to him or her. God continuously works through your actions or the actions of

His people to prepare the way for your witness. You never know who watches your good deeds or who has formed an opinion about your God because of His acts through you. You do not know who has prayed that God reveal Himself to them so they may believe. For this reason, we should not only be careful about how we represent God but we should also freely engage others with the confidence that our presence or conversation may answer their prayer to know God.

Have you ever met someone who had sought after God and your conversation helped him or her to trust Jesus? If so, describe that event. If not, how would you apply this possibility to your actions today?

_____

_____

_____

Read Joshua 2:8–11a. Before the men went to sleep and after the king's men had exited the city, Rahab went on the roof to talk to her hidden guests. She explained why she had risked her life by lying to the king's men. Summarize her reason here:

_____

_____

Rahab heard with the rest of the city about the mighty acts of God. News of the parting of the Red Sea and the defeat of their neighbors (Num. 21:21–31) had reached Jericho. As other travelers passed through her house,

she had firsthand accounts of the acts of Israel's God, Yahweh, or Jehovah (vv. 8–10). She also told them that great fear had fallen on the people of Jericho because of what they had heard (v. 11a).

Read the second part of verse 11. Highlight the phrase that begins with "for the LORD." This phrase is Rahab's confession of faith in the LORD. The primary god of Canaan was Baal, a fertility god. Rahab, however, confessed that Yahweh, the God of Israel, was "God in heaven above and on the earth below."

Read verses 12–13. Based on her confession of faith in Yahweh she asked that the spies spare her and her family. She asked them to swear that they would protect her and give her a sign of their word. Since she had shown kindness to them she asked that they show kindness to her.

Read verse 14. Underline the promise the spies made to Rahab. The spies agreed to return her kindness by sparing her and her family when they returned to take the land

and the city. They promised their life for her life. Make a short list of some of the things you have heard from others that either led you to trust Jesus as Lord or that strengthened your faith in Him.

_____

_____

## 21.3 Sign of Protection

The final miracle God enacted in Egypt was the death of first born sons. The death angel passed over the land and took the life of the first heir of every family; every family except those who had sprinkled the blood of a lamb on the doorpost of their home (Ex. 12:7). This sign of sacrifice marked the home as one in which the family trusted God's words and lived in obedience to do what He commanded. This miracle came to be known as the Passover—when the death angel passed over the families with blood on the entrances to their homes. This event points those of us who read the Bible from this side of the cross to God's plan to rescue all people through the final blood sacrifice of Jesus.

Compare and contrast the events of Exodus 12 with Mark 14:12–26 and Mark 15:21–39. What acts are common, and how did Jesus' Last Supper and death on the cross "fulfill" the Passover promise of God for all people?

_____

_____

Read Joshua 2:15–16. Notice how Rahab fulfilled her promise to the spies.

Read verses 17–21, and notice what the spies told her to do. Highlight what they told her to tie in her window.

The spies told Rahab to tie a scarlet cord in the window through which she lowered them and to gather her family into her home when the Israelites returned for war. Everyone in the house marked by the scarlet cord would be safe from the invading army. Anyone who left the house lost any guarantee of protection.

The scarlet cord Rahab tied to her window was a type of the red blood of the Passover that the Israelites spread on their doorposts. Both created a covering that brought protection from death by those who trusted the words of God through His representatives. Both required not just belief in God, but also an active trust by those who heard the promise.

How are both the Passover and Rahab's scarlet cord similar to Jesus' death on the cross? What do these events tell us about the primary plotline of His-story? Write your thoughts here:

_____

_____

Read Joshua 2:22–24. Underline the spies' announcement to Joshua after they hid in the mountains for three days.

The witness of God's works in His-story caused Rahab to

confess her trust in Yahweh above all other gods. She trusted the witness of the spies and acted out her faith by tying a scarlet cord in her window. She was later saved when Israel took the city. How is this pattern of witness and trust similar to our witness to others? Take a moment to consider how you came to trust Christ's eternal protection for you.

## 21.4 Waiting on the Promises

Sometimes the time between when we trust God's promise and God's fulfillment of that promise is lengthy. We hope for God's Word to come true like when we hoped to get what we wanted through birthday wishes or lists we gave Santa Claus as children. We forget that God gives us His Word to grant us confident hope, not happiness. The time between promise and fulfillment is a season of trust as we wait with anticipation for God's Word to manifest. Waiting requires hope, and God's Word is a source of that hope.

Rahab hung the scarlet cord in her window but some time lapsed before the armies of Israel rescued her from the destruction of the city. The red cord hanging from her window may have given a sign to travelers of where to find a woman like her—the precursor to a "red light district"—when it actually gave a sign of trust in God.

Imagine what Rahab must have thought as she waited for Israel to cross the Jordan and surround her city? How did her faith strengthen or waiver the closer the troops got to the walls? What do you believe she did during the six days the Israelites walked around the city?

How was her waiting experience similar to your own experiences of waiting on God to fulfill His promises? Write your thoughts here:

_____

_____

_____

Read Joshua 6:17, 22–24. Highlight from what Israel would spare Rahab. Underline why Israel would spare her.

God introduced the practice of "devotion to the Lord" when Israel took Jericho. To "devote" a city to the Lord meant to completely destroy the town or people in order to remove them as an obstacle to God and His people. This practice may seem ruthless to us, but God used it not only to clear the way for His people to occupy the land but also as an act of trust by the people that God would provide even when they destroyed everything useable to them on their journey. Because of her act
of faith—hanging the scarlet cord in the window and gathering her family into her house—Joshua and his army spared Rahab.

Read Joshua 6:25. The storyteller concluded his account of Rahab by noting the Canaanite "prostitute" lived among the chosen people of Yahweh "to this day." The most unlikely citizen of Jericho lived among God's people as a reminder of God's kindness toward those who put their trust in Him.

Rahab waited in faith, and her trust was rewarded by her rescue. Take time to say or write a prayer to thank God for the hope He has given you in His promise of your rescue from destruction through your trust in Jesus.

## 21.5 Famous Faith

Rahab's act of trust still held significance for the New Testament writers. As God inspired them to look back over His-story and take note of the plotline that led to Jesus, Rahab's name came up several times. She played a key role in Jesus' genealogy and gave an example of what faith in action looks like for all followers of Jesus.

Read Matthew 1:5. What is the context of her name here? How does this verse describe her? Highlight her name and the name of her son. Also, highlight the names of the other three women (besides Mary) recorded in Jesus' genealogy (vv. 3, 5, 6). Use a Bible dictionary to find out more about Tamar, Ruth, and Uriah's wife.

Read Hebrew 11:31. What is the context of her name in this passage? Underline what the writer recorded about Rahab in the list of famous people of faith.

Read James 2:25. What did James write about when he used Rahab as an illustration? Why did he claim she was "considered righteous"? What does this teach you about the true nature of faith?

_____

_____

Rahab, a foreigner and a prostitute, is an example of anyone who will trust God's Word and act upon it. God spared her because she trusted His promise through His people. Rahab stepped into the stream of Abraham's descendants whose lineage led to Jesus, the Son of God, whose final blood sacrifice rescues those who trust Him. She risked her life with her own people and with the spies, but her risk of faith resulted in her salvation. Rahab provides an example for all who risk trusting God and His Word.

Take some time and write out how your observation of Rahab's life has influenced your trust in God. What has she inspired you to do? How has she taught you to trust? How much do you really risk because you trust God?

_____

_____

_____

**For further study:**
- **Daniel 6**
- **Hebrews 11**

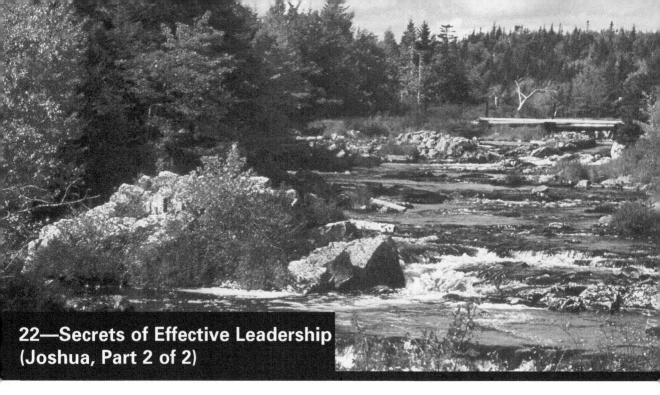

In recent years the word leadership has become more that just a buzz word. It has become the passion of CEOs, pastors, and business professionals.

The Bible describes effective leadership as servant leadership. As we studied in week 20, Jesus described His model for leadership in Mark 10:42–44 and directed His followers not to "lord it over" others, but to serve others.

Effective servant leadership requires absolute resolve to complete God's mission no matter how absurd it may seem. Moses trained Joshua in the ways of God in the wilderness. Joshua had experienced the power of God in the crossing of the Jordan River and now it came time to take the first major city of the promised land. He had defeated lesser foes on his way to Canaan, but Jericho lay as his biggest challenge yet. How would he lead the people to take a walled city? They had no training in

siege warfare. He had no choice but to listen to God's plan—a plan that sounds strange to modern ears and must have been just as hard to grasp when Joshua heard it the first time.

The Memory Verse for this chapter is Hebrews 11:30. The writer of the Letter to the Hebrews honored Joshua for completing God's battle plan to take Jericho without hesitation.

Our question to consider this week is: Does God ever tell us to do something that seems to make no sense? Joshua's leadership to defeat the king of Jericho would say yes, but does God still ask His leaders to do things that seem to make no sense to those who follow?

## 22.1 Accepting Orders

God is in the business of asking His leaders to do things in unconventional ways so that they, those they lead, and those who do not believe know the results came from Him alone. God paired down Gideon's army from 32,000 to 300 to show His power (Judg. 7). Elijah's odds were 450 to one when he asked God to show Himself by raining fire on an altar soaked with water (1 Kings 18). Jesus confounded His disciples when He told them to seat 5,000 for dinner when they had nothing to offer (Matt. 14:13–21). Biblical servant-leaders soon learn that the mission they lead is more about God getting credit for completing His rescue plan than about their skills as leaders.

What other biblical examples come to your mind as you remember odd things God asked His leaders to do to show His power? Describe them in the space below.

_____

_____

If you cannot think of any others, read the passages listed above to see what God did in each story. Read Joshua 6:1. Jericho "was tightly shut up." Why was that so? What information from the bigger context of the passage helps you understand this phrase? List a passage or two here that explains this condition of the city:

_____

_____

Joshua 2:8–10 tell of Jericho's fear of Israel and their God. The invaders now camped outside the city. The fear of rumors had turned into the fear of reality.

Read Joshua 6:2–5. Underline the promises of God in verses 2 and 5. The verses between those promises list a battle plan. Describe the plan in the space below.

_____

_____

Seven priests carrying ram's horns would march in front of the ark of the covenant followed by all the armed men. (See Exodus 25:10–22 for the makeup of the ark.) No one must say anything while they marched around the city. Only the trumpets would sound. After one pass around the city they would return to the camp. They must do this for six straight days. On the seventh, they would march around the city seven times and on the last pass they would blow the horns and the people would shout. God said the walls would simply collapse. God's promise was that the city and its king already belonged to Joshua.

Every servant-leader of God must decide when given God's plan to fully accept it or to add his or her own twist to it. Or if something seems irrelevant or ineffective, he or she may omit or replace parts of it with something that had before worked for the group. Effective servant-leadership accepts God's plan and executes it as He has revealed it—no matter how strange it may seem to those who follow.

## 22.2 Risk Factor

The risk of biblical servant leadership involves telling those you lead what you know as God's plan for them—especially when the plan goes beyond their experience. Many leaders fail in the execution of God's plan because they know what God has called them to do, yet they cannot find the courage to relate God's plan to those they lead. They fear that those who hear them will find the idea so absurd they would never do it.

For example, let's say God puts it on the heart of a leader to meet the needs of a neighborhood in a certain part of town. It is known as a low-income, high-crime area. No new members or funds would come from the area, and it would take both volunteer hours and ministry money away from the programs of the church. But God's prompting will not leave the leader's heart.

The leader now stands in the place Joshua stood when God gave him the plan to take Jericho. God's message was clear, but how would it "sale" with the people?

Read Joshua 6:6–7. Highlight the two groups to whom he gave orders.

Joshua did not hesitate to give God's orders to the priests or to the people. Along with the promises God gave Joshua in verses 2 and 5, for what other reasons could Joshua so confidently turn and give the odd military orders to the people?

_____

_____

Previous experience with God provides a source of confidence for the servant-leader. Read Joshua 3:14–17. God parted the swollen Jordan River when the priests carrying the ark of the covenant put their feet in the water, and the people crossed on dry land to the other side. God's use of the ark to demonstrate His power was nothing new, and the Israelites had positive memories from their last experience with it. God had used the ark as a symbol of His presence and power before, and Joshua felt comfortable telling the people again to follow it in order to experience the power of God.

God's promise and Joshua's previous experience with God were two things that gave Joshua the confidence to turn and tell the people God's plan to take Jericho.

What experiences have you had with God that give you confidence if He were to ask you to do something out of the ordinary you would risk doing it? Describe one or two of your experiences in the space below. Pause and pray, thanking God for the demonstration of His presence in your life.

_____

_____

## 22.3 Working God's Plan

The challenge of biblical servant leadership involves motivating the people to do what God has told the leader they must do. God had a unique plan for taking Jericho, but Joshua did not hesitate and ordered the priests and people to follow. The moment of effective leadership happened when the priests picked up the ark and the people followed them around the walled city. This is different than what happened with Moses after the 10 spies deemed entering the promised land as too risky. Moses had to spend time convincing the people that even though entering the land seemed like a huge risk, they needed to move forward and trust God's plan.

Return to the leader who sensed God wanted the church to engage the needs of the neighborhood. Out of obedience to God's call the leader must at some time invite the people to join what God wants to do in that neighborhood to meet its needs in the name of Jesus. What are some possible negative responses the church may give to God's call? What are some positive responses to the idea? Write your thoughts here:

_____

_____

Read Joshua 6:8–11. Highlight the different characters in this scene. What new command did Joshua give the people (v. 10)? Underline the response to his orders. Read Joshua 6:12–14. Consider the sounds of the circling crowd.

The only sounds Jericho heard were the shuffling of feet and of trumpets as the invaders walked around the city once and then returned to their camp. This went on for six days straight.

Joshua embraced God's plan as did the priests and the military leaders. We know the people did also, but put yourself in the place of an Israelite not in leadership.

What comments would you have by the fifth or sixth day of walking quietly around a walled city when you wanted the army to attack and get it over with?

_____

_____

Effective servant leadership requires those who follow to carry out the plan until its completion—no matter how unreasonable it may seem.

Have you ever done anything that seemed out of the ordinary but that you felt led to do either through the Bible, prayer, or a spiritual leader? What did you do and how did you experience God in doing it? If not, what spiritual discipline such as obedience, fasting, or simplicity may God call you to do consistently for a period of time?

_____

_____

_____

## 22.4 Blessed Leadership

God told Joshua His plan to defeat the walled city of Jericho by God's power, not by his army or leadership. Without hesitation Joshua commanded his leaders and the people to follow God's plan. Everyone responded although the idea seemed strange and an unlikely way to overcome the defenses of such a huge city. When servant-leaders humbly lead people in God's plans, God can do mighty and wonderful things through them.

Our imaginary leader risked telling the church of God's plan for the neighborhood. The leadership and church embraced the concept and put a plan together to meet the needs of after-school care and tutoring for the neighborhood. They teamed up with local groups and worked alongside them to meet this need. What are some possible outcomes of such a situation? Have you experienced similar opportunities with your church or group?

_____

_____

God blesses effective servant leadership because the leader and those who follow have made themselves servants to God's plan. God gets the credit in this situation because what happens usually has no other explanation than, "God did it!"

Read Joshua 6:15–16. Underline the final instructions of Joshua to the people.

Read Joshua 6:20–21, 24. Notice the result of Joshua's command.

God's promises became reality. God gave the people the city—not by conventional warfare, but by a miraculous demonstration of God's power. On the seventh day and on the seventh revolution, the people shouted and the walls fell. Every man charged into the city and took it without resistance (v. 20). The confidence of those in Jericho collapsed with their defenses, and the courage of the Israelites soared when the walls fell.

The people also practiced the "devotion" of all things in the city to the LORD. This purge of the city would serve as an example to all of God's enemies that the land belonged to Israel's tribes not to its inhabitants. The items of value taken started a storehouse of currency to support Israel as it continued its conquest of the land (v. 24).

You can see how the hostilities between Israel and those who lived in Canaan before them could have grown up. Those same hostilities exist today between Israel and its neighbors. The battles in the Middle East persist over land and who occupies it.

God miraculously removed the defenses of Jericho in order for Israel to receive its inheritance of the land. While the actions of the military were violent according to modern rules of engagement, they served to give notice to the God of Israel, Yahweh, as a powerful foe.

Pause and seek to know the heart of God in these actions of His people. Thank Him for the inheritance of the land that led to the birth of His Son and your rescue by Him.

## 22.5 A Famous Work of God

We have talked about what makes someone "great," but what makes someone "famous"? Jeffrey Dahmer and Suddam Hussein are famous, but few would call them great. Mel Gibson and Jennifer Aniston are famous, but not so much great. A person can be famous and not great, or vice versa. Fame is a tricky label that sticks to those who may or may not desire it, and those who have it are not always glad their wishes came true.

Read Joshua 6:26. Summarize Joshua's curse on the city of Jericho in the space below.

_____

_____

Joshua completed the absolute destruction of Jericho by making an oath before God that anyone who tries to rebuild its walls will lose his first born son and whomever tries to reset the city gates will lose their youngest.

Read Joshua 6:27. Underline the two phrases that conclude this episode of His-story.

Our storyteller observed that after the fall and destruction of Jericho one could clearly see "the LORD was with Joshua." After such a display of God's power through His humble servant, who couldn't see that? The second observation was that "his fame spread throughout the land." The natural reading of the phrase would make Joshua the antecedent of "his," however you could also read it as "Yahweh's fame spread throughout the land."

Joshua's victory and Yahweh's power existed as one in the same. To know one meant to experience the other. Whether or not "his" refers to Joshua or Yahweh proves inconsequential to the fact that what happened at Jericho spread like wildfire over the hills and valleys of Canaan.

Our question to consider this week was: Does God ever tell us to do something that seems to make no sense? Based on your observations of God's instructions to Joshua, how would you answer this question?

_____

_____

Read Hebrews 11:30. Underline why the walls of Jericho fell according to the writer.

"By faith" they fell, not by Joshua's leadership skills or the military's might or the people's numbers. The walls fell because all from Joshua to the last family in the procession around the city trusted God's words that if they did what He told them to do the city would belong to them. Faith activates the power of God to complete His plan.

Take time to quietly listen for God's voice. Jericho's fall was a huge event, and you may wonder what it has to do with your life today. As you sit quietly, ask God to strengthen your faith in Him so He can do whatever He wants through you. Don't worry if you don't hear anything. Review this chapter and trust that God can create such a defining moment in your life.

**For further study:**
- **Joshua 5:13–15; 7:1–26**
- **Joshua 8:1–29**

# 23—God Uses Imperfect People (Judge Gideon, Part 1 of 2)

Does God use flawed people? If so, how? This week's study gives us insight into this question.

Israel went beyond Jericho to settle by tribes into the land God promised them. They did not completely drive out those who lived there, and they intermarried with the locals and began to mix their worship of Yahweh with that of Baal. The focus of the invaders got fuzzy as they settled into their new homes. God allowed neighboring clans to harass Israel because of their disobedience. But, staying true to His promises, God raised up occasional leaders to unite the tribes and drive back their foes. This period of His-story is called the time of the "judges." Gideon was a "judge." He was also a reluctant servant-leader. Like Moses to whom God came in solitude and in troubled times, Gideon became a hero in Israel not because of who he was but by what God did through him. His reluctance reminds us of ourselves when God

calls, but his eventual obedience to God's words gives us hope that God can use us if we trust him. Gideon, cautious in his faith and small in stature and influence, did not seem like someone we would choose to solve our biggest problems. Yet, God used this imperfect man to lead His people into battle to defeat those who harassed them in the promised land.

The Memory Verses for this chapter are Judges 6:15–16. These verses pose the ideal combination of our reluctance and God's assurance when He calls us.

Our question to consider this week is: Should we use Gideon's example of "putting out a fleece" to discover God's will? We will not look at this incident directly in our study, but what he did to test the words of God does raise the question of how we truly know what God wants us to do. Read Judges 6:36–40 and see what Gideon did.

## 23.1 A Dance with Danger

When I was in the first grade, I lived across the street from the elementary school I attended. I would walk down the street from my house to a crosswalk guarded by fifth and sixth graders. I would tremble every time I would come to the crossing if a certain sixth grader stood at patrol. A rumor spread among us first graders that the sixth grader told a kid to stop once and the kid talked back, so he cut the kid's tongue out. Of course, no one had ever seen the kid without a tongue and the sixth grader was still in school, but the fear of him really existed. I always felt thankful once I sat in my classroom whenever he patrolled the crosswalk.

Did you have a perceived or real bully growing up? What was his or her name and what did he or she do to you? How did you overcome your fear to combat your bully's influence on you?

_____

_____

Israel had real bullies, but not because every story has a villain who brings hard times to the main character. In His-story, things happen because the Author either allows or ordains them.

Our storyteller in the Book of Judges described how Israel and God had fallen into a dance of disobedience, judgment, repentance, and rescue. The steps grew so familiar that some writers call the dance the "cycle of the judges."

Read Judges 2:11–19. Write some of the dance steps in the space below.

_____

_____

Read Judges 6:1–6, the setting of this episode in His-story. Underline the parts of this introduction to Gideon that correspond with the dance steps we see in Judges 2.

Israel sinned (Judg. 6:1). God allowed the Midianites to harass them (vv. 2–5). Israel cried out to God for help (v. 6). God sent a prophet to remind them of what He had done for them and the covenant agreements they had broken (vv. 7–10).

God, however, refused to leave His people in their sin. He had chosen to use them to He reveal Himself to all the nations. So, God sent an angel to an unlikely hero, who felt as discouraged and unsure as the rest of Israel.

Read Judges 6:11–12. Highlight the names in these verses and look them up in a Bible dictionary to discover more details about them. Underline the highlighted name of the one who plays the main character in this episode and what the angel said to him.

God sent an angel to tell Gideon, the son of Joash the Abiezrite, His plans to rescue Israel from the marauding Midianites. Gideon threshed wheat in a winepress—a clear indication of the fear that had come over the people as they hid their produce from their enemies. Things had gotten bad—real bad, but God had a plan.

Reflect on Israel's pattern of sin and repentance and God's response to them. How is this like your relationship with God? What does this tell you about your life? What does it tell you about God?

_____

_____

## 23.2 You Want Me to Do What?

As Israel settled into Canaan, God called judges, or leaders, to unite the tribes of Israel against their enemies. They did not hold any particular position of leadership. God chose them to restore Israel back to a place He could use them as His covenant people. God raised up servant-leaders like Othniel (Judg. 3:7–11) and Deborah (Judg. 4) who carried out God's mission for the sake of God's plan to rescue all peoples from destruction. In this episode of His-story God called an unlikely servant-leader, Gideon. The first thing the angel did was promise Gideon God's presence and call him "mighty warrior" (Judg. 6:12).

Read Judges 6:13. Summarize Gideon's response to God's call through the angel in the space below.

_____

_____

Often when people sense God's call to serve in leadership, they quickly retort with the circumstances they find themselves in as reasons the call seems foolish or ill-timed. They point out how bad things look and how silly God's call seems. Gideon mocked the angel's words with his narrow picture of reality and rebuffed every word the angel said.

Read Judges 6:14. Check one or two other translations of this verse. Choose one that best helps you understand God's response to Gideon's excuses for not leading. Write the other translation here:

_____

_____

The LORD would not hear Gideon's excuses, and He made His call even clearer. The question at the end of verse 14, "Am I not sending you?" can be made into the statement, "I AM is sending you." The strength of Gideon's call rested in I AM, not Gideon or a group of people who called him to engage the enemies of Israel.

Read Judges 6:15. Notice Gideon's second excuse for not making himself a servant to God's call on his life. How is that excuse like some you have made to God for not

doing what He has called you to do?

Gideon could not see himself as God saw him. Circle the personal pronouns "I" in verse 15. What does that say about where Gideon had his focus?

_____

Read verse 16. Underline God's response to Gideon's excuse. Again, God did not answer Gideon's response. God basically said, "This isn't about you. It's about Me. I will be with you, and you will succeed because of who I am, not who you think you are."

Compare Moses' response to God's call in Exodus 3 with Gideon's response here. Compare and contrast how God answered both leaders' questions. Record your findings on another sheet of paper or in your journal.

End today's moment with God by listing your excuses for not saying yes to God and some responses God has given you through His Word or Spirit or others in community with you.

## 23.3 Strategy, God-Style

The servant part of servant leadership begins when you make yourself a servant to the mission call of God. You may answer with a reluctant yes to God's call but you eventually will step out and lead those God has assigned to you down the path of His purposes. The leadership aspect of servant leadership begins when you invite others to join you in God's call to complete the mission.

Most people define successful leadership as the ability to

get the appropriate number of people moving together toward a shared vision. A misunderstanding of biblical servant leadership, however, is that God calls a leader and then leaves it up to that leader to make things happen. That is never the case in His-story. God always accomplishes His mission through a willing servant, but God's power saves the day, not that of the leader.

Read Judges 7:1. Consider the setting of this episode. Consult a Bible handbook or commentary to gain a fuller image of the Israelite camp and that of the Midianites. Highlight Gideon's Canaanite name. This gives another example how Israel tried to fit in with the local culture.

Read Judges 7:2. For what reason did God reduce the number of warriors with Gideon? How would that make you feel as a leader of the army?

_____

_____

_____

God told Gideon He did not want Israel to have the opportunity to boast that they had defeated the Midianites in their own strength. God did not want them to depend on their power. God wanted them to learn to trust in His strength alone. This lesson shows how God leads those He calls.

Read Judges 7:3. How did God tell Gideon to thin out his numbers that day? Do the math. How many went home, how many remained, and how many did Gideon start with?

Twenty-two thousand went home as soon as Gideon said, "If you are afraid, you can leave." List some ways this was a good thing. Consider some feelings Gideon may have had as he watched them leave and go home. What gave him confidence although his army shrunk? What aspects of this part of the story connect with your life? Is it your confidence in God's power? Pause and pray for God to give you the heart of Gideon to continue no matter the numbers around you.

## 23.4 A Lean Focus

"Lighter is better" in the sport of ultra running—and in most sports for that matter. I had a friend I trained with for awhile who wanted to lose five pounds before his next run. I could not see where he had five pounds on his body to lose, so I asked him why he wanted to lose weight. He looked fit to me. He told me those five pounds would feel like someone handing him a five-pound backpack at the starting line and asking him to carry it for the next 50 miles. I said, "Oh, I get it." I then started thinking of ways in which I could lose five pounds so I wouldn't have to carry the extra weight with me on my next run. Dead weight slows down a runner, an organization, and a team. Lighter is often better because in any sport agility and speed matter.

When have you ever intentionally lost weight—either physical weight or weight in your schedule in order to lighten up to accomplish something?

Read Judges 7:4. Underline God's assessment of the number of men in Gideon's army.

God said 10,000 men were too many for Him to receive credit for what He would soon do. The army still weighed too much. But compared to the size of the Midianite army the Israelites looked thin enough. God, however, knew better. God told Gideon to take the remaining fighters down to the river and tell them to get a drink of water. There God said He would sift them for Gideon. God told Gideon He would let him know which of the men would go with him into battle.

Read verse 5. Underline how Gideon would separate the warriors.

Commentators have had different ideas about why God chose those who raised the water to their mouths rather than those who got down on their knees and lapped directly from the river. Some say that those who held the water in their hands were more alert to their surroundings and made better fighters. Others claimed these men were ready for battle because they kept an eye on the Midianite camp as they drank. Whatever the practical suggestions for why God separated the men this way, God took a natural tendency to drink as the benchmark of whom He chose for battle. This seems odd when choosing an army. You would think He would put them through some sort of skills test to find the best fighters. But this did not concern the fighters' numbers or skills. This concerned God's power to deliver.

Read verse 6. How many drank from their hands? Write the number here: _____

God guided Gideon to whittle the number of warriors to make the army the right size for God to do His work.

Gideon must have wondered what was going on when less than one third of one tenth of those at the river fulfilled God's requirements to fight the battle with him. God told Isaiah, "My thoughts are not your thoughts, neither are your ways my ways" (Isa. 55:8). Gideon surely felt the impact of that truth on his life.

When has lighter is better held true in your relationship with God? Has God ever called you to reduce the number of people involved in something to stamp out any confusion about who was the Victor?

## 23.5 God's Signposts

God told Gideon to send the 9,700 men who drank directly from the river to their homes (Judg. 7:7). He then stood with the 300 surrounded by "the provisions and trumpets of the others" (v. 8). Three hundred and one men stood by the pile of provisions and trumpets of over 9,000 who dropped them all off on their way home. That must have made quite a sight. Consider what went on in their minds at the time. What was the level of their confidence?

Have you ever been left "holding the bag" in a desperate situation while others made their way home to comfort and protection? If so, write your experience here:

_____

Gideon stood in a moment of confident uncertainty. He felt confident of God's clear call and instructions, and he had seen God purposefully reduce the number of fighters in his army. Yet, there he stood with 300 others waiting

on his next orders from his Commander.

Before Gideon may not have been so confident in the LORD. Our question to consider this week was: Should we use Gideon's example of "putting out a fleece" to discover God's will? Read Judges 6:36–40 if you have not already. Write your initial answer to the question here:

_____

How have you heard the practice of "putting out a fleece" taught before? Was it "the way," "a way," or "no way" to know God's will? Consider the implications of reading the passage any of these ways.

God graciously gave Gideon the signs he needed to overcome his hesitancy to step up to God's call on his life. But do not assume that what God did for one person He will do for everyone. Because God defeated an army of thousands with 300 men doesn't mean you can. But you can be assured that God will respond to your request for help.

Gideon's trust in God changed from "I need proof to trust you" to "I'll wait here with this pile of stuff and these 300 men until I hear from you." Time in a relationship with God had changed his response to God's instructions in his life. How has your trust in God changed since the first time He broke into your life until today?

**For further study:**
• **Judges 2:6–19; Judges 6–8**
• **Exodus 3:7–12; 4:10–12; Galatians 6:1–5**

## 24—God Uses Imperfect People (Judge Samson, Part 2 of 2)

So if God uses imperfect, reluctant leaders like Gideon, does He use people who have committed sins as well? Maybe you have been inspired by a leader in the past and later found out that the leader had done something immoral. When you heard that the leader had fallen into sin you may have asked yourself, "Was the work God did in my life as a result of this leader real?" This week's study will help us to explore this question and others.

Israel continued its dance of rebellion with God, and God continued to discipline them and to rescue them through the "judges" he called out to lead the people. Through this waltz of sin, judgment, and rescue Israel learned about Yahweh's great love for His people. God showed His covenant love for them in that while they rebelled He sent a leader to rescue them from their enemies. Samson is probably the most recognizable of

the judges. He represented the physical model of a man, and his seduction by Delilah is notorious in any ancient history book. His character lacked in so many ways, but in spite of his self-centeredness, God used him to deliver Israel from their archenemy, the Philistines.

The Memory Verse for this chapter is 2 Timothy 2:4. God called Samson as a servant-leader with the mission to rescue Israel from its enemy.

Our question to consider this week is: Who does God use more to accomplish His will, righteous or unrighteous people? This question could fall into the "trick question" category. Think about it, and then we will talk at the end of the chapter.

## 24.1 God was Up To Something

Marriage begins with a vow of separation to someone you love. You promise "to love and to cherish . . . 'til death do us part." You promise to forsake all others and to love no matter the circumstances of life. Rings display the outward signs of the vows in most weddings. The ring made of special metal worn publicly serves as a sign to others of the vow you made before God, friends, and family to separate yourself from all others for your spouse alone. The ring symbolizes of the vow, and the vow a spoken promise of the love in your heart.

If you are married, what specific vows did you share on your wedding day? How have they guarded your relationship with your spouse through the years? If you are not married, what promises of separation have you made in life? Some may include, for example, sexual purity or no "fermented drinks." Describe your vows and the impact they have made on your life in the space below.

_____

_____

God had a plan to rescue Israel from the Philistines. That plan in His-story involved vows placed on a boy's life before his birth. The strength he would have in his life to complete God's mission call on his life required that he remain faithful to those vows.

Read Judges 13:1. Highlight the people whom God allowed to attack Israel.

The dance of the judges went another round. Israel rebelled, and God allowed the Philistines, a migrating "sea people," to dominate them for 40 years. (Refer to a Bible handbook or dictionary to learn more about these people.) But God would not abandon His covenant people. He began their rescue through the birth of a very special boy.

Read Judges 13:2–5. Highlight the characters in this episode of His-story. Underline what the boy would be and what he would do.

An angel came to a nameless, barren woman to reveal to her that she would become pregnant. She must avoid certain drinks and foods because she would give birth to a son who would live as a Nazirite from birth. The Nazirite vow consisted of a voluntary promise in which a person separated him or herself to the LORD. The outward signs of the vow required that they not drink any fermented drink, not cut their hair, and not go near or touch a dead body (Num. 6:1–8). This boy would be set apart from birth because God would use him to deliver Israel "from the hands of the Philistines" (v. 5).

Read Luke 1:26–38. Compare the angel's visit to Mary with that of Manoah's wife in Judges 13:2–3. What is both similar and different about the details? What is similar about God's intention for the boys' lives?

_____

_____

_____

After the angel's visit, the nameless woman told her husband what the angel promised her (vv. 6–7). The plan began unfolding. God was up to something.

## 24.2 An Issue of Character

Temptation reveals true character. Whether you feel tempted to make an unethical deal to gain more money or whether someone tempts you to compromise your marriage vows, your character will either keep you from crossing the line or it will let you slip into sin. Character is the firewall around the CPU of your heart. Temptation is the Hacker's virus to shut it down.

Samson lacked character. Although God used him to cause chaos among the Philistines and to lead Israel for 20 years, his sexual behavior—not a warrior or army—brought him down. Early in his adult life he developed a lust for foreign women (Judg. 14:1). Judges 16 opens with Samson going to see a prostitute in the Philistine town of Gaza after he killed a thousand men with the jawbone of a donkey. War and women dominated his interests.

What character flaws that you know of in your own life do you constantly have to monitor in order to keep the firewall of character updated? What patterns of behavior have you developed that could lead you to fall morally? You do not need to write these down anywhere, but allow God's Spirit to guide your thoughts. Pray for Him to expose the truth of your habits and for the power of His Spirit to change them.

Read Judges 16:4. Highlight the two main characters in this episode. Underline what the storyteller said happened to Samson. Use a Bible handbook to learn more about the location of Sorek.

This marks the first time Samson's biographer has told us Samson is in love. He had married before, but "he fell in love with" Delilah. This was the common Hebrew word for human and divine love. This was the real deal to him. Delilah, the object of his newly found affection, must have been known in influential circles because the "rulers of the Philistines" soon came to her with an offer to help them capture the Israelite strong man (v. 5).

Read Judges 16:5. Underline the rulers' offer to Delilah. "Eleven hundred shekels" equals about 28 pounds or 13 kilograms, a great sum of silver for the secret of Samson's strength.

Delilah also lacked character. She willingly served as the bait for the trap of those who offered to pay for her services. She had no interest in Samson. She wanted the money. She happily played her part in the rulers' little theatre of deception in order to further her influence and bank account.

Read Proverbs 7:6–27. Meditate on God's instructions to stay away from women who sell their bodies for money. If you are a parent, have you taken time to teach this passage to your son(s)? If you are a woman, apply these teachings to protecting your heart from men who use women for their own gain.

## 24.3 The Thrill of Seduction

To tease temptation is like an "Xtreme" junkie who tries one more jump beyond the last one because the thrill must heighten—unless, of course, he or she crashes the next try and never rides again. To give into one temptation and not experience immediate consequences makes the next jump more enticing and exciting. The problem is that with each successful trip you bring yourself closer to disaster. The thrill of the jump overrides the reality of the danger.

Again, you do not need to write anything unless you want, but what temptations have you allowed yourself to give in to because of the thrill that followed? What consequences resulted from your "jump"? Guilt? Shame? Nothing? Pause and listen to your heart and the Spirit concerning these things.

Read Judges 16:6–9. Write out your own version of the conversation between Samson and Delilah.

_____

_____

_____

She had no interest in Samson. How do we know? Verse 6 begins with "So Delilah said to Samson . . ." The "so" points back to the rulers' monetary offer to her if she would get Samson's secret of strength. She worked as their hired hand in the plot to capture the Israelite pest. What does this reality tell you about getting involved in someone else's scheme for the money?

Notice the result of the rulers' actions to tie Samson up with seven fresh thongs. Imagine the emotions of both Delilah and Samson when this happened.

Read Judges 16:10–14. Delilah continued her seduction of Samson in these verses. Highlight their names to keep up with the dialogue. Underline the result of each action.

Samson toyed with Delilah like he did earlier with his wife's relatives (Judg. 14:10–14). He was clever but without character. Each answer to her seductive questions marked one more jump in the extreme game of attraction. While Delilah played her role for the rulers, Samson jumped closer to his destruction with each answer. He wanted the Philistine woman and would eventually give up his strength in order to have her—a reality that never happened.

Samson not only toyed with Delilah, but he did not respect the source of his strength. By now in the story, Samson used his strength and wit for his own purposes, but God had made him strong for His purposes. Samson's delight in Delilah's efforts to uncover the source of his strength showed he claimed God's gift as his own. He had lost what was at stake. He had forgotten the angel's message before his birth and the source of who he was.

What gifts that you know are God's gift to you have you taken for granted as your own? What abilities and strengths that make up part of who you are have you claimed as your own rather than giving God the credit for what you can do?

## 24.4 The Wisdom of Distance

Resistance to temptation works best from a distance. You stand a better chance of saying no to the tempter and yes to what is right if you are not in the room with the one tempting you. Samson never left the room because his desire for Delilah outweighed his devotion to God. Rather than flee his "evil desires of youth" (2 Tim. 2:22), he stayed close, and lust won in the end.

Recall a time when you know that if you had left a situation you would have overcome the temptation. Read 1 Corinthians 15:33 and apply it to the situation you remember. How was this principle true in your situation?

_____

_____

Read Judges 16:15–16. How would you describe Delilah's tactics this time? Underline verse 16 as an example of what staying near temptation will do to a person.

No one knows the tone of Delilah's voice in verse 15, but you can imagine it was not sweet. She had grown tired of Samson's games. She wanted her money, so she turned to what eventually wore down Samson—nagging.

Read Judges 14:16. Observe how his wife got the answer to his riddle out of him.

Read Judges 16:17. The verse begins with the word "so." What does that tell us about why Samson would tell Delilah what he did?

_____

_____

Samson told Delilah the secret of his strength. In fact, his uncut hair did not provide the source of his strength anymore than a wedding ring provides the source of fidelity in a marriage. Samson was strong because of God's power and presence in his life, not because he never went to a barber. His hair only gave an outward sign of God's power. He betrayed God's blessing on his life.

Read Judges 16:18–21. Consider what happened after Samson turned his back completely on God. Delilah perceived this time that Samson told the truth and called the rulers to return with her money. Underline the last sentence in verse 19.

We know that Samson broke his vow when he touched the dead body of the lion (Judg. 14:8–9). We do not have any indication that he drank fermented drink, but when Delilah had Samson's hair cut he willfully denied the signs of God's blessings and his strength left.

What things in your life do you need to keep at a distance? Ask God to show you things you desire so much that you may miss the real danger they place on your life. If you have an accountability partner, he or she may help you in this. Pray that when God reveals these to you, you will act to separate yourself from them.

## 24.5 Samson's Payback

God accomplishes His plans in His-story no matter the choices we make. The incredible nature of God's love is that no matter your mistakes or willful decisions to rebel, He can redeem them for His purposes. Make a list of biblical characters you know who sinned against God, but who God still used for His purposes. Include characters like King David, the Apostle Paul, and Samson. Write your list of names and what they did here:

_____

Read Judges 16:26–30. Underline Samson's prayer (v. 28). How would you describe his cry to God? Compare it to Jesus' prayer in the garden in Matthew 26:42.

Samson's capture and humiliation did not humble him in any way. In his last prayer he requested revenge for what the Philistines had done to him. He prayed nothing about God or the country God chose him to deliver. His death prayer was to get payback for what his enemies had done to him, not for what God could do through him.

Underline the last sentence in verse 30. How many Philistines died with Samson? Write your answer here: _____ (See verse 27.)

He killed more in his death than in all his battles. Even though Samson remained self-centered to the end, God still used him to accomplish His purposes. Recall what the angel told Samson's mother he would do. (See Judges 13:5.) In his death, Samson fulfilled God's plan for his life. He did "begin the deliverance of Israel from the hands of the Philistines." This task remained incomplete until David became king, but God's word came true although Samson was an imperfect savior.

Our question to consider this week was: Who does God use more to accomplish His will, righteous or unrighteous people? Given Samson's story, how would you answer this question?

_____

End this chapter with a prayer of thanksgiving that God is sovereign and that no matter your sin, willful or otherwise, He can accomplish His purposes through your life.

**For further study:**

- **Judges 13:8–25; Judges 14–15; 16:1–3, 31**
- **Numbers 6:1–21; Proverbs 7:6–27**

## 25—Dealing with Heartache (Ruth)

One of the most powerful attributes of the Bible is that it helps us to deal with real-life issues. The Bible records real human history and shows us how God seeks not only to reconcile people to Himself, but also to relate personally to each human being. While the Bible is God-centered, it is also people-centered because people are His treasure.

The story of Ruth comes as a sub-plot in His-story that places a major character into the storyline. At first reading you do not understand why God has preserved the out-of-the-way episode through the centuries. On the surface it appears to tell a simple story of loyalty, love, and provision for the less fortunate.

But, when you poke around the edges of its message you can see both the foreshadowing of a new covenant and the mystery of how God works no matter the circumstances that swirl around a character's life. Ruth, like Rahab, came to find her place in the lineage of Jesus, and that alone makes her story worth following. She also provides for us an example of how to deal with the troubles that life brings.

The Memory Verses for this chapter are Philippians 2:3–4. Stories of people in the Bible often illustrate principles in the Bible. Ruth exemplifies these verses, so as you become familiar with them keep her actions and attitudes toward Naomi in mind.

Our question to consider this week is: Why does God sometimes bring us to a point of emptiness before using us? Why doesn't God use us when we are on our game or in the spotlight? What is it about tough times that God uses to set us up to complete His purposes? Begin to answer these questions, then observe Ruth's story.

## 25.1 When Hardship Strikes

You might feel that if family members die, famine hits, and you end up in a foreign country among strangers, there is no way God was at work in writing His-story. Somehow an evil editor must have stolen the manuscript and began to write in his or her own twist to the plot. You feel like either the unluckiest people on the planet or like you have done something to deserve God's punishment. When Hurricane Katrina hit the Gulf Coast many people migrated to the Dallas-Fort Worth area where I live. Many came with what they could carry on short notice, leaving behind their homes, jobs, and belongings. As we served those God sent our way, the stories sounded much like the opening paragraphs in the Book of Ruth.

What hard times have you experienced? How did you feel about God's involvement? How did you cope with the stress of the situation and where did you go for help?

_____

_____

_____

Read Ruth 1:1–2. Highlight the names of people and places. Use a Bible dictionary and map or commentary to know more about the people and to locate the places mentioned. The details play an important part because they connect the people and events in the story with His-story and God's rescue mission toward Israel.

The story takes place during the time of the judges (about 1380 B.C. to 1050 B.C.), and it tells about a family in the tribe of Ephraim who lived in Bethlehem, Judah. Famine crippled the land, so the family of four loaded up their lives and moved to nearby Moab in order to survive.

Read Ruth 1:3–5. Highlight the new characters in the story and underline what happened to the men in the story.

Somewhere in the events of days Naomi's husband, Elimelech, died. Her two sons married, which took some of the sting out of her husband's death, but not long after his death, they died as well. We can only imagine the pain of losing a spouse and two sons—all this while in a foreign land away from extended family. Naomi and her two daughters-in-law found themselves alone and without support.

Read Ruth 1:6–7. What news came to Naomi? What did she decide to do? Write your description here:

_____

_____

_____

Naomi heard that "the LORD had come to the aid of his people" (v. 6). Note the storyteller gave God, not nature, credit for Israel's turn of fortune. We read the Bible with faith that God purposefully guides the events of history to accomplish His purposes. When Naomi heard the good news, she prepared to return home with her two daughters by marriage.

Take time to empathize with Naomi's situation. Prayerfully enter her emotions and sense of loss. If you have experienced similar losses, ask God to come into the situation and show you His presence in both this ancient story of hope and the story you find yourself in.

## 25.2 When You Don't Want to Say Goodbye

I remember the day we left our oldest daughter at college for the first time. We had anticipated the moment for years. We talked about it, saved, and planned for the time we would leave her to live on her own. We arrived at her dorm's steps at 6:30 that morning and had her moved in with all the furnishing hung and stashed by noon. We went to lunch and then returned to say goodbye. I do not care how much you prepare yourself for a goodbye; it is almost impossible with someone you love. I remember taking my wife's hand after we had both hugged our daughter and turning to walk to the car. I said, "Don't look back," but we both did. With tears in our eyes and lumps in our throats, we waved one more time and got in the car for the three-hour drive home. Neither of us said anything for about an hour and then memories and hopes flooded our conversation. Our first child had started the next chapter of her story.

Describe a memorable goodbye from your life. Write some of your feelings and memories of the event in the space below.

_____

_____

Read Ruth 1:8–10. Underline Naomi's two wishes for her daughters-in-law. How did they respond to her request for them to stay in Moab?

Read verses 11–15. How would you describe Naomi's retort to the two women who said they wanted to go with her to Judah? Was it reasonable or unfounded? What do you know about the culture that would make her request sensible? Which woman heeded Naomi's request? Write her name here: _____

Read verses 16–18. Highlight verses 16–17. Ruth promised to stay with Naomi no matter what. She committed herself not only to Naomi but also to her God, the LORD, or Yahweh. These are some of the most beautiful words in Scripture.

The Moabite woman pledged her loyalty to Naomi, forsaking her home and embracing the people and the God of the one she loved. (Read 1 Samuel 18:3–4 for a description of David and Jonathan's love for each other.) Naomi gave in and accepted that Ruth would not leave her but would accompany her on the journey back home.

Read John 14:1–4. Meditate on Jesus' words to His disciples as a promise that He would never leave nor forsake them. If you are a follower of Jesus, His words speak specifically to you.

## 25.3 The Touch of Kindness

Feeding the poor is part of a Christian's way of life. Jesus taught His apprentices the right motives to give alms to the poor (Matt. 6:2–4). The Apostle Paul made sure during his trips to collect funds for the poor in Jerusalem (Rom. 15:25–27). God gave Israel specific instructions not to reap to the edges of their fields so the poor who did not own fields could harvest grain for their families (Lev. 23:22). Jesus also taught, "From everyone who has been given much, much will be demanded; and from the one who has been entrusted with much, much more will be asked" (Luke 12:48). Rich Christians in an age of hunger have a responsibility to feed the poor.

What have you or your church done to live out the teachings of Jesus and the Bible in regard to feeding the poor? Take some time to allow God to give you more ideas to feed those who are hungry.

_____

_____

Read Ruth 2:8–10. Describe the essence of Boaz's instructions to Ruth. How did she react to his kindness? (v. 10)

Our storyteller introduces the eventual husband of Ruth, Boaz, as chapter 2 opens. He was a relative of Naomi and a "man of standing" (v. 1). Boaz made it possible for Ruth to pick up grain after his servant girls so she would have food for Naomi and herself. Boaz followed God's command for the treatment of a foreigner or alien living among the Israelites (See Leviticus 19:33–34 and1 Peter 2:10–12 about God's command for treating foreigners.)

Read Ruth 2:11–12. When Boaz saw her gracious response, he blessed her. He acknowledged the kindness she had shown his relative, Naomi. Highlight the names for God in verse 12.

Also read Psalm 36:6–8. How do these verses echo Boaz's description of Ruth's decision to find refuge with the God of Israel? How does this picture of God's care deepen your understanding of God?

Read Ruth 2:13. Ruth acknowledged Boaz' kindness—especially as a foreigner, a Moabite, she held a lower status than his servants. Boaz was a righteous man and showed Ruth the kindness God's people should demonstrate to those who did not belong to their family.

Boaz' kindness toward Ruth gives an example of God's kindness toward all people. God rescued Israel out of Egypt so the nations would know Him. Jesus rescued those who trust Him so all would know Him. Your acts of kindness are a powerful witness to others about God.

End your moment with God today by asking Him to make you aware of ways you can show His love to those who do not yet trust Him. Thank God for the kindness He has shown you. Meditate on Psalm 36:6–8.

## 25.4 God's Actions and Our Participation

A fine line exists between our dependence upon God for all that happens and our efforts to make things happen. One way of looking at life can lead to the assumption that you can lie on the couch all day and God will bring all you need. The other idea can drive you to trust your efforts alone to realize the good things in our lives. God is the Author of His-story, and He has created us to participate in the plot. We have a role to play but we must never see ourselves as Author or Creator. A life of faith is balanced between God's sovereign work and our humble participation.

How do you respond to the concept in the above paragraph? Can you describe an incident in which you trusted God to have given you the opportunity while your efforts played a role in the results?

_____

_____

_____

Read Ruth 3:1–6. Naomi watched Boaz' kindness toward Ruth and she saw an opportunity for her widowed daughter-in-law to find "a home" and "be well provided for" (v. 1). We do not know how prevalent Naomi's plan was among her people, but we will see that Boaz responded as she expected he would. Ruth followed her mother-in-law's instructions. She put herself under the wing of Yahweh when she came to Judah (Ruth 2:12), now she would put herself under the wing/skirt of one of Yahweh's sons, Boaz.

Read 3:7–13. Ruth carried out the plan to lie at the feet of Boaz after he had celebrated the harvest. Highlight why she asked him to "spread the corner of your garment over me" in verse 9. Underline Boaz' explanation of his part in the redemption process.

Ruth understood Boaz to be her "kinsman-redeemer." God made provision for members of a clan who became poor to be "redeemed" by another family member (Lev. 25:25, 39–43). The law also required a kinsman-redeemer to marry a widow in order to produce an heir for the deceased man. This was the case with Naomi's daughter-in-law Ruth, who through marriage was related to Boaz.

Boaz accepted his responsibility as a kinsman-redeemer. Although there was one "nearer" than him, he would see to it that Ruth had her needs cared for.

As you read this episode of Ruth's story, what aspects of it did God clearly orchestrate and what parts did the people in the story execute? In the middle of both, God provided a redeemer for the foreigner so she could become part of God's forever family. Apply your observations to your live now. What opportunities have come to you by God's goodness alone, and what have you done to make the most of those?

_____

_____

_____

## 25.5 God's Love Story

His-story is essentially a love story; a love story between God who seeks out and rescues those He loves so they can live "happily ever after."

The exodus was a major scene in God's rescuing love for Israel. Even the wilderness wandering was part of God's disciplining love that trained Israel to trust Him and live in His ways. The judges served as God's representative rescuers who united the tribes of Israel to rid the land of their enemies. Even Ruth's short story presents a love story within the bigger love Story of God.

You and I as readers on this side of the cross can see how God orchestrated the events of her life as a foreigner, widowed and living among strangers, to become part of the lineage of Abraham which birthed the new covenant God would make with His people in order to bring the Final Rescuer into His-story.

Read Ruth 4:1–12 for the ancient process through which Boaz redeemed the land and made Ruth his wife. Verse 13 says that Ruth gave birth to a son.

Read Ruth 4:17. Highlight the names in the verse. If you have a study Bible, use the references in the center column or in the footnotes to see the next references to the characters listed in verse 17. The most obvious will be David, who was to rule as the second king of Israel.

Boaz redeemed and married Ruth. From that marriage continued the covenant promise of God, which birthed the promised King.

Read Matthew 1:5. Highlight Ruth's name. Ruth, the widowed Moabite, was one of only four women (other than Mary) listed in "the genealogy of Jesus Christ the son of David, the son of Abraham" (v. 1). Like Tamar, Rahab, and Bathsheba, Ruth seems an unlikely candidate to serve God's purposes. But His-story has many such characters.

Boaz was Ruth's kinsman-redeemer. Christ is your Redeemer. Read Galatians 3:13, 14, Colossians 1:13, and Titus 3:3–7. Circle the action words that describe what Christ did for you. (Answers: redeemed; rescued; saved)

Take time in the days ahead to read through the short story of Ruth in one sitting. Remember its place in the bigger Story and the nature of the story. It is a love story first, and a clue to Jesus' genealogy second. Read it as a love story and rejoice that Christ, like Boaz did for Ruth, has redeemed you as His own. Also, get familiar with the Memory Verses for this chapter: Philippians 2:3–4.

Take time to reflect on our question to consider this week: Why does God sometimes bring us to a point of emptiness before using us? After studying Ruth, how would you answer this question?

_____

_____

_____

**For further study:**

• Ruth 4

• Philippians 3–4

# 26— When God Seems Silent (Hannah)

How do you respond to times when God seems far away? Or when, despite your best effort, your soul seems unable to tune into God's frequency and the Bible seems to only consist of random words on pages of thin paper? This week's study will help provide insight into how a godly woman dealt with this issue. The story begins toward the end of God's silence.

The era of the judges came to a close with the person of Samuel. This priest and prophet was Israel's final judge before Israel's first king, Saul. As with other major characters in His-story like Isaac, Moses, and Samson, the Bible records the story of his birth. The first two chapters of 1 Samuel tell how God answered the persistent prayers of a childless woman to bring the next significant player on stage in the saga to capture the hearts of men and women for God. Samuel's mother Hannah, whose name means "gracious," played the main character of this episode. She

could not have children but longed to have them. She remained faithful in her worship of God, yet God did not answer her prayer to have a child for a long time. Her defining moment with God came when Eli, the priest of Shiloh, told her God would answer her prayer. Her faithfulness gives an example for all who wait upon the Lord.

The Memory Verses for this chapter are 1 Samuel 1:27–28. These verses record Hannah's commitment of Samuel to the LORD. Her words declare God's provision and her faithful response of her promise to God.

Our question to consider this week is: How should I respond when I feel like God is not listening to my prayer? To wait on God often challenges your concept of prayer and your relationship with Him. Write your initial answers to this question, and then we will return to it after we have observed Hannah's struggle of prayer.

## 26.1 Facing Rivals

"You can't know the players without a program,"
I barked as I tried to sell programs at the football games
at my alma mater. The service organization I joined sold
programs, and the non-winning record we held made it
a tough job. But a program does give you stats about the
people on the field no matter the sport, and the game gets
more personal when you know the personnel. We still
sold many copies to those who cared to know the players
and the stats of the team.

What were some of your college activities? Were you a
sports fan, club member, or did you spend most of your
time on academic pursuits? Write your memories here:

_____

_____

The Book of 1 Samuel opens with a list of players on
the field. These names are important because of their
connection to the covenant people God chose to
represent His love to all nations.

Read 1 Samuel 1:1–2. Highlight each name in the verses.

From this introduction to the characters in this episode
of His-story we learn a man named Elkanah, a Levite
(1 Chron. 6:26–27), had two wives, Hannah and
Peninnah. The characters are in place and a problem
is laid out on the table: Hannah could not have any
children while Peninnah could have as many children
as Elkanah desired.

Read 1 Samuel 1:3–5. Underline what Elkanah did for
Hannah when they traveled to worship in Shiloh.

Elkanah was a man of faith. "Year after year" he took his
family to the worship center of Israel in Shiloh (v. 3). Eli
served as the lead priest there, but his two sons, Hophni
and Phinehas, did not have good reputations (1 Sam.
2:12). Elkanah showed favor to his barren wife by giving
her a double portion of the sacrificial meat.

Read 1 Samuel 1:6–8. Peninnah's harassment of Hannah
would overcome her husband's special care. Hannah wept
openly because she could not have children.

Have you ever experienced constant harassment from a
rival for a condition you suffered from or a perceived
lack of performance? Has that person ever driven you to
tears because of his or her constant badgering? Use your
experience to empathize with Hannah's emotions.

Infertility remains a real-life issue for many couples
today. Many Christian couples long to have children but
cannot. This condition can drive them to tears as well as
to wonder where God is in their situation. If you know of
a couple who struggles with infertility, pray for them and
continue to comfort them—even when they cry out or
feel less significant because they cannot bear children.

## 26.2 Anguished Prayer

Prayer is a conversation between God and the petitioner.
Sometimes it may feel as if you are the only one talking,
and prayer becomes a monologue before a silent God.
You ask, listen, and look. You ask again. You wake up

and hope today is the day you see the answer to your prayer. You remind yourself that you asked for good things like a job, health, and children who will grow into godly adults. It is not like you asked to win the lottery or something. Finally, over time you may come to the place where you either quit asking or get so angry with God that your soul gets bitter and your love for God fades. Or you make a deal with God that if He will answer your prayer you will do such and such just to make it happen. But we only hear silence.

In what ways can you relate to this description of prayer? What prayer have you prayed that has gone unanswered? What sentences in the above paragraph describe how you feel now? Underline those sentences now.

Read 1 Samuel 1:9–10. Underline the words in verse 10 that describe Hannah's emotional and spiritual condition.

On one of the family's annual trips to Shiloh to worship and after the meal of sacrifice, Hannah stood up to pray. Eli, the priest at Shiloh, sat near the door of the Temple. Verse 10 describes Hannah, "in bitterness of soul." She "wept much and prayed." Hannah had reached the end of her emotional rope over her infertility, yet she continued to pray to God. Have you ever found yourself in a similar situation before?

_____

_____

_____

_____

Read verse 11. Circle the words "if" and "then." These words explain the conditions of the vow Hannah made to God. (See Numbers 6:1–21 for the Nazirite instructions.)

Hannah prayed that if God gave her a son, then she would give that son back to God. Her prayers for her personal desires turned into a prayer of submission for what God would want with her son. Hannah's vow was not a bargaining chip to get God to respond. She did not make a "deal" with God. Her promise served as a release of what she longed for to the ownership of God's purposes. Prayer is ultimately about our submission to God's ways rather than the fulfillment of our hopes and dreams. This was her defining moment with God.

Have you ever come to God with a prayer like Hannah's? If so, in what circumstances? What were the "if-then" parts of your prayer? Did you pray to bargain with God or to submit to God's plan? Write your prayer here:

_____

_____

_____

## 26.3 Passionate Prayer

Jesus told a story of a persistent widow who came to a wicked judge often with her request (Luke 18:1–8). At first he refused to hear her, but she showed up day after day to ask that he grant her justice against her adversary. Finally, although he feared neither God nor man, he granted her request "because this widow keeps bothering me" (v. 5). Jesus concluded, ". . . will not God bring about justice for his chosen ones, who cry out to him day and night?" (v. 7) Luke said Jesus told the story, to show His disciples that "they should always pray and not give up" (v. 1). According to Jesus, one quality of authentic prayer is persistence.

Apply Jesus' teaching on prayer to a current situation you face. What do His words teach you about praying in these circumstances? How does His story give you hope?

_____

_____

Read 1 Samuel 1:12–14. Underline Eli's words to Hannah.

Eli watched Hannah pray as she stood in the Temple. Her lips moved, but she spoke no words. We know from verse 10 that she was crying. No wonder he concluded she may have been drunk. Some religious festivals in those days included drinking (Judg. 9:27; Isa. 28:7) (Kline). Eli thought Hannah had participated in excess during her worship. He told her to put away her wine.

Have you ever prayed so passionately that someone would have wondered if you were OK? (This question is not to prescribe this kind of emotion in prayer, but to connect you with the depth of Hannah's hurt and desire for God to answer her petition.) Write your thoughts here:

_____

_____

Read 1 Samuel 1:15–18. Underline the last phrase in verse 15 and Eli's answer in verse 17.

Hannah said she was not drunk but that she was "pouring out" her soul "to the LORD" (v. 15). Her worship was a cry from the depths of her soul. She cried out of her "great anguish and grief" because of her barrenness; she was not a "wicked" drunk (v. 16). (See Acts 2:13; When Peter stood up to speak at Pentecost some also accused him of drunkenness.) Eli understood, and he blessed her (v. 17). The priest's blessing calmed her heart, and she went and ate something. Our storyteller observed, ". . . her face was no longer downcast" (v. 18).

Hannah's countenance changed after Eli's blessing. She knew God would answer her prayers. Are you currently praying seriously about something? Circle the word that best describes your situation. After you have done this, pause and pray again to God for your need.

| | | |
|---|---|---|
| asked once | frustrated | wondering |
| grieving | weeping | at peace |

## 26.4 Answered Prayer

Every ministry goes through times of growth and times of struggle. I remember one season that presented a time of turmoil. We chose to update the church's constitution and bylaws, and we experienced as much enthusiasm as we did resistance to the process. After a tough meeting to explain the whys and hows of the update, I found myself in tears and prayer with two other ministry associates. I asked God to show me the spiritual nature of what was going on. I did not want to read or hear any more advice on leading through change. I needed God's perspective. In that time of extended prayer, God revealed to me that the spiritual issue dealt with authority—who had it and how they shared it so that the church could be the church and carry out its mission to help people trust Jesus.

I believe God answered my prayer because it served to form and empower His church to make an impact in its mission field. You may not have experienced as an exact or immediate answer to prayer as this one, but describe a time God clearly answered your prayers for His purposes.

_____

Read 1 Samuel 1:19–20. Highlight the name Hannah gave her son. Underline what the name meant.

God answered Hannah's prayer, and she soon became pregnant with a son. She named him Samuel because she "asked the LORD for him." His name sounds similar to the word for "heard of God." Hannah remembered her pledge to God, and her son's name would always serve as a reminder to him and others that he was God's answer to his mother's prayer.

Hannah honored God with the name of her son, but one other part of her pledge still awaited fulfillment. She promised to give him to the LORD for His service. Would her faith go that far? Have you ever balked on a promise you made God after He answered your prayer?

Read 1 Samuel 1:21–23. Underline Hannah's decision about the family's annual pilgrimage to Shiloh. Underline Elkanah's response to her.

When it came time to return to Shiloh, Hannah said she would not go until Samuel was weaned. Some mothers in ancient times may have nursed their children as long as three years (Kline, 3). Elkanah told her to do what she thought best, but he added, ". . . and may the LORD help you keep your promise" (v. 23 NLT). Hannah's husband wanted to make sure she was not looking for a way out of her promise. He desired only that "the LORD confirm His word" through Eli (NASB).

Part of prayer is obedience to what we hear God tell us through His Word, His Spirit, or a spiritual friend or advisor. As you pray today, promise God you will remain faithful to Him as He is faithful to you.

## 26.5 Responding to Answered Prayer

As followers of Jesus we do not offer animal sacrifices to a priest at a temple. This is because Jesus served as the "once for all time" sacrifice for our sins (Heb. 10:10–14). We no longer need to bring gifts of our possessions to be made right with God. Jesus accomplished our righteousness before Holy God through His death, burial, and Resurrection. Under the previous covenant between God and His people in His-story, God required sacrifices for atonement and as acts of worship. (See Leviticus 16 for an example.) Hannah followed God's prescribed ways of dedicating her son to the LORD when she came to offer him to Eli.

Read 1 Samuel 1:24–25. Circle the offerings Hannah and Elkanah brought to sacrifice to God. (See Leviticus 1:1–29 for instructions of a burnt offering.)

Read verses 26–28. How did Hannah complete her commitment to the LORD before Eli? What was the length of her commitment to the LORD (v. 28)?

Hannah remained faithful to her promise to God. She gave the son she always wanted to God as a full-time player in His-story. Her peace did not rest in the fact that she had a son so she could compete with her rival Peninnah. She worshiped God joyfully because she knew her son surely had a special place in the purpose of God (Read 1 Samuel 2:1–11 for her song to the LORD.)

The Memory Verses for this chapter are 1 Samuel 1:27–28. Reflect on Hannah's words as a way to honor God with the commitments you make to Him. Rewrite Hannah's message to Eli in your own words as a way to make them relevant to a situation you may face now.

The Book of Psalms is a collection of songs in the key of life. They represent every emotion and spiritual condition you encounter as you live out your part in His-story. Psalm 42 honestly portrays one's longing to know God and hear His voice. Read this song and allow it to speak the prayer of your heart to God. Make note of it for the days that will come as you struggle in prayer with God.

Hannah struggled in prayer with God. She made a promise to God that she would dedicate God's answer to Him for the length of the child's life. God answered her prayer and brought into the storyline of His-story the last "judge" and the bridge person between the judges and the kings of Israel.

**For further study:**
- **1 Samuel 2:1–21**
- **Psalm 51; Psalm 55**

_____

_____

_____

## 27—Hearing God's Voice (Samuel)

Times when God seems silent are often accompanied by questions. Most likely we will wonder how we can discern God's voice. Or we may ask, "Is God actually speaking and I just do not know how to listen?" This week's study will explore how one young follower of God learned how to recognize God's voice.

Samuel was God's answer to Hannah's prayer for a child. Hannah remained faithful to her promise to dedicate her son to Yahweh, and she gave the child to Eli, the priest, so he could serve with God's leader. Samuel was a young child at the time of his dedication, and he grew up in the Temple at Shiloh. This chapter in His-story tells how Samuel learned to recognize the voice of God.

Eli mentored Samuel as a boy, and he taught him many things—most importantly how to hear the voice of

God. Samuel grew up to become the spiritual leader in Israel whom God used to give Israel its first king. Hearing God's voice played a key role in his leadership and his relationship with God. We have much to learn from Samuel because all of us need to know how to discern God's voice in order to influence those around us. Confidence in God's directions provides freedom to serve Him and others.

The Memory Verse for this chapter is 1 Samuel 3:10. Samuel's words in this verse model for us how to receive God's prompting.

Our question to consider this week is: How can I know God's voice in the midst of daily life? God does not always speak in an audible voice like He did to Samuel. This question is important to anyone who desires to know God and follow Him.

## 27.1 The Influence of a Mentor

Almost every Wednesday for the past six years I have met with Ray. He is a retired pastor and denominational executive and 20-plus years older than me. We met when he moved here with his wife to live closer to their children and grandchildren. God had prompted me at the time to find a mentor, or someone farther down the road of ministry who could guide me. After our first meeting, I knew I could trust Ray and that he would be open and honest with me about the situations going on in my life. Over the years, Ray has been what I call a "mentor of presence." He does not give me five things to do each month to solve a problem. He simply listens to me rant or rejoice, asks some questions, and pays for lunch every other time. Ray is a constant in my chaotic cosmos of ministry. He has taught me much simply because he is there for me and available.

Do you have a mentor or someone farther down the road of life whom you can go to for guidance? If so, write his or her name here: _____ Offer a prayer of thanksgiving for that person. If you do not, ask God if this would be the season for someone more mature than you to guide you.

Read 1 Samuel 3:1. Highlight the names in the verses and underline the storyteller's description of the times.

Samuel grew up as he served, or ministered, before Yahweh under the leadership of Eli, his mentor. Like the time between the Old and New Testaments, God seemed silent while the people settled in their new land and their religion. (See Joel 2:28–32 for God's promise to pour out His Spirit, and Acts 2:17–21 for the fulfillment.)

Read 1 Samuel 3:2–5. Verses 2–3 provide the setting of the action to follow. Verses 4–5 record Yahweh's call and Samuel's response. Setting and action creates the context for God's words. Understanding these components is essential to accurate biblical interpretation.

"One night" Eli, who had become nearly blind due to old age, slept in his usual place (v. 2). Our storyteller notes that the "lamp of God had not yet gone out" and Samuel slept near the "ark of God" (v. 3). The lamp may indicate the lamp stand Moses prescribed in Exodus 25:31–40. The ark of God was the ark of the covenant, or testimony, that Moses ordered in Exodus 25:10–22. Both were housed in the Temple at Shiloh.

In this routine setting for both Samuel and Eli, a voice came in the night. It was the voice of God calling Samuel's name. The boy jumped up and ran to his mentor, who drowsily told his trainee he did not call him and sent him back to bed.

Look back over the verses in today's moment with God. Which of the descriptions or actions seem similar to the ones you experience today? Has God's voice been rare? Is your faith routine? Do those who should know the voice of God seem unsure about what they have heard?

_____

_____

_____

_____

## 27.2 The Need for Discernment

How do you know the difference between the voice of God and your own thoughts? Samuel did not know either. As we continue in this episode of His-story, you will see a young boy running back and forth to his mentor in the night. Someone called him, and he wanted to know who woke him up. When he came to the elder priest a second time, Eli gave him the same answer, "I did not call; go back and lie down" (1 Sam. 3:6). Both mentor and apprentice were in the dark as to the nature of the voice. Why?

Read 1 Samuel 3:7. Summarize in the space below why Samuel did not know it was God who called his name.

_____

_____

The key word in the verse is "revealed." Revelation is the biblical explanation of how we know God. Human beings know God by the revelation of Himself through the written and spoken gospel (Rom. 1:17) and through His Spirit (1 Cor. 2:9–11). God comes to people to show Himself and His purposes. As with Samuel, some people may need a more mature disciple to help discern God's revelation from human thoughts (1 Sam. 3:8–9). We live in a world where personal reason and experience define truth for the individual. In a biblical worldview, however, God's revealed Word serves as the objective truth by which people know God and live according to His purposes for their lives.

Read verse 10. Underline Samuel's response to God's call.

God came to Samuel a third time and called his name. This time he responded as Eli had instructed him to speak. He answered, "Speak, for your servant is listening." This was Samuel's defining moment with God. Samuel humbled himself before God. He made himself a servant to the call of God. His submission to God's call set the course of his life as a prophet and priest of God.

Those whom God used greatly considered themselves servants of God. (Read about Moses in Deuteronomy 34:5, Joshua in Judges 2:8, and Paul in Romans 1:1; Jesus claimed He lived a life of service in Mark 10:45.) Submission to God's call marks the beginning of servant leadership among God's people.

First Samuel 3:10 is our Memory Verse for this chapter. Take time to familiarize yourself with this verse. Say it softly several times as your confession to God's leadership in your life. Use it throughout the day as a prayer of commitment to God and His purposes in your life.

## 27.3 Sharing the Truth

I work as a volunteer chaplain for my city's police and fire departments. The most enjoyable part of my community service is getting to know the officers and fire fighters as they serve our citizens. The hard part of the job is making a death notification to a loved one or debriefing personnel after a critical incident. The truth of the situation hurts the one who receives it so deeply I often wish I did not have to do that part of the job. But someone has to tell the truth so everyone can live in reality. Sometimes truth hurts because it changes how you see and live your life.

Have you ever had to tell someone the truth even though you knew it would hurt him or her? How long did it take you to tell the person? What did you do to prepare yourself to tell the truth? How did that person react? Briefly describe your experience in the space below.

_____

_____

_____

Read 1 Samuel 3:11–14. Samuel surely got excited when he heard God's first words to him. Who would not want to have a part in something that would "make the ears of everyone who hears of it tingle" (v. 11). However, the news included judgment on his mentor's family. (Read 1 Samuel 2:12–34 for the background of God's judgment.) Samuel had to bear the burden of hard news for the one who had raised him and shown him the ways of God. The revelation of God's truth is not always a day at an amusement park.

Read 1 Samuel 3:15–18. Samuel went back to bed after God gave him the message for Eli. The next morning he arose as usual to open the Temple for worship. But this day was different, and his life would never be the same.

Eli called for Samuel to tell him what God had said. He knew God always spoke truth. Eli could tell Samuel had heard harmful news about his family from God, but he insisted his apprentice tell it all to him (v. 17). To trust God means to trust everything God says, not just what makes you live better according to your own values.

Read verse 18 and underline Eli's reply. The elder priest submitted to the words of God because "He is the Lord." This is the confession of every true believer for it conveys a trust in God and that His ways are true and just—even if they mean God's judgment on you and your family.

Read Paul's warning to his apprentice, Timothy, in 2 Timothy 4:2–4. What did the older disciple teach his younger partner in ministry about speaking God's Word above all else? Consider this teaching as you walk through Scripture and come to things that may convict you or challenge certain values in your life.

## 27.4 Increased Credibility

To grow up is to build your reputation. Your accomplishments, the teams you played on, and the organizations you joined all added up to create your reputation as a student. As an adult, you continue to build your influence through your achievements and those with whom you associate. In the end your reputation on earth sums up what you have done and those you have known.

What accomplishments and people are you associated with that make up your reputation? How would you describe your reputation at home, at work, and in the church? Write your answers in the space below. (See Philippians 3:7–9 for how the Apostle Paul saw his achievements in comparison to knowing Christ.)

_____

_____

_____

Read 1 Samuel 3:19–21. These verses record Samuel's reputation among the Israelites. List the characteristics of his life that gave him his standing among the people.

Verse 19 _____

_____

Verse 20 _____

_____

Verse 21 _____

_____

Our storyteller recorded that Samuel's reputation consisted of the facts that "the LORD . . . let none of his words fall to the ground," that he was known as a "prophet of the LORD," and that God "revealed himself to Samuel through his word." He became a trusted leader in Israel due to God's presence and power in his life.

Notice that none of these facts have to do with Samuel's giftedness or abilities. Samuel had this standing with the people because of who God was, not because of who he was or what he did. A godly reputation is built upon who God is, not what we can do.

Eli trained Samuel to know and hear Yahweh, but he failed to train his sons in the ways of God. Eli had a tainted reputation because of the evil his sons did, and God judged him for that. As Eli's life faded into the background, Samuel's ministry emerged for him to take center stage as God's spokesman and leader.

Compare and contrast the reputations of Eli and Samuel. In what ways are they similar? In what ways are they different? What can you learn from their reputations about your own? Write some of your thoughts on another piece of paper or in your journal. End your moment with God in a prayer for God to give you a godly reputation as you submit to His call on your life to follow Him.

## 27.5 Faithfully Stewarding God's Message

Servant-leaders serve those on mission with them. They are responsible for the well-being and training of those who follow them. Biblical servant-leaders strive to live as men and women of integrity in which no one can accuse them of betraying the trust of those who follow them. (The Bible calls this "above reproach"—1 Timothy 3:2). These people act the same in private as they do in public.

Leaders lose credibility and influence with those they lead when they begin to serve themselves rather than the mission and those who serve with them. Classic business scandals like the crash of Enron and government debacles like Watergate that ended in President Nixon's resignation give proof that leadership can become more about serving the leader than those he or she leads.

Name a leader in your life who you would describe as "above reproach." Write the name of a leader in whom you put your trust but he or she lost that trust by an act of indiscretion or impropriety. Take some time to process your feelings toward both the leader of integrity and the one who lacked it.

_____

_____

_____

Much has happened since the last episode in His-story. 1 Samuel 4–11 records how Israel got its first king and his years of leadership. Chapter 12 records Samuel's farewell speech to the people. He still had several significant things to do in God's Story with Israel, but he had given them the king they wanted in Saul, and he was ready to pass his leadership on to the king.

Read 1 Samuel 12:1–5. Summarize his message to the people. What conclusion did they both agree to?

_____

_____

_____

Samuel desired to establish that he served the people by

giving them the king they wanted and by not betraying their trust through acting dishonest in any way. A leader's character is sometimes all he or she has to stand on when those who follow have their own opinions as to where they want to go. Samuel had a reputation of honesty and service to the people. This would serve him well in the months ahead as he spoke God's words to Saul and anointed David as king.

Our question to consider this week was: How can I know God's voice in the midst of daily life? After your study of this episode in God's Story, how would you answer the question now? Write your thoughts here:

_____

_____

Initial answers to our question include through God's Word recorded in the Bible, through God's Holy Spirit, and through a mentor like Eli. Look for other ways God guides you through the day.

**For further study:**
- **1 Samuel 2:18–21, 26**
- **2 Timothy 3:14–17**

# 28—Mishandling Holy Things (King Saul)

The word holy is an interesting word. It is typically not a word we use every day. We reserve it for church settings. Yet, God has commanded Christ-followers to be "holy" and to live "holy" lives (1 Pet. 1:15). The biblical perspective of the word holy signifies something or someone set apart for special purposes. In some way, the idea of Special Forces withing the military communicates the meaning. This week's study will explore the concept of acting properly or improperly with what God considers holy.

Saul was the first king of Israel. He ruled for 42 years. God used him to unify the twelve tribes of Israel who had entered the promised land under Joshua. God chose Samuel to bridge God's rule over Israel through judges to kings. Samuel served as God's voice to King Saul during his reign. Problems started when Saul took matters into his own hands rather than obeying the words of God through Samuel. Saul's actions serve as a warning to live out God-given positions in life under His leadership. Christ-followers are to live out God's clear words revealed in Scripture.

The Memory Verse for this chapter is 1 Samuel 13:14. This is not a verse you will print and post on your mirror to read every morning. It records God's judgment on Saul for his disobedience. But it offers a significant reminder of how when you willfully go against God's commands, you will experience consequences—both immediate and eternal.

Our question to consider this week is: How do you determine what is holy and what is not? Read this question in the context of Saul's decision to offer a sacrifice after Samuel did not show up when the king thought he would.

## 28.1 The Plight of Fear

I do not frighten easily, but I do remember when I lived in the panhandle of Florida as a boy a tornado spawned by a hurricane came through our neighborhood. The wind sounded like the mythical train engine racing closer by the second. My mother shouted above the roar, "Downstairs!" All five of us children leapt down the stairs as the wind lifted the roof off the walls for a moment. I remember seeing trashcans and bicycles flying horizontally past the sliding glass doors as we crouched behind a sofa. It ended in 30 seconds, but I had nightmares for a year. I know what fear feels like from that experience, and occasionally this tornado-in-the-backyard fear visits me. Fear makes you do things you may not do otherwise.

What experience of fear do you have from your childhood? How did you respond to it?

_____

_____

As king, Saul led the army of Israel against its primary foe, the Philistines. These sea-going settlers made powerful enemies and wanted the same land Israel claimed as its own. War inevitably followed.

Read 1 Samuel 13:5. Highlight the two nations mentioned in the verse. You may want to read the previous verses for more details. Use the notes in a study Bible, Bible handbook, or commentary to discover the geography of the setting. Underline the description of the Philistine army. Compare it to that of Israel's army in verse 2 of this chapter.

Read 1 Samuel 13:6–7. Circle the verbs in these verses that describe the response of the Israelites to their circumstances. Circle words like "hard pressed," "crossed," and "quaking with fear."

In your opinion, were the actions of the Israelites justified? If so, why? If not, why? Consider these questions from the biblical perspective: where God is the Victor no matter the odds. Also, consider them from a natural perspective: where you alone are responsible for the outcome against the odds you face.

_____

_____

Saul found himself in a desperate situation. The storm clouds of his enemies formed on the horizon. He chose to wait in Gilgal where Samuel confirmed him as king while his troops hid in caves and retreated from their potential death.

What situations have you found yourself in similar to that of Saul and his army? What were the odds of your downfall? How did you respond? What kind of fear did this raise in you? Write about your experience in the space below and relate some of your feelings to that of Saul and his army.

_____

_____

_____

## 28.2 Stepping Out-of-Bounds

I am told that the difference between a foul ball and a home run in baseball is timing. The best batters wait for the ideal moment to put the bat on the ball in order to get a hit. Those of you who cannot get out of the Little League stall at the batting cages know this concept only in theory. You, however, do enjoy watching it happen live or on television. Waiting that creates ideal timing also holds true in spiritual matters.

Read Psalm 27:14. King David offered this advice as he cried out to the LORD for help in one of his battles. What does this verse teach you about waiting on God even when circumstances press upon you? How much is up to you and how much is up to God when things get tight?

_____

_____

Read 1 Samuel 13:8. Underline how long Saul had waited for Samuel and what Saul's men began to do. What would such actions create in the heart of a commander if his army began to do this? Read verse 9. Highlight Saul's response to this situation.

Saul was a man of action, and he fulfilled his kingly role by mustering and attacking the enemies of Israel (1 Sam. 11:1–11). When Samuel did not show up when he said he would and Saul's troops began to scatter, the king took matters into his own hands and offered sacrifices to Yahweh in order to gain His favor. When Samuel arrived (v. 10), he was appalled that Saul had done such a thing. The priest asked, "What have you done?" (v. 11a;

See Genesis 3:13, in which God asked Eve the same question.) Saul had crossed the line by performing a priestly function.

Read 1 Samuel 13:11b–12. List Saul's reasons for offering the sacrifice.

1. _____

2. _____

3. _____

Saul explained he felt "compelled" to offer the sacrifice because his men were scattering. He added that Samuel did not arrive when he said he would, implying that this was essentially his fault. Finally, Saul said the Philistines were preparing for battle and he needed to do the same, so he offered the sacrifice in order to get going. All of these were legitimate reasons for taking action. The problem rested in the fact that Saul took action God had not authorized him to do. Even as king, he must not to perform the duties of a priest.

Describe a situation in which you felt you had no choice but to act. What consequences, both positive and negative, resulted from your choices? Return to Psalm 27:14 and meditate on the promise of God's Word. What difference does waiting make?

_____

_____

_____

## 28.3 The Balance of Truth

Parenting is a balance between correction and encouragement. To build character you must correct your child, but you must also encourage your child so he or she will try again and improve. Too much correction can create a negative self-image and too much encouragement produces a false picture of your child's abilities.

If you are a parent, describe a time you balanced these two actions well. When did you not?

_____

_____

Samuel's job as prophet and priest worked much like that of a parent. He had to correct and encourage Saul in order to accomplish the purposes of God. In this episode, Samuel corrected Saul because he crossed the line of his responsibility as king and took up the practices of a priest. Samuel did little to encourage the king in this situation, and he spoke clearly the consequences of Saul's actions.

Read 1 Samuel 13:13. What did Samuel say God would have done if Saul had kept God's words?

_____

_____

Read verse 14. Notice what had God already done to replace Saul as king. Underline in verses 13–14 the phrase "you have not kept the LORD's command."

Because Saul violated God's command through Samuel, he would experience two consequences. First, God would not establish Saul's kingdom forever. Remember, His-story focuses on the covenant God made with Abraham, Isaac, and Jacob to reveal Himself to the world. God was going make an everlasting covenant with David (2 Sam. 23:5), but according to Samuel that could have happened with Saul. Samuel also said God had already chosen someone to replace Saul as king. (See 1 Sam. 16:1–13 for the actual choice of David.) These came as hard truths for Saul, but they were the consequences of Saul's willful choice to cross the lines God had put in place for kings and priests.

Samuel told Saul the hard truth of his actions. The king mishandled the holy things of God, and he would pay the consequences. When has a friend spelled out the consequences of your actions? Or when have you spoken with enough honesty to tell a friend the truth about a his or her life? Take time to allow God's Spirit to reveal any sin you have overlooked and the potential damage it could bring. Write your thoughts here:

_____

## 28.4 Excuses for Disobedience

Obedience means doing what you are told to do. People tend to see the Bible as a book of good advice. They like to see themselves see as the center of the universe. The result is that they have difficulty doing exactly what God's Word tells them to do.

For example, God calls His people to be holy, set apart for His purposes, and to "not conform to the evil desires you had when you lived in ignorance" (1 Pet. 1:13–16). These instructions read clearly. However, we often neglect them. Possibly because our disobedience does not affect us immediately or we have relegated God's words to one of many voices we listen to on how to live our lives.

In what areas of your life have you become lax in following God's clear instructions? Write 1 Peter 1:13–16 in your own words in the space below. Seek to live by these verses today.

_____

_____

Samuel gave Saul clear instructions regarding what to do with the Amalekites after he defeated them (1 Sam. 15:1–3). Read 1 Samuel 15:4–9 to see how Saul followed those instructions. What did he do and not do?

_____

Read 1 Samuel 15:10–11. Highlight the phrase "the word of the LORD." (You may want to do a word search on this phrase to get an understanding of its importance in the biblical record.) Underline God's message to Samuel and circle the words that describe Samuel's response to it.

God came directly to Samuel and told His servant He was "grieved" ("sorry," NLT; "regret," NKJV) that He had ever made Saul king. (See Genesis 6:6 and Psalm 78:39–41 for other examples of God "grieving" for the sin of His people.) God did not rethink His decision. God grieved because Saul did not obey. Samuel shared God's grief and stayed up all night crying out to God.

Have you ever grieved over the sin of others—not for the purpose of judgment but to share God's heartache?

Read 1 Samuel 15:20–21 and notice Saul's excuses for doing what he did.

Read verses 22–26 for Samuel's response to Saul. Underline the phrases in verse 26 that declare the judgment of God to Saul.

God rejected Saul as king of Israel because he would not do exactly what God commanded him to do. Reflect on your understanding about the character of God from these verses? How do they apply to your life today?

Take time to prayerfully write your responses in your journal or on another piece of paper.

## 28.5 And So It Was

This episode in His-story does not end with a "and they lived happily ever after." Saul was to fall on his sword, and the next king, David, would wait for years to take the throne. Saul's mishandling of holy things caused trouble for all who followed him.

God's judgment on Saul seems harsh from a non-biblical perspective. You could argue that Saul did not hurt anyone when he offered the sacrifices. He actually worshiped God before he left to go into battle. That's good. You could argue that Saul essentially did what God told him to do by crushing the Amalekites. He simply kept the best to honor God with what his army captured. It belonged to God. They would give the best to God and use the rest.

In what ways do these thoughts reflect your thinking about following God's words? In what ways do they not?

Read 1 Samuel 15:22–23 again. Read the verses from several translations. Use the cross references in your study Bible or footnotes to see where similar instructions occur in the Bible. Summarize Samuel's message to Saul in the space below.

_____

_____

God needed a king to follow Him without compromise or question. The king, after all, served as God's leader to write His-story. To not obey God was to jeopardize how God wanted His purposes revealed to all.

Our question to consider this week was: How do you determine what is holy and what is not? After studying Saul's actions, how would you answer this question?

_____

_____

_____

**For further study:**
- **Genesis 17:15–16; Deuteronomy 17:14–20**
- **1 Samuel 8–11; 13–15**

## 29—The Art of Friendship (David and Jonathan, Part 1 of 3)

God rejected Saul as the king of Israel because of his disobedience, but he remained king while God led Samuel to anoint the next leader—a young man named David. God's favor was obvious to the people of Israel because of the success David experienced fighting the enemies of God. But Saul became increasingly frustrated at David's success and growing popularity. He resolved to kill David. God protected David from Saul's anger through his friend, Jonathan, who was also Saul's son.

Through Saul's vengeance a true friendship was born. David and Jonathan's friendship not only saved David's life but it also gave him hope in very dark days.

Their gift of friendship is an example of God's provision for those on the journey of faith. Their friendship also shows how followers of Jesus should love one another.

We live in the digital age. In the workplace, people commonly send emails to a coworkers in offices just down the hall and rarely have a face-to-face conversation. We also live in a transient culture where families are spread out geographically and live in one place for shorter periods of time. Studying this picture of real friendship will help all of us to see the value of real friendship.

The Memory Verse this chapter is John 13:35. Authentic Christ-followers are known by their love. They love each other like David and Jonathan.

Our question to consider this week is: What is a "true friend"? Describe the characteristics of a true friend and write the name of someone who has been that to you. See how David and Jonathan's friendship expands your concept of friendship as you observe their relationship.

## 29.1 Issue of the Heart

Do you know what you call a nerd in high school after you both graduate from college? Boss. That old joke may remind you that a person's appearance and lack of social skills does not determine his or her success in life. It is hard to tell who will emerge as a leader simply by his or her looks or ability to fit in. Add to that reality the mystery of God's choice of leaders based upon what He sees in their hearts, and you never know whom you may find yourself sitting next to on the train in to work tomorrow.

What person do you remember from high school who you were certain would never amount to much but who is now a leader? Write his or her name and something about that person in the space below.

_____

_____

God sent Samuel to Bethlehem to anoint a new king after God rejected Saul. Read 1 Samuel 16:1–5 for how Samuel came to the "House of Bread," the home of Jesse and his eight sons. Remember Ruth was Jesse's grand-mother (Ruth 4:21–22). His-story holds together through intentional relationships as God unveils His plans.

Embedded in this narrative is the truth of how God sees and judges people. Read 1 Samuel 16:7. Underline the last sentence of the verse. Consider what it reveals about the character of God. Also, apply how God views us to how we should see others.

Read 1 Samuel 16:8–10. Highlight the names in these verses. Jesse paraded all seven sons before the prophet of God, but Samuel did not hear the voice of God tell him to anoint any of them. Samuel felt certain God had not yet spoken. Jesse then admitted he had the youngest son out watching sheep, so Samuel sent for him (v. 11).

Read 1 Samuel 16:12–13. Underline how our storyteller described David. While this phrase only presents his outward appearance, God saw his heart. (Read 1 Samuel 13:14 for a description of David's heart for God.)

Underline what the storyteller said happened after Samuel anointed David. Recall how the "Spirit of the LORD" came upon the judges as God chose them to lead. (For examples of this, see Judges 3:10; 6:34; 11:29; 14:6.)

David was his family's last choice to be a king. However, God knew his heart and his potential as a leader. Samuel had learned to recognize the voice of God as a youth. He waited until he heard God tell him to anoint the ruddy-faced shepherd boy rather than deciding on his own as Saul had done at Shiloh.

What hope does this story give you for your life? If you are a parent, what does it tell you about your children's potential in the eyes of the LORD? Write some of your thoughts here:

_____

_____

_____

## 29.2 A Troubled Saul

I like different kinds of music for different kinds of moods. For example, as I write I like to have classical music playing in the background. In spin class, I prefer rock-n-roll or techno with a constant beat. When I run or ride I don't listen to music. For worship, I like acoustic sounds for more meditative moments and multiple-instrument bands for energetic praise. Music is the language of the soul and a gift of God that affects us in many ways.

What kind of music do you prefer for different moods? Or do you think of music as simply a background sound?

_____

_____

Read 1 Samuel 16:14. Underline the two spirits mentioned in the verse.

The removal of God's Spirit from Saul may sit better with your knowledge of the ways of God than the fact that God sent an "evil spirit" to torment the king. You may wonder if God acted vindictively, but remember two things concerning His decisions like this. God told Isaiah, "neither are your ways my ways . . . so are my ways higher than your ways" (Isa. 55:8–9). We cannot fully comprehend why God does what He does. Secondly, time after time God does nothing that will not move His-story along in order to accomplish His plan. In the next verses the evil spirit's torment brought David to Saul's house. God arranged for David to have insight into the kingship he would not have experienced as a shep-

herd.

What other insights do you have about the impact of God sending an evil spirit to torture Saul? What does this teach you about the character and power of God? How does a promise like Romans 8:28 add to your understanding? Write your thoughts here:

_____

_____

_____

Read 1 Samuel 16:15–20. These verses describe how David came into the service of Saul. Underline the servant's description of David in verse 18. Use a Bible dictionary, encyclopedia, or handbook to learn more about the harp mentioned in these verses. (Also, find psalms written by David, like Psalm 57 that mentions the harp—v. 8.) Write what you find here:

_____

The music of the harp, a hand-held stringed instrument, soothed the soul of Saul when the spirit disturbed him. His servants offered to find someone who they could call on to play. A servant heard—by chance?—one of Jesse's sons play the harp and offered him to play for the king. Saul sent word to the family, and David's father, knowing David was the anointed king of Israel, sent his son to Saul.

Put on some of your favorite music for prayer or praise and spend some time allowing the words and sounds to move your heart toward God. Thank God for the gift of music and those He has talented to play it so carefully to guide your heart toward Him.

## 29.3 Little Big Things

I was teaching an adult Sunday school class while working for a Christian camping organization when a former student in my youth ministry called. I knew he served as a youth minister at a church in a nearby suburb, and I felt proud that a student who grew up in my ministry now served as a leader of a similar ministry. He called to ask if I wanted to preach for his church because the pastor had resigned and they needed someone to preach for awhile. I said goodbye to my class and preached for the church on a Memorial Day weekend. Ten months later, they called me to serve as their pastor. Twenty years later, I still pastor that church. One phone call from a former student set in motion the ministry position I would serve for the majority of my adult life.

What seemingly small connections in your past have turned into major avenues of service or work in your life? How have the unexpected moves resulted in either positive or negative experiences? When you look over your past, how have you seen God's hand in your connections and in the decisions you have made?

Read 1 Samuel 16:21–22. Describe the progression of David's status with the king. An armor-bearer personally attended to the king's needs on and off of the battle field. This person was a highly trusted servant of the king.

_____

Read verse 23. How did God use David to help the king? "The spirit from God" is the same spirit introduced in verse 14. God used David's talent to play the harp to soothe the king's soul.

An unnamed servant remembered a shepherd boy who could play the harp. The king sent for the young man and he lived up to his reputation. Soon he not only played for the king when "the spirit from God" came upon him, but he also became the king's trusted confidant, his armor-bearer. God placed David in training to become king before he ever took the throne through the "chance" of someone's memory.

Recall how God used Pharaoh's cupbearer to bring Joseph into the presence of royalty to exercise God's gift to interpret dreams and ultimately to serve as second in command in the most powerful country in the world at that time (Gen. 41:9–14). God used Joseph's connections while in prison and the memory of one of them to get the Israelite where God needed him in order to save God's covenant people from starvation.

Reflect upon the people and ways God has brought you to where you are in life. Joseph's life can remind you that God can even use places like prison to get you to where He can use you most. David's rise into the palace tells us God can use our talents to place us where He desires to use us. Ask God to reveal His purposes to you as you reflect on the journey that brought you where you are.

## 29.4 A Friendship is Born

Kent is one of my best friends. We met when we joined the same service organization in college. We quickly became friends through all the shared experiences of those four years of service together. We were in one another's wedding, and our families have vacationed together every other year for the past 30 years and have seen each other at our college homecoming almost every year. Kent and I even worked together after college for a private Christian foundation that owned and operated camps and conference centers. Little did we know that when we met our lives would stay connected for so long. Friends like Kent are hard to come by, and he and his family are one of God's best blessings in my life.

Who is your best friend? How did you meet and how long have you known one another? How has this friend helped you in your faith? Write one characteristic of your friend that you appreciate the most.

_____

_____

Favored status with an emotionally tormented king is never guaranteed. Read 1 Samuel 17–18 to see how David's defeat of Goliath made him a hero throughout Israel and how Saul came to resent his armor-bearer's new fame. These events set up the importance of David and Jonathan's friendship.

Read 1 Samuel 19:1–3. What had Saul commanded concerning David? Underline how our storyteller described Jonathan's relationship with David? What did he propose to do because of his friendship with him?

The storyteller wrote that Jonathan "greatly delighted in David" (v. 1; NASB, the most literal translation). We learned in an earlier episode that Jonathan loved David "as himself" (1 Sam. 18:1–3). The Great Commandment insists Christians "love your neighbor as yourself" (Matt. 19:19). (See also John 21:15–17 for Jesus' questions to Peter about his love for Him.)

Read 1 Samuel 19:4–7. List some of Jonathan's reasons for his father not to kill David in the space below. What did Saul do in response?

_____

_____

"The spirit from God" was absent and Saul received his son's requests. The king swore he would not have David killed, and he accepted his former armor-bearer back into royal service. Jonathan risked his life by approaching the king, but he loved his friend so much that he willingly took that risk.

Jonathan demonstrated his love for David by risking his life for him. This is the same love Jesus showed us when He called His followers "friends" and said, "Greater love has no one than this, that he lay down his life for his friends" (John 15:13). Reflect on Christ's love for you and the demonstration of that love by His death in your place. Write some of your thoughts and feelings here:

_____

_____

_____

## 29.5 A Willingness to Sacrifice

Saul's emotional and spiritual roller coaster continued, and he decided again to have David killed. Jonathan, his son, tried again and again to protect his friend, the anointed king of Israel. Saul's condition affected both the country and his family. Have you ever lived with an emotionally unstable person? If the answer is yes, use some of your experiences to identify with Jonathan's situation. What would you add to the storyline to help readers know the struggles Jonathan faced as he sought to respect his father and still protect his friend?

_____

_____

Read 1 Samuel 20:30–34. Observe Saul's response to David's absence at the festival meal. Why was David not

there? (See 1 Samuel 20:1–29 for the answer.) Verse 34 describes Jonathan's reaction to his father's actions. He grieved at the potential loss he would experience if his father killed his best friend.

The Memory Verse for this chapter is John 13:35. Jesus told His followers that people will know they are His apprentices by the love they show one another. David and Jonathan's friendship gives an Old Testament example of the kind of love Jesus talked about. You and I should look out for, take risks for, and defend fellow followers of Jesus just as Jonathan did for David. Write out other ways in which people who observe Christ-followers would see the love of Jesus between believers.

_____

_____

_____

Our question to consider this week was: What is a "true friend"? Now that you have observed the friendship of the king's son and the anointed king, take time to write your description of a "true friend." Add to this description Jesus' love toward you as His friend, which He proved by dying on the cross in your place. (See Romans 5:8 as another expression of Christ's love for you.)

**For further study:**
- **1 Samuel 12:1–11; 18–20**
- **John 13:34–35**

David and Goliath show up in speeches and literature today to represent the little guy taking on a giant in most any area of life. People love it when the underdog wins and the long-standing giant falls. But, the story does not focus on the agility and innovation of a shepherd boy who outwitted a military machine. Instead, the story tells how God empowered a young man who had a heart completely sold out to God in order to show His greatness and power to an unbelieving people. Israel had two kings at the time of the battle: Saul, the ruling king, and David, the anointed one. God blessed David and eventually made an eternal covenant with him in order to bring on stage the main character of His-story, Jesus. God felt drawn to David's heart, not his strength or appearance. In biblical terms, the heart does not refer to the physical organ that beats within us. Instead, the heart refers to the seat of our emotions and the place where our innermost thoughts reside.

Jesus had much to say about the condition of our hearts. In Luke 6:45 He taught that the mouth speaks from the heart. He emphasized that what you have stored up in your heart will come out and reveal the type of person that you actually are (Mark 7:20).

The Memory Verse for this chapter is Acts 13:22. When Paul spoke in the synagogue in Pisidian Antioch he recalled the description of David's heart for God from the Old Testament (1 Sam. 13:14). Acts 13:16–41 retells His-story for the Jews and God-fearing people who had gathered on that Sabbath.

Our question to consider this week is: What does it mean to seek God's heart? We will observe the life of David to discover an answer to this question.

## 30.1 Facing Goliath

Every army will eventually face a Goliath. Every person will have to stand up to a bully. Goliath was not a mythical figure. He was a real giant of a man who threatened God's rescue mission for all people. Israel had a king and an army but no one trusted their God enough to engage the Philistine warrior.

No one, but David. He was the youngest of eight from an out-of-the-way town who watched sheep while his brothers fought in the big war. Who would have picked him to bring down the nine-foot warrior? What significant fact of David's life do you know from His-story prior to this event? How could this fact make a difference in the battle to come? (See 1 Samuel 16.)

_____

_____

Read 1 Samuel 17:1–16 for the setting of our focal verses. Highlight the names of the people and places. Use Bible study helps to learn more about the geography and point in the time of the events. Underline verse 11, which describes the mood of the troops and the apparent hopelessness of the situation.

Read 1 Samuel 17:17–22. What circumstances surrounded David's entrance onto the battlefield? How would you describe David's emotions from verse 22? Was he eager to see the battle or more like the soldiers described in verse 11?

Jesse sent his youngest son on a routine trip to check on his sons who served in the army of Israel. What began as a trip to bring supplies and return with updates on the troops turned into a defining moment with God.

What circumstances surrounded your last encounter with a "Goliath"? Did it come in a routine event or during a unique time in your life? Did you approach the danger like David did when he heard the battle cries, or did you feel somewhat like the other soldiers? Invite God's Spirit into the situation. Picture His presence and the difference it made in your battle. Write your thoughts here:

_____

_____

## 30.2 Young, but Brave

Youth has its advantages. We are usually in better physical shape at a young age. Most of our youth-filled options were still open to us as teens. Dreams were still possibilities. Youth tend to have an I-can't-be-hurt attitude in their decisions, and they tend to live without fear of the future or authority. Youthfulness can be the fuel for innovation and new horizons. But the lack of knowledge, skill, and experience ends life prematurely.

Describe the attitude you had toward life as a teenager. What were your dreams? How did you view the future. What did you anticipate your life would be like when you grew up?

Write some of your memories in the space below. Whether you felt optimistic or not about the days ahead, take time to engage your youth-filled days so you may get a sense of David's attitude toward the future he faced.

_____

_____

_____

Read 1 Samuel 17:32–33. In the space below, write the conversation between David and Saul in your own words.

_____

_____

David offered to slay the giant since no one else would. Read verse 25 for a possible motivation of his desire to take on the giant. Highlight who accused David of this motive in verse 28. King Saul, the seasoned warrior and leader, tried to give the enthusiastic boy some perspective. David was a shepherd boy. Goliath was a veteran soldier, not to mention about four times David's size and strength!

Read verses 34–37 for David's response. What did he base his courage on? Naiveté? Foolishness? Trust that God would empower him like He did while he kept sheep all alone? Underline verse 37, which gives David's reason for his confidence.

David did not make his offer for money and fame as his older brother accused him of doing. He did not do it because he was naïve to the situation he faced. David offered to fight Goliath because he was convinced that the same God who empowered him as he fought off animals to protect his family's sheep would give him the ability to defeat this enemy of Israel. He did not do this out of youthful exuberance. He did it out of faith.

As you end your moment with God today, look back over your story to recall the times God has empowered you to make it boldly through a situation. Think of those experiences as the "lion and bear" victories that give you faith for the "Goliath" you may face today.

## 30.3 Who Gets the Credit?

I love it when a professional athlete on a national stage gives God credit for a victory. It impresses me that he or she would take the focus off him or herself and give it to God. There have been some big wins in which an athlete who has a proven relationship with God has made an impact on people because of his or her witness. On the other hand, it does not impress me when an athlete who makes a shot or scores a goal points up to the sky or kneels down on the field. I do not know if he or she is giving God the credit, pointing to his or her deceased grandmother, or posing for the cover of a sports magazine. Whatever the trendy sign of devotion may be that season, only a witness backed by a godly lifestyle can truly help others trust Jesus.

How do you feel about celebrities who have an "out front" witness about their relationship with God? How do you feel about public displays of attention toward God?

Write some of your thoughts here:

_____

_____

_____

Read 1 Samuel 17:45. Circle the word "but" in the middle of the sentence and underline the phrase on either side of it. What are the different "weapons" David said Goliath and he brought to the battle? Highlight the names for God in this verse.

Read verses 46–47. After the LORD gave him the victory, what did David tell the armies they would know? (v. 47) The victory, David said, would reflect the greatness of Israel's God, not the strength of their army.

As you read David's declaration to Goliath, note he used the personal name of Israel's God in front of the polytheistic Philistines. He declared he came in the name of Yahweh, the LORD Almighty, and that his God would bring victory to God's people on the battlefield.

David placed not only his life but the reputation of his God on the line with his confession. When have you had enough boldness to make a declaration in public that put your witness on the line with a group of people? How did you feel?

Read verses 48–50. Verses 48–49 describe the short battle between the boy and the giant. Agility and long-range accuracy proved superior to stability and armor. Our storyteller wrote that David won with just "a sling and

a stone" and did not carry a sword, the common instrument of war. This reinforced the fact that the battle was won by the power of God through His servant David.

David gave God all the credit for his victory over Goliath. Yes, he was young and skilled in the use of lightweight, agile weapons, but David confessed that God and God alone won the battle. Would you do the same for all your victories?

## 30.4 Reflection on His-Story

Remember Cliff Notes®? We used them when we were supposed to write a book report but did not want to take the time to actually read the book. I still use the online version to recall or grow familiar with the seminal stories of culture. At the front of the notes is a synopsis of the story. It gives the user the storyline and main events that shape the story of the book. You could get the overall gist of the book from the synopsis, but you could never get an

"A" on your report without reading the book. A synopsis helps the reader grasp the overall point of the story.

What is your favorite story recorded in a book or film? Write the title here:

_____

Write a brief synopsis of the story and why you love it so much.

_____

_____

_____

Often in the biblical record you will run across a brief synopsis of His-story. In one or two sentences either the storyteller or a main character will summarize what all the action and characters are about. David's prayer to God records such a summary.

David became king years after Samuel anointed him (2 Sam. 3:1). As with Joseph, those years behind the scenes molded his character for the major role he would play in His-story. When he had conquered Jerusalem (2 Sam. 5:6–12) and brought the ark of the covenant there (2 Sam. 6), he built a palace for himself and desired to build a temple for the ark (2 Sam. 7:1–2).

God told David that his son would build the Temple, but through the king's "house" He would establish His eternal covenant (2 Sam. 1:3–17).

Read 2 Samuel 7:18–21. Highlight every time David used the name of God in his prayer. What kind of attitude did David have in this prayer? Write a one-word description here: _____ David's prayer gives an example of a servant-leader who has made himself servant to the mission call of God on his life. David was humbled by God's choice of his family, yet he committed to carry out the part God wanted him to play.

Read 2 Samuel 7:22–24. Underline the phrases in verse 23 that describe the actions of God.

Embedded in David's prayer is a synopsis of His-story up to this point in time. David recapped all that God had done to establish Israel as Yahweh's people since the king's ancestor, Abraham. David "got it." He understood what God was up to and how he played a part of the bigger Story of God's redemption of all people. God's choice and redemption of Israel makes up the Old Testament story. The exodus was Israel's defining moment with God.

Write the synopsis of His-story up to this point in time in your own words. Look back over the biblical story you have interacted with so far with this summary in mind. How does it help you understand the movement of His-story? What does it tell you about God?

_____

_____

_____

_____

## 30.5 The Heart Revealed

King David was a servant-leader of God. His set his heart on giving God the honor for all he did, and he humbled himself to do whatever it took to play his part in the epic of redemption for all people. David showed his heart for God as he continued his prayer for God's blessing on him and his family.

Read 2 Samuel 7:25–26. Underline verse 26. For this reason David asked that God's promise come true. He desired to be the "house" through which God brought forth His eternal covenant. To him it was more than simply building a temple for God. This a good example for all who follow Jesus and feel tempted to build buildings rather than building into the lives of the people they serve for God.

Read verses 27–28. Why did David say he had courage to ask God's blessing for his family? David was a servant-leader who only asked for God's blessing as it pertained to God's promise, not his personal happiness or wealth. David demonstrated the perspective of one who has a heart for God: Life is about God and His-story. We only act as supporting cast whom He writes in and out of the plot to move the epic along to its culmination. Jesus is the main character.

One piece of evidence proving Jesus as the main character and Son of God is the fulfillment of prophecy made about Him centuries before He entered His-story on earth. God's covenant with David to "establish his house forever" came about a thousand years before Jesus was born. The writer's of the New Testament of Jesus caught this truth and made note of it in His-story.

Read Luke 1:32–33 and Luke 2:4. How do these verses connect Jesus with God's promise to David? Jesus would reign as the "the King eternal, immortal, invisible, the only God" God promised through David (1 Tim. 1:15–17).

Our Memory Verse, Acts 13:22, notes God's use of David because of his heart for God. This verse is part of a synopsis of His-story up until that time (Acts 13:16–41). The old covenant stories are best understood when viewed through the person of Jesus, God's new and final covenant with those who trust Him.

Our question to consider this week was: What does it mean to seek God's heart? After having observed David's actions and prayers in the episodes of this chapter, write your answer to this question. Consider making those characteristics part of your trust relationship with God.

_____

_____

_____

**For further study:**
- **1 Samuel 13:14; 16:1–13; 17:1–58**
- **1 Samuel 18:5–23; 24:3–7; 26:9–11**

## 31—Our Vulnerability to Sin (King David, Part 3 of 3)

God made a covenant with David and his family to make them the lineage through which the promised Messiah would come. God chose him because David had a heart for God, but that same heart when left unaccountable wandered from its passion for God to lust for another man's wife. The story of David and Bathsheba is a tragic subplot in His-story that illustrates how one act of passion can wreak havoc on many lives. It also paints a picture of God's forgiving grace no matter the sin. God's rescue mission would not get sidetracked by the selfish desires of His chosen.

The Memory Verses for this chapter are 1 Corinthians 6:19–20. Paul reminded us that our bodies are the temples of the Holy Spirit and we, therefore, should honor God with our bodies. Sexual purity is part of God's design for our lives.

Our question to consider this week is: How does my sin affect other people? David's sin caused enough trouble for himself, but it also affected his family and the entire kingdom of Israel. Watch for the ways David's decision affected others in this episode of His-story.

# 31.1 The Peril of Idleness

"An idle mind is the devil's workshop," is a proverb I heard some time in my family's past. Although not a biblical proverb, it reflects a biblical truth similar to I Timothy 5:13, "Besides, they get into the habit of being idle and going about from house to house. And not only do they become idlers, but also gossips and busybodies, saying things they ought not to." Paul warned Timothy to be careful who he put on the list of widows because if the church cared for them completely they may grow idle and turn into "gossips and busybodies." An idle life will find something to do, and given human nature, that something is often neither healthy nor helpful.

How has this truth played out in your life? What does the garden of idleness grow in your life?

_____

_____

Read 2 Samuel 11:1. Highlight the names and look them up in a study help if needed. Underline the two phrases that describe David's actions.

What an innocuous beginning to a story: "In the spring, at the time when kings go off to war . . ." It is spring, snow melts and life returns to the earth. Kings wage war because of the dry ground and the warm weather. Life continues as it always has—even for the king of Israel. After this innocent beginning, the story turns. David, the king who led his troops to war, sent Joab to fight instead, and he "remained in Jerusalem."

What warning signs tell you moral trouble could be on the horizon for the king? What were the consequences of the king staying in the capital while his troops fought his war? Apply David's choices to your own life.

_____

Read 2 Samuel 11:2–5. Highlight the woman's name. Circle the verbs that tell David's actions. For example, he "got up," "walked around," and "saw" (v. 2). Each act led to "he slept with her" in verse 4. And each act presented an opportunity to stop the progression of events. Underline Bathsheba's message to David in verse 5.

Write the steps that led to their adultery. As you do, suggest what David could have done to turn away from the willful act of sleeping with another man's wife. Do the same from Bathsheba's place in the decision. Suspend the position she had no choice because he was the king and sent for her. Consider how she felt when she realized she was pregnant.

_____

_____

_____

David delegated his responsibility as the country's military leader to one of his generals. Nothing is inherently wrong with this act. But what did he do while he should have been at war? He laid in bed in the evening! He was idle, and no accountability around him. Idle with no accountability—a formula for moral failure.

Your turn: What impact does idleness and laziness, not rest, have upon your moral decision? Be honest. Let the Holy Spirit sit with you as you consider these things. Write your thoughts in your journal or on another piece of paper.

## 31.2 Attempts to Bury Sin

After people sin they most often try to cover it up. They erase the history on their Internet browser. They throw away the magazines. They do not call that person any more. They pray for forgiveness and try to hide whatever would give away their sin to those closest to them. But the gnawing presence of guilt and shame will not go away. And when something as obvious as a pregnancy is involved, hiding the evidence of their actions gets complicated. Sometimes people spend more energy on covering sin than it took to commit it.

We all sin, and we all try to deal with it on our own. In what ways do you try to cover your willful decisions that you know are wrong? If you have children, what have they taught you about human nature's will to cover up transgressions?

Read 2 Samuel 11:6–9. Describe David's plan to cover Bathsheba's pregnancy in the space below. What part of the plan kept it from working?

_____

_____

_____

David tried to cover his tracks by sending for Bathsheba's husband who was at the battle front. He hoped the man who had been away from his wife for some time would spend the night with her, and the problem of the baby would go away. The problem, however, turned out to be that Uriah was a man of integrity and loyalty. As long as his men could not sleep with their wives, neither would he. David's cover up did not go as planned.

Read 2 Samuel 11:10–12 for David's second effort to cover his sin. How did that turn out for him?

The tragedy of this episode is that "the man after God's own heart" found himself trapped in a web of deceit and hypocrisy that he created himself. His heart for God turned to lust for another man's wife and to schemes to hide his sin.

There is nothing pretty or uplifting in David's situation. The king of God's chosen people sat in his palace while the wife of one of his generals sat pregnant with his child and her husband slept outside on a mat. Let the scene fade out there.

Take time to put yourself in that setting. Allow the darkness of the moment rest on you. Sin is dark and complicated. Even those chosen to play major roles in His-story felt it. Call upon the Spirit of God to reveal to you the pain sin brings to Him.

## 31.3 Sin Leads to More Sin

I believe people watch soap operas because they want to see people act in ways they never would on their own. A woman's sinful side wants to slap the one who stole her boyfriend, run her rival off the road, or tell the family secret at the dinner party. Many people allow the murder of someone to cross the screen because they know they would never do that, but that guy got what he deserved. They love it when the dramatic chord sounds as their favorite character exposes the heroine's cheating. I do not endorse watching soaps, but they do strike a cord with millions of viewers.

What about television soap operas appeals to so many? Is it the on-going story? The characters? Is it a life people would want for themselves? Write your opinions here:

_____

_____

Second Samuel 11:14–15 reads like a soap opera plot. Surely, a biblical character would not do such a thing. But, David used his authority and position as God's anointed king to formulate the murder of Uriah, his own general. Underline David's orders in verse 15. What happened as a result of his order? (vv. 16–17)

When David's plan to cover up his sin by orchestrating Uriah and Bathsheba to sleep together did not work, he conceived and executed a plan to kill Uriah. David misused his power as king, and he killed an innocent man so he could have the man's wife as his own. And do not miss the slimy, insincere comment by the king to Joab in verse 25, "Don't let this upset you; the sword devours one as well as another." Joab knew the plan; he executed it and reported the results back to his commander-in-chief. David's consolation was a farce.

Read 2 Samuel 26–27. Underline the action verbs in this passage. What happened after Uriah's murder? Underline the last sentence of verse 27.

David got his way, and he married Bathsheba. He was convinced the affair had ended. David falsely believed everyone else thought Bathsheba carried her husband's baby, Uriah tragically died in battle for the king, and the king graciously took Uriah's wife as his own to care for her because of her husband's loyal service to the king. But God and you know better.

Use your journal to summarize the truth of the situation, not how David perceived things. Write some thoughts about how sin clouds ones perception of reality and how people tend to believe their own lies as they go deeper with sin.

A footnote to His-story: By her marriage to David, Bathsheba, a Hittite and adulteress, became part of the "house" of David whom God chose to bring forth the Main Character, the Messiah, into His-story to rescue all people. She is the fourth and final notorious woman in the genealogy of Jesus (Matt. 1:6).

## 31.4 Confronted with Sin

I worked out once a week with a couple of guys for about two years. We met at the local gym, went through our workout regimen, and headed to a nearby coffee shop to share life together. One day, I got a call from one of them to say the other guy had been having an affair for the last several years—even while we supposedly lived life together as a small band of brothers. His son exposed his lie. When confronted with the truth he first denied it, then he said it was true and left the house. I wish I could tell you that I found the guy, prayed with him, and led him to repentance and reconciliation with his wife and family, but I can't. He chose the woman he had the affair with and left his wife and children. It created a mess, and to the writing of this story, he has neither repented nor reconciled as far as I know.

The point of the story is not the man's sin but the way in which we posed as brothers in Christ while never getting to who we really were and what we did beyond church and coffee. It took a truth-seeking son to expose the lie. Have you ever found yourself in a similar situation? Did someone you love expose your lie? How did you respond or how have you seen others respond?

_____

Read 2 Samuel 12:1–6. God graciously sent Nathan, the king's trusted and faithful prophet, to tell David a parable (vv. 1–4).

How did the king respond to the story? (vv. 5–6) How would you describe his response given what he believed was reality?

How would you describe his response given what Nathan and you knew as true?

_____

_____

Read 2 Samuel 12:7–10. Underline the first sentence Nathan spoke to David after the king's declaration of justice. Pause after that sentence and reflect on how David must have felt after hearing those four words.

Read each verse separately and paraphrase—restate it in a way to give its meaning a different form—God's message to David through Nathan.

Verse 8_____

Verse 9_____

Verse 10_____

God reminded David of His grace shown through all He had given him (v. 8). God stated the truth in no uncertain terms: David murdered Uriah and took his wife as his own (v. 9). The consequences of his actions would plague his house (v. 10). These were tough words spoken in love to expose the lie David lived. The craziness of the situation was David believed his secret was secure, that his messengers would not tell anyone. But our sins like scenes in a soap opera will always get played on public TV. Anything you need to confess to God today before your friend Nathan shows up?

## 31.5 Experiencing Forgiveness

God forgave David (v. 13b), but the consequences of his actions were both immediate and long-lasting. Read 2 Samuel 12:11–12 for what consequences he would face.

The difference between my friend who was caught in adultery and David is that David confessed the reality of the situation: "I have sinned against the LORD" (v. 13a). David admitted his actions were first against God. My friend told how he had felt cheated sexually and how this woman fulfilled his needs. He never got around to David's confession. We have two options when God exposes our sin: agree we have sinned against God or give excuses for our self-centered choices.

Read Psalm 51. David wrote this song of confession and repentance after Nathan came to him. Grow familiar with David's heart in order to use this psalm when you have sinned against the LORD. Your sin does not need to include adultery and murder for his God-inspired words to guide your heart to repentance.

Read 2 Samuel 12:14–18. Nathan prophesied the death of the child conceived in adultery, and it came to pass. Observe David's actions during the illness of the child and his actions after its death (2 Sam. 12:19–23). Summarize his reasoning here and write how his responses can serve as models of prayer and grieving for you.

_____

_____

Our question to consider this week was: How does my sin affect other people? Write what you have observed from this episode in His-story. Also, see 1 Corinthians 5:1–9 for how Paul told the church in Corinth to deal with one who flaunted his sin in front of the church. He wrote this because sin does affect other people.

_____

_____

David still had a heart for God. His quiet confession and Psalm 51 prove it. God forgave him and took away his sin, but the sins' consequences remained. God kept his promise to David. The birth of Solomon and Matthew 1 prove that. However, David and his family would never out live the consequences of his sin.

As you close this dark chapter in His-story, write what you have learned about yourself, sin, sin's consequences, and God's love and forgiveness. Use the space below, your journal, or a separate piece of paper record what God has revealed to you.

_____

_____

**For further study:**
- **2 Samuel 11:1–13:39; 15:1–37; 18:1–33**
- **Romans 3:23–24; 6:23; 1 Corinthians 5:1–9; 6:19–20**

# 32—Guarding Your Heart (King Solomon)

Solomon was Israel's third king. He had more wealth, wisdom, and power than his father David or any king who followed. He consolidated his power early by removing his rivals and extended his kingdom by politically astute alliances through marriages with neighboring countries. Solomon brought wealth and prestige to Israel like it had never known before or since. Foreign royalty traveled to hear his wisdom and see his wealth (1 Kings 4:34). Many still read daily the proverbs he wrote to guide his people. God had chose Solomon as king, but the wise king chose to serve and protect the worship of foreign gods, and God judged him for that. Like his father, David, the king had a heart for God. Still, his heart wandered from God to chase after the things of the world.

The Memory Verse for this chapter is Matthew 6:21. Solomon is an example of Jesus' proverb that our hearts follow what we treasure. While he knew the need to guard his heart (Prov. 4:23), he allowed his love for foreign wives to become the treasure that led his heart away from his first love, the God of Israel.

Our question to consider this week is: How can my relationships with other people compromise my relationship with God? The answer to this question will grow more clear as you observe the rule of Solomon. Take notes. We will talk at the end of the chapter.

**Yahweh—Divine Encounters** in the Old Testament

## 32.1 Asking for Wisdom

What would you say to God if He came to you in a dream and said, "Ask for whatever you want me to give you?" That's a bigger question than the small group ice breaker question. Go ahead and write your answer here:

_____

Before you say, "God would never say that to anyone," know that He did. You will read the person's answer in this episode of His-story.

Solomon was the second son of David and Bathsheba. Nathan, the prophet, gave him the name Jedidiah (2 Sam. 12:25). Solomon established his rule over Israel after his father named him king instead of his brother, Adonijah, who had begun to act as if he were king, and after Solomon assassinated his brother and a rival military leader and priest from David's reign (1 Kings 2:13–46). While Solomon held a God-given position, he performed ungodly acts to secure and keep his place in the government. Once a kingdom is established it must be kept whole.

Read 1 Kings 3:1–5. Underline the phrase "high place(s)" wherever it occurs in these verses. A "high place" in this context refers to an elevated place used for Canaanite worship of pagan gods. Also, circle the word "except" in verse 3.

Consider how Solomon showed "his love for the LORD." Notice the exception to his love for God. Highlight where Solomon went to worship in verse 4, and underline God's question to him in verse 5.

Read 1 Kings 3:6–10. Outline Solomon's prayer in the space below. Circle the word "servant" in the verses, and Underline the first sentence in verse 9, which tells his specific request. How did God react in verse 10?

_____

_____

Solomon acknowledged God's goodness to his father, David, and that God had remained faithful in His promises to give him an heir (v. 6). The king then stated his need: he was inexperienced and like a child when it came to being king and he ruled among a people too numerous to count. He saw himself as a servant-leader of the LORD, fulfilling the mission given him (vv. 7–8). He requested, then, that God give him "a discerning heart to govern [God's] people and to distinguish between right and wrong" (v. 9). God felt pleased with his answer (v. 10). Solomon's request of God was the king's defining moment with God.

If you were in Solomon's position, would you have asked the same thing? What about his request surprised you? Would you answer God this way in the story you find yourself in now? Why or why not? Write an honest prayer to God as your answer to His promise made through His Son, Jesus, recorded in Mark 11:22–24.

## 32.2 The Giver of Wisdom

Jesus told a story of a man who harvested a bumper crop of grain (Luke 12:16–21). The man said to himself he would tear down his existing barns and build bigger ones. He would then sit back and enjoy his wealth. God came to him in the night and said, "'You fool! This very night your life will be demanded from you. Then who will get what you have prepared for yourself?'" (v. 20) Luke wrote that Jesus told the story to show "how it will be with anyone who stores up things for himself but is not rich toward God" (v. 21).

Apply Jesus' teaching to your own attitude toward wealth. Compare those with Solomon's value on things when God allowed him to ask for whatever he wanted. (Before you say, "Yeah, but the king was rich already," remember that we can serve money no matter how much we have.)

Read 1 Kings 3:11–15. Underline what God noted Solomon did not ask for. Circle what God acknowledged he did ask God for; that is, "discernment to understand justice" (v. 11; NASB). Underline the kind of heart God said He would give Solomon (v. 12) and what God said He would give the king because he did not ask for it when he could (v. 13).

What blessing did God add to Solomon in verse 14? Based on what conditions? Paraphrase God's promise in verse 14 here:

_____

_____

_____

Solomon's request for help to carry out God's role for his life proved he was a true servant-leader. His prayer

did not focus on himself except as it related to his place in God's Story concerning Israel. He desired wisdom over wealth and to discern justice more than to defeat his enemies. God saw his heart and heard his request. God granted him a wise and discerning heart and a long life if he would remain true to God's commands. Solomon, the servant-king, humbled himself before God to ask for what only God could give him.

Read verse 15. How did Solomon react to God's answer? Why is worship a proper response to an encounter with God?

_____

_____

_____

End this moment with God by thanking God for all He has provided that you have not even asked for. Read Proverbs 8 which describes wisdom and its power in a person's life as God's words for you today.

## 32.3 God Keeps His Promise

One way to read a story is by skimming the storyline in order to get the broad events before settling down to read word-for-word. To read ahead and find out what will happen sometimes helps you see more clearly what you are reading. This is not a good idea when reading a novel. But when reading His-story it is a helpful way to gain context to what you are reading at the time in order to comprehend the bigger Story of God.

**Yahweh—Divine Encounters** in the Old Testament

What story did you last skim over? Was it a story you have not read before or a favorite story you skimmed simply to remember the parts you like so well?

_____

_____

You can read the Bible in the same way. With the help of headings in many translations, you can follow the plot of His-story for some time without reading an entire paragraph or passage. The topic headings allow you to move along with the story or to stop whenever you like to read a single verse or study a passage. Let's give reading the story of Solomon by skimming a try before we get to the focal passage of today's time with God. Find a translation of the Bible with topic headings in the text. For example, the NIV has "The Queen of Sheba Visits Solomon" at the beginning of 1 Kings 10. These headings are not part of the original text, but they can help you grow familiar with the story.

Skim 1 Kings 3:16–10:22 by reading the headings provided by the editors of your translation of the Bible. If you would like to list them as you read, you can create a timeline from Solomon's prayer for wisdom to the summary statement in today's verses. List them in the space below. Highlight a topic you would like to return to later to study or read completely before you move on in the story.

_____

_____

Read 1 Kings 10:23–25. These verses give a summary statement of all that had before been described. They fall under the heading, "Solomon's Splendor." (Read 1 Kings 4:29–34 for a similar summary statement.) Underline some of the superlative statements the storyteller used to describe the wisdom and wealth of King Solomon. You can clearly see through skimming the previous chapters and these summary verses that God did what He said He would do (1 Kings 3:11–14).

Wealth and power followed the king's God-given wisdom. The Queen of Sheba's visit to see the wealth and experience the wisdom of Solomon gives just one example of the world-wide notoriety of what God gave him. God kept His promise to make the everlasting covenant He made with Solomon's father, David (1 Kings 9:4–5). But, would Solomon keep his?

## 32.4 Wisdom, Marriage, and Comprise

Marriage involves compromise. My wife and I will be married 32 years the summer of the year in which I write this sentence. We have never come close to divorce because we learned early on in our relationship the art of compromise. That does not mean to negotiate core values and beliefs in order to keep the peace. Too many marriages fail when that happens. We learned that we cannot change the other person into what we want him or her to be. We discovered that God can redeem any decision we make or action we take, and found there is always a "middle road" we both can agree to walk on. The art of compromise is finding that "middle road."

What roll does compromise play in your relationships? Have you learned the lessons we have learned? What others have you learned that help your marriage last?

_____

_____

_____

Read 1 Kings 11:1–3. Highlight the names of the places from where Solomon got his wives and the names of their gods. Use a Bible handbook to find out more about both. Circle the number of wives and concubines.

Underline verses 4 and 6. These verses tell how his relationship with non-Israelite wives affected his devotion to God. With whom did the storyteller contrast his disobedience? Write his name here: _____

Solomon did what many kings have done through the ages. They married to create alliances with other countries or leaders. Solomon clearly adopted this practice as his primary foreign policy strategy.

Solomon's marriages led him to compromise with his wives in order to find the "middle road" for their faith, but this meant to compromise a core value and belief, which went against God's direction.

Read 1 Kings 3:7–8. What else did Solomon practice that led his heart away from full devotion to God? Solomon worshiped at the "high places" and allowed his foreign wives to worship the gods of their homelands. This negotiated "middle road" may have kept peace at home, but it brought God's judgment on a wise king's reign. Read 1 Kings 11:9–13 for God's response to Solomon's compromise.

Consider how compromise of God's clear guidelines has affected your relationship with God and others? What core values and beliefs have you felt tempted to negotiate in order to achieve something you wanted or thought you needed?

_____

_____

_____

Listen for God's Spirit to reveal to you areas in which you have wandered away from His perfect direction for your life.

## 32.5 Holding on to Wisdom

God granted Solomon wisdom, wealth, and world-wide influence. God established the same eternal covenant He made with King David with David's son. Solomon, like his father, wrote much of the wisdom literature in the Bible which serves as a guide for godly living for Christ-followers today. If you have not read the Book of Proverbs, mark some time to do so. It is a guide for living a godly life in so many arenas.

One particularly insightful axiom is Proverbs 4:23. Read the proverb and paraphrase its meaning here:

_____

_____

Solomon knew the wisdom of guarding one's heart because it is the source of life. Did Solomon learn this proverb early or late in life? In other words, did God reveal it to him early so he could guard his life from the influence of foreign wives and their gods, or did God reveal this truth to him at the end of his life when he realized he had not guarded his heart and had let his devotion fade toward God? Either way, you benefit from God's revealed wisdom to a person who knew the truth firsthand.

According to Jesus, your heart follows what you treasure. (This is found in Matthew 6:21, our Memory Verse.) Solomon's heart followed his treasure of foreign wives, which led him to compromise his devotion to God.

You know Solomon's story now, and you have his wise counsel and Jesus' direct teaching on the matter. Take some time to apply God's wisdom to your current situation. What do you treasure? How can you guard your heart? How have you seen both truths lived out in your experience?

Our question to consider this week was: How can my relationships with other people compromise my relationship with God? You should have this answer by now. The Apostle Paul warned the Christians in Corinth that "Bad company corrupts good character" (1 Cor. 15:33).

Who are some people in your life who may cause you to compromise your relationship with God? Combine this question with the truth of Proverbs 4:23. What can you do to guard your heart from their influence? Prayerfully ask God to show you how they seduce your heart from God and how you can show them grace and mercy while distancing yourself from their influence. Thank God for the relationships in your life that involve people who keep you devoted to God and your role in His-story. Consider asking one of these people for advice on guarding your heart.

**For further study:**
- **Exodus 34:15–16; 2 Samuel 12:24–25**
- **1 Kings 1:5, 11–40; 4:29–34; 10:1–9; 11:28–37**

## 33—Trusting God to Provide (Prophet Elijah, Part 1 of 2)

God revealed His covenant plans through individuals like Abraham, Isaac, and Jacob. He then raised leaders called judges to unite the tribes of Israel against their enemies. God allowed Israel to have a king, but when the kings stopped living faithful to God, He raised up prophets to speak His words to the people.

Elijah was a prophet who served as God's spokesperson during the reign of an unfaithful king, Ahab. Just as God chose David to demonstrate His power when the shepherd boy brought down towering Goliath, God selected Elijah to show His superiority over the god of Canaan, Baal. Elijah's story tells of courage, danger, and God's provision for one He chose to speak for Him in some very dark days.

The Memory Verse for this chapter is 1 Kings 17:16. This verse serves as a reminder that God provides for those whom He calls.

Our question to consider this week is: How do difficult circumstances affect my trust in God? Life is tough. Life can be the crucible that purifies your trust in God or the oven that melts away your desire to serve Him. Observe how tough times affected the faith of Elijah in the verses you study this week.

## 33.1 Trusting the Story Writer

God's plans are perfect, but human beings are not. Still, people are part of His plan even when they bring chaos through making wrong choices. His-story involves God working in apparent chaos to complete the next era of His rescue mission for all people. The mission of the church I pastor is "We help people trust Jesus." We chose this wording after we prayerfully agreed our reason for existing was Jesus' co-mission with us to make disciples (Matt. 28:19–20). Through the years we have made choices related to how we live out that mission. Sometimes those choices resulted in growth; other times they created painful chaos. The good news is that God is still in control despite our mistakes and we are still seeking to serve Him. God writes and edits His-story so that all may know the storyline and its Main Character, Jesus. Every Christ-follower can find hope in this reality.

What decisions have you made that resulted in chaos? Could you see God's work despite those decisions to bring about His purposes? Write some of your decisions and the way God used them in the space below.

_____

_____

_____

Solomon reigned as the third and last king of the united kingdom of Israel. His son, Rehoboam, added to the misery of the people by taxing them more than his father, so they rebelled and forced him to retreat to Jerusalem (1 Kings 12:1–24). Jeroboam, a self-appointed ruler, sided with the people, and they made him their king. He ruled Israel in northern Israel from Shechem (1 Kings 12:25–33). From those days until the exile, the kingdom of God's people stayed divided: Israel in the north and Judah in the south. God used a succession of kings and prophets to continue His-story in the midst of moral and social chaos. (Read 1 Kings 13–15 for the leaders and events that led up to this episode.)

Read 1 Kings 16:29–34. Highlight the names of the characters that entered the stage of His-story. Underline the description of Ahab in verse 30.

Read 1 Kings 17:1. Highlight the names in this verse and underline the prophet's message to Ahab. By whose authority did Elijah speak this message? (See the opening words of his statement.) Use a Bible handbook to locate Gilead.

Ahab ruled the northern kingdom of Israel from about 869–850 B.C., and he married a foreign wife, Jezebel. He regularly worshiped Baal, the primary god of the Canaanites. Our storyteller wrote he "did more evil in the eyes of the LORD than any of [the kings] before him" (1 Kings 16:30). To bring judgment and show He still had control, Yahweh raised up Elijah. God's prophet, or spokesperson, boldly went to the king of the north and said that it would not rain until God said it would.

When has God asked you to speak His Word to a person who did not live his or her life for God? How did you respond? From whom or what did you find your confidence?

## 33.2 The Coming of the Word

In the biblical record of His-story, "the word of the LORD" designated that what was heard or said came from God. This designation is important in a story where the actors learn the Author's intentions through a revealed script, not by human reason or intuition. (Read John 1:1–5, 14 for the phrase's biblical connection to Jesus. Jesus is the living Word of the LORD.) The Author guided His chosen leaders and prophets by revelation of Himself and His desires to them through His words.

Review the times "the word of Yahweh" guided a leader in the verses below. Read the passage and highlight the person's name and record the "word" God revealed to him in the space following the reference.

Genesis 15:1 _____

_____

Deuteronomy 5:5–7 _____

_____

1 Samuel 15:10–11 _____

_____

1 Kings 6:11–12 _____

_____

Read 1 Kings 17:2–4. Highlight "Elijah" and underline God's words to him.

From Abraham to the prophet Elijah, God revealed His purposes to the key players by direct revelation. "The word of the LORD" came to Elijah, a new character in the Story of God. Yahweh told him to go to a nearby wadi or ravine, and God would provide for him there. A riverbed would conceal him from Ahab's henchmen. God revealed a public word for the king and the kingdom (v. 1), which brought a word of judgment. He also revealed a private message for Elijah, which gave a word of promise to care for him (vv. 2–4). Elijah obeyed both words from God. He spoke to the king and then left for the river. God provided for Elijah with water from the river and ravens that brought him meat and bread twice a day.

Read Leviticus 11:13–19. Highlight the bird in that list that is also in this story of Elijah. Circle the words in verse 13 that describe the list of birds. These birds lived as scavengers, and unlike the "clean" birds, they were carnivorous.

**Yahweh—Divine Encounters** in the Old Testament

God used "detestable" or abhorrent birds to feed His called servant. Did God violate His own Word by feeding Elijah in this way? Other than the unsanitary nature of the food by modern standards, would you have had any reason to not accept the food offered by ravens?

## 33.3 When Provisions Run Dry

We went through a season of ministry in the church where I was pastor in which we could not pay all the staff we asked to serve with us. Attendance and giving had dropped to the point that we had to ask some of them to find other places of ministry. I personally took a cut in salary to demonstrate I still stood committed to our mission but that I also shared the responsibility of our situation. Those were painful days, and many of us wondered, "We are trying to do what God wants us to do! How did we get here?" No, no one embezzled any money, had an affair, or preached heresy. We trusted God, but God said, "This is all there is for now." We did what we believed God wanted us to do as clearly as we understood it, yet God's provisions did not match our plans.

Have you experienced a time in your epic with God where you felt convinced you were living according to the "word of the LORD" as you knew it, but the things that you thought should be normal were not? How did you respond to God? To others?

_____

_____

Read 1 Kings 17:7–9. Highlight the place God told Elijah to go, and underline God's directions to him.

God remained true to His words, and no rain fell. The river that had provided for Elijah dried up. Even God's chosen felt the affects of God's judgment on others. "The word of the LORD" came to the prophet, and God directed him to a specific place and person. Use a Bible dictionary to learn more about the place God sent him. God sent him into the country from which Ahab chose his Baal-believing wife, Jezebel.

Read 1 Kings 17:10–12. Underline the first sentence in verse 10. What does this say about Elijah's trust in God's words to him?

Underline, too, the first phrase in verse 12. What does "the LORD" stand for in the NIV? Paraphrase what the widow may have meant by her response to Elijah here:

_____

_____

Elijah obeyed God's call, and he went to Zarephath. When he called to a Phoenician widow while she gathered sticks to start a fire, she responded with her own confession, "As surely as Yahweh your God lives . . ." She recognized Elijah as an Israelite, and swore on his God that she was at the end of her supplies and would soon die. She felt desperate and had only a foreigner to tell her story to. The widow had only enough food for one meal. She was convinced she and her son would die soon. How can you explain to a person in a similar situation that God will provide? Have you ever had to comfort a person who had come to the end of all of his or her resources? What did you say or do? How did you use God's promises to encourage that person?

_____

_____

## 33.4 God Provides

A miracle happens when God steps into the world He created and restores someone. The example is what God uses to help people trust Him. The miracles of His-story give prompts to those on stage that God is still Writer and Editor and that the storyline is still the rescue mission of all people through Jesus Christ. Miracles, as John, the Gospel writer, described them, are "signs" that help people trust Jesus. They are in no way designed to puff up the one through whom they happened. Miracles can range from as big as the parting of the Red Sea to as seemingly insignificant as a widow and a prophet having enough food to survive a drought.

Write your definition of a miracle in the space below. You may want to list some familiar miracles you know from the Bible or from your own life. How do these events help you trust Jesus, or have they caused you to wonder
if they are possible?

_____

_____

Read 1 Kings 17:13–16. Highlight the name "LORD" and the phrases connected to it.

Few of us have been asked to give our last piece of bread to someone before feeding our family. But, the widow was this desperate when Elijah asked her to feed him first. She had to choose whether or not she trusted the words of the Israelite God. Should she take care of her son and her own needs before cooking for the stranger? This was her defining moment with God. Elijah assured her by first telling her not to be afraid (v. 13), and then he simply repeated Yahweh's message to her (v. 14). "The day the LORD" (v. 14) and "the word of the LORD" (v. 16) both designate Yahweh as the One God behind the message Elijah shared with the woman. The miracle of the continuous flour and oil was not only to feed Elijah, Yahweh's chosen prophet. God did this to help the Baal-worshiping widow trust the God of Israel.

Read Matthew 10:25–31. Circle the word "afraid" in the verses. Underline those things Jesus told His apprentices not to fear.

Read Matthew 14:15–21. How were Jesus' actions similar to the bread and oil multiplying with Elijah?

Elijah's private encounter with the widow foreshadowed the Messiah's coming ministry. Jesus told His followers John the Baptist was like the prophet Elijah who prepared the way for the Messiah (Matt. 17:11–13). Jesus and Elijah met on earth when Jesus changed in appearance on a mountain with His followers (Matt. 17:1–3). I wonder if they swapped stories about the bread and flour?

**Yahweh—Divine Encounters** in the Old Testament

## 33.5 Learning to Trust

Our Memory Verse for this chapter is 1 Kings 17:16. How does this description of events help you trust God? What ways can you apply it to your life? Write some of your thoughts here:

_____

_____

You may have heard a preacher or teacher use the story of the widow's act of trust in this episode as an example of the kind of faith you must have. They may have said that you must give to God—even if it is your last penny—to show your trust in Him, but if you do that God will provide for you like the unending flour and oil in the jars. The application is that if you trust God like the widow, God will act the same way toward you, and you will have all you need.

Miracles like the widow's bottomless jars describe God's work to provide for His servants and to help people trust Him. They, however, are not prescriptive for everyone. This passage presents a narrative that describes the work of God in His-story. Though He always acts in a way that is consistent with His character, the details of the events are not necessarily transferable to your life. For example, there was only one burning bush. Yet, God still speaks through His Word, the Spirit, and future acts of God.

On the other hand, God's instructions through Jesus to "love your neighbor as yourself," for example, are prescriptive for all who call Him their Master. In other words, just because God performed this miracle through Elijah does not mean that God will do the exact same thing for you. God raised His Son, Jesus, from the dead as the ultimate miracle so you will trust Him. Jesus' promises that God will provide your daily needs (Matt. 6:25–34) prove superior for faith over mimicking the actions of a widow who responded to Elijah, the prophet.

Our question to consider this week was: How do difficult circumstances affect my trust in God? You have observed the difficult times Elijah faced in this episode of His-story. Write your answer to our question based on your observations in space below:

_____

_____

_____

One more observation: God used "unclean" ravens and a non-Israelite widow to provide for His messenger. Both made the "do not touch" list of God's people, but God used them as players in this episode. Never discount any person or thing of God's creation to do His work. Do not categorically write off someone because they are not "one of the chosen." God may invite him or her into the storyline so he or she can trust Him like you do.

**For further study:**
- **1 Kings 16:29–34**
- **Matthew 6:28–34**

# 34—Facing Depression (Prophet Elijah, Part 2 of 2)

People who make a difference for God always face opposition. Moses did. King David did. The Apostle Paul did. Jesus certainly did. So what makes you think you will not face conflict as you live out the Author's role for your life among those who call on other gods? Serving God by its very nature creates conflict. As you lead toward the mission call of God, you disturb the status quo of those you call to join you; and since most people like things the way they have made them, any challenge to change brings opposition. God often empowers His servant-leader to endure such push back, but the constant rebuffs of others can take its toll on the leader. We will see in this episode of Elijah's story how God empowered His servant for victory and cared for His messenger when he ran in fear and wanted to kill himself.

The Memory Verses for this chapter are James 5:17–18. God inspired James to remember Elijah as a man like everyone else. However, Elijah passionately sought God and was used greatly by Him. We will apply James' teaching to your life this week.

Our question to consider this week is: How does God feel when I face depression? Begin to formulate your answer as you observe how God acted toward Elijah in this episode of His-story.

## 34.1 A Showdown

The 1881 "Shootout at the O.K. Corral" became a symbolic battle between law and order, and lawlessness in the Old West. The battle included famous characters such as Wyatt Earp and his brothers, as well as Doc Holliday and the McLaury brothers. The U.S. Marshals won the day. This gunfight was one of many that eventually brought the rule of law to the wild, wild American West. Good defeated evil. The town folk walked safer streets, and the rustlers received their deserved justice.

What is your favorite scene from history or a film that portrays good overcoming evil? Who were the characters? Why does that scene stand out so clearly in your mind?

_____

_____

Read 1 Kings 18:16–40 as you would a historical novel. Picture the scene and events as you read. When you have read the story through once, go back and highlight the characters in the story. Circle the number of prophets of Baal and Asherah (v. 19). Underline the people's confession in verse 39. In the space below, record any other details that stand out to you in the events.

_____

_____

Elijah's showdown on Mount Carmel with the 850 prophets of Baal and Asherah was one of Israel's defining

moments with God. When the people saw Yahweh's altar-consuming response to His one-against-850 prophets, they cried, "Yahweh—he is God!" (1 Kings 18:39), and they followed Elijah's instructions to kill those who represented the false god, Baal (v. 40). You could not ask for a more dramatic demonstration of the Living God of Israel to draw a nation back to the God of the covenant and away from the false gods they worshiped.

God revealed Himself to His unfaithful people in a huge way that day on Mount Carmel. God demonstrated His power to show that the people had foolishly worshiped a non-existent and worthless god. You may wish God would do something like that so others would trust Him and your faith would grow.

Read Matthew 27:45–56 in the same way you read about Elijah. Put yourself at the foot of the cross with those mentioned in verse 56. What did you see, hear, and feel as you watched Jesus die? What does this event in His-story tell you about God's interest in your life and those who worship false gods? Record some of your Spirit-directed thoughts here:

_____

_____

## 34.2 Dealing with a Threat

I worked one summer between semesters at college on a labor crew where my father worked as a chemist at the refinery. Now, I am more like Jacob who hung out in his mother's tents than like Esau who hunted wild game. So when another laborer started pushing on me and calling me "Preacher Boy," rather than taking him out with a right hook, I turned and walked as fast as I could to the foreman. I wish I could tell you I did that because Jesus said to "love your enemies" and "turn the other cheek," but I really did it because I got scared and ran! The guy was huge and could have injured me, injured me bad. They say fear brings on either "fight" or "flight." I flew fast that day.

When have you faced someone who threatened you and you got scared and ran? What was at stake? Why did you choose to run instead of stay and confront the person? (Please understand that I am not making light of life-threatening situations. If you have suffered a life-threatening encounter pause and invite the Holy Spirit into your memories to bring peace to your heart and to the situation.)

Read 1 Kings 19:1–2. Underline Jezebel's threat to Elijah. The queen's threat to kill Elijah was real, and he knew it. He had heard what she had done to other prophets of Yahweh (1 Kings 18:4).

Read verses 3–5. Highlight the places to where Elijah ran and underline his cry to God in verse 4.

As soon as the royal messenger told him the queen's intentions, the prophet took off in a sprint to put as much distance between him and her as he could. He ran to Beersheba in Judah (consult your maps to find this location), and then went another day's journey into the desert (v. 3, 4a). Our storyteller wrote that Elijah had "had enough" and wanted to die (v. 4b).

Read 1 Kings 19:5–9. How did God respond to Elijah's desire to die? What would you expect God to do?

_____

_____

God did not scold or tell His prophet to get up and quit whining. God sent an angel to minister to him. Rather than "unclean" ravens who dropped meat and bread beside him, God sent an angel to prepare a hot meal. God let Elijah rest and make his way to Mount Horeb. When he arrived, he crawled into a cave and fell asleep.

Elijah ran from God's victory on Mount Carmel many miles away to hide in a cave on Mount Horeb. Record some of your observations of Elijah, God's messenger, and God Himself in this episode in the space below. How can you empathize with Elijah? What can you learn about God in this story?

_____

_____

_____

## 34.3 Feeling Alone

My oldest daughter called me one day from college and said, "I think I'm the only one in my class who believes in God!" We talked about the professor's philosophy and how my daughter's biblical worldview was out of sync with his and that of her classmates. She had chosen a state university, which had a large Christian community, but a secular culture and classrooms. She did not expect special treatment as a follower of Jesus going in and we had prayed she would be a witness wherever God led her. But she had grew frustrated at being what seemed to her the "only one" who tried to stand up for biblical values in her class. Of course other Christian students did the same, but she felt alone and I had the opportunity as her father to encourage her no matter how she felt.

Have you ever felt like the "only one" who was a witness to the things of God where you worked or went to school? Describe the setting and what led you to feel that way in the space below.

Read 1 Kings 19:10. Highlight the name of God. Summarize Elijah's response to God's question here:

_____

_____

Why did he say he felt he was the only one serving God?

_____

Read 1 Kings 19:9b. Underline God's question to Elijah. Since God is all knowing—the theological word for this characteristic of God is omniscient—why do you think God asked Elijah that question?

_____

Confession is not telling God something He does not already know but agreeing with God on how He sees things. (See 1 John 1:9 about confessing to God.) God's question to Elijah was not one to inform, but one of self-disclosure in which the prophet could say aloud to God how he felt so God could guide him to see things from God's perspective. The first step in any recovery involves a confession of truth and helplessness to overcome the situation. God did not taunt Elijah. God lovingly gave him an opportunity to share his true feelings with God.

Elijah honored God with God's name and then laid out the facts of why he hid in the cave. He acknowledged the reality of the situation and spoke the truth when he said his enemies were out to kill him, too. The prophet did not whine. He stated facts, but came to the wrong conclusion. He thought he was the only person who remained faithful to God.

End your moment with God by reading Psalm 22. This prayer offers a call to God to deliver God's servant out of desperate situations and concludes with praise. (See Mark 15:34 for Jesus' cry from the cross.)

## 34.4 A Gentle Whisper

I love to watch a storm front come through town. In North Texas spring storms can be particularly violent. They tend to form up in the northwest and move southeast across the open plains. A wall of black and blue clouds swirling over the suburban landscape can ruin a sunny day but spark excitement in my soul. I like to stand in my back yard as long as I can without getting drenched to feel the whipping wind, see the bolts of lightning, and hear the booming thunder. Yes, I feel in the presence of God when I stand below a surging storm front, but I seldom feel like I hear God in the storm. I sense God's voice in the early morning darkness when the house is quiet and the skies are calm and the candle that sits near my computer burns without a flicker. Storms energize me. Stillness lets me hear God.

How do you respond when storms come to town? Are you a storm chaser, or do you head under the nearest roof when they come close to you? Where do you hear the voice of God best? Record your thoughts here:

_____

_____

_____

Read 1 Kings 19:11–12. Highlight the name of God in these verses. Circle the elements that came upon the mountain where Elijah hid. Underline the last two words of verse 12.

When God heard Elijah's complaint, He called him out of his cave to stand on the side of the mountain in "the presence of the LORD" (v. 11). God's command is reminiscent of Exodus 33:18–22, when God revealed Himself to Moses on same mountain. Wind, earthquake, and fire pummeled the hillside, but Yahweh was not present in them. Finally, Elijah heard a "gentle whisper," a "still small voice" (v. 12, KJV).

Read verses 13–14. How did Elijah respond to the whisper of God? What did God ask him, and how did Elijah respond again?

The whisper of God caused Elijah to cover his head and step to the mouth of the cave. God asked him a second time why he was there instead of back in Israel where God had appointed him to go.

Elijah responded exactly the same as before (v. 14; see v. 10). He still felt convinced he was the only one left who truly served Yahweh in a land that worshiped Baal. Even the demonstration of God's presence in the elements did not change his countenance.

Jesus went often to quiet places to pray and listen to the voice of the Father. Read Luke 9:28–36 to see what God said to His Son on that mountainside.

## 34.5 Returning to Work

Depression can immobilize any of God's leaders for a season. These times of discouragement can cause a servant-leader to disengage and run from his or her responsibilities. Rather than hide in a cave on a mountainside, some retreat under bed covers and refuse to come out. The weight of the work weighs too heavy. The turbulence of the storms is anything other than the presence of God! Elijah's story of running for his life and his subsequent desire to die allows the rest of us feel OK with the fact that even someone God chose to bring fire down from heaven got depressed and wanted to quit. Slowing down and retreating from the work of ministry is part of God's Story with people.

God allowed Elijah a respite from his work. God ministered to him in that season of recovery. God gave His prophet a chance to say how he felt and then He revealed Himself to Elijah in the whisper of His voice. After this God sent His servant back into the fray of cleaning Israel from its worship of false gods.

Seasons of ministry, like seasons in nature, create times of enthusiastic engagement. Times of retreat keep the servant of God whole and humble.

Read 1 Kings 19:15–18. Highlight the names and places. Use your Bible study helps to identify the names and places. Consider what God told Elijah to do. Circle the number of those God had "reserved" in Israel and underline what was unique about them.

Elijah, famous for the showdown on Mount Carmel with the prophets of Baal and Asherah, returned to Israel to anoint a new king for both Syria and Israel. Both men had chosen to remain faithful to Yahweh alone and would cleanse their countries from those who had not. Elisha would succeed Elijah as God's primary prophet in Israel. And, by the way, Elijah was not the only one who had remained faithful to Yahweh in Israel. God told him

7,000 others had not "bowed down to Baal" and their "mouths have not kissed him" (v. 18).

Our Memory Verses for this chapter are James 5:17–18. Read James 5:13–18 for the full context of the verses. James remembered Elijah as a normal man who prayed, and then God stopped the rain for over three years. How can you apply James' teaching on prayer to your life? Write some applications here:

_____

_____

Our question to consider this week was: How does God feel when I face depression? You have observed how God responded to Elijah's depression and desertion of his duties. Based on your observations of how God treated Elijah, how would you answer this question? Write some of your thoughts here:

_____

_____

_____

**For further study:**
- **1 Kings 18:1–46; 19:1–9**
- **James 5:17–18**

# 35—Choosing a Mentor (Prophet Elisha)

In a previous moment with God we saw how Moses passed the leadership of God's people to Joshua, one of the two spies who trusted God to take the promised land. Moses had invited Joshua into leadership on different occasions and had mentored him in the ways of God. We saw how God came alongside Joshua and promised to remain in his life just as He had in his mentor's life (Josh. 1).

This chapter of Elijah's life records the transition of spiritual leadership from Elijah to Elisha. God would be with the younger as He had been with the elder. The miraculous and the mundane mix to give us a vivid picture of how God passed the cloak of leadership from one man to another and how an apprentice became the master in the work of God.

The Memory Verse for this chapter is 1 Thessalonians 5:24. God who calls you is faithful to do what He called you to do. This promise offers confidence in tough times.

Our question to consider this week is: How do I become qualified for God's service? Do not think of full-time job training here. Apply it to your life now. All of life's experiences are qualifying tasks for servant leadership. Observe Elisha as we walk through this episode together.

## 35.1 Passing on the Mantle

One axiom in life is "don't burn your bridges." It means to keep all of your options open and your relationships in good condition as you build your career. You never know when you may need to fall back on companies you have worked for or call on a former coworker for help if the choices you make do not work out. The proverb makes good sense in an uncertain job market. Bridges work great to cover your mistakes, but they are of little use when it comes to God's call on your life.

How do you evaluate this piece of advice? How have you practiced it in your career? Have you ever had a time when you "burned your bridges" intentionally or unintentionally? What were the results?

_____

_____

Read 1 Kings 19:19. Highlight the place where Elijah found Elisha. Underline what Elijah found Elisha doing and circle what the elder prophet did to the younger one.

God instructed Elijah to make his way from Mount Horeb to Israel where he would anoint Elisha as his successor (1 Kings 19:16). He found him in a field plowing with a team of oxen and 11 other teams. Elijah walked by him and laid his cloak over Elisha's shoulders. In the King's English of 1611, the phrase reads, "and Elijah passed by him, and cast his mantle upon him" (KJV). Yes, this is the source of the metaphor for transferring leadership or "passing the mantle." Elijah identified Elisha as his successor by placing his coat around him.

Read 1 Kings 19:20. Underline Elisha's response and Elijah's answer to him.

The younger prophet understood completely what the older prophet meant by his actions, and he ran after him. A kiss would show endearment and acceptance of the offer, but he also wanted to say goodbye to his parents. Elijah allowed his protégé to return, but I wonder what tone of voice he used. Does it sound something like Jesus' response to those who asked to go home and say goodbye before they would follow Him? (Luke 9:61–62)

Read verse 21 and underline the verbs that tell what Elisha did with his yoke and oxen. Circle what Elisha became to his mentor at the end of the verse.

Elisha "slaughtered" his oxen to show his total commitment to God's call on his life to follow in Elijah's footsteps. He shared the food with the people so they would be witnesses to his decision and to worship the God of his calling. Our storyteller said that Elisha caught up with the prophet and became his "attendant" (NIV) or that he "ministered to him" (NASB).

Take a moment to reflect on the bridges or oxen you have kept in your life for safety and security. Do you have anything you need to burn as a sacrifice to God to show your complete devotion to Him?

_____

_____

_____

## 35.2 Guides on the Path of Life

Mentors are guides. They agree to show you the way. You humble yourself under their leadership and trust them to guide you in whatever area you share in common. Parents, teachers, seasoned adult followers of Jesus, a boss, or a friend can be a mentor. The relationship can be formal or informal, with high expectations or low. His-story records some key mentoring relationships. Paul mentored Timothy; for example, 2 Timothy 3:14–16. Jesus mentored Peter; for example, Matthew 16:17–19. Elijah mentored Elisha. Every great leader prepared a successor to carry on the mission after his departure.

We saw at the end of 1 Kings 19 how Elijah identified Elisha as his apprentice. Now, let's observe how Elisha did as the one being mentored.

Read 2 Kings 2:1–6. Underline the opening phrase of the chapter. Highlight the places mentioned and paraphrase Elisha's response to Elijah when his leader told him to stay in a place. Highlight the phrase "company of the prophets" when it occurs in the passage.

Our storyteller introduced the time of this episode with the phrase "When the LORD was about to take Elijah up to heaven in a whirlwind" (v. 1). We will not see that happen until verse 11 of this chapter, but the phrase gives us a hint as to why Elijah went where he did and whom he saw along the way.

When Elijah told Elisha to wait for him in Gilgal instead of following him to Bethel, Elisha said, "I will not leave you" (v. 2).

Given the setting from verse 1, why would he have responded this way? Write your thoughts here:

_____

_____

Note the path Elijah took. Reverse his path from Gilgal, Bethel, Jericho, and the Jordan River (v. 6). What route does that remind you of from the early days of Israel in Canaan? (Josh. 1–8)

Each town had a "company of the prophets" or "sons of the prophets" (NKJV) who came out to see the two men of God. We know Elisha is aware of what would soon happen by his responses to them. What does this tell us about why Elijah met with the groups of prophets?

_____

_____

Mentoring relationships require closeness of time and space. Elisha wanted to stay near the one who chose him to lead. He may have sensed the end was near for the one he followed, or he may have grown so close to his leader he would not miss an opportunity to learn from him. Why do you think Elisha wanted to stay near Elijah? What are some advantages of spending time with someone older and more experienced than you in the things of God?

End this moment with God by thanking Him for a mentor in your life or by asking Him if He desires for you to have a mentor in your life now.

## 35.3 Sources of Learning

Mentors often guide more than one person. Sometimes they lead groups of people who seek to learn from them the skills of their trade or pattern for living. Communities or groups of followers grow up around a teacher or mentor for encouragement and learning. Traditionally, this was accomplished through formal education or a trade school, but in recent years less institutionalized ways of learning from a mentor or a mentoring organization have emerged. Teaching churches, conferences, and networks have surfaced as sources to learn new ways of seeing and living life. Students of the Bible, for example, may choose to take occasional courses from a parachurch group than enroll in a Bible college or seminary. The "what" of the Christian life has not changed, but how we learn it has changed dramatically.

What are some sources for how you have learned the Bible? How does your church aid your knowing the things of God? What seminars or conferences have you attended that have helped you in your relationship with God through Christ Jesus?

_____

_____

_____

Read 2 Kings 2:7–8. Circle the number of men in the "company of the prophets" and underline what happened when Elijah struck the river with his cloak.

Elijah and Elisha's journey from Gilgal to the Jordan River had created interest among the communities of prophets. Along the way, 50 of them stood and watched the senior prophet and his apprentice approach the river. Elijah most likely knew and mentored some in this group throughout his lifetime, and they wanted to see him as he came by.

When Elijah hit the water with his cloak, it "divided to the right and to the left, and the two of them crossed over on dry ground" (v. 8). Read Exodus 14:15–29 and Joshua 3:7–17 for other times in which the river parted for one of God's servant-leaders. Write the leaders' names here: _____ and _____

Read verses 9–10. What question do you have about the dialogue between the two prophets?

_____

_____

What other source(s) do you have other than this book to find the answer to your question? List one or two sources and write some answers you have found here:

_____

_____

The intriguing thing to me was Elisha's request for a "double portion" of blessing from his mentor. I wondered if that was a selfish request until I looked the term up in a Bible concordance and found that a law in Deuteronomy 21:17 said a father should give his firstborn a "double share" of his wealth. Since Elisha called Elijah his "father" (2 Kings 2:12), he saw himself as heir to Elijah's wealth of God's Spirit to aid him in the new role he will play as God's chief spokesperson.

What did you find? Have you ever prayed for God to give you a "double portion" of His Spirit since you are an heir as a child of God (Rom. 8:16–17)?

## 35.4 When the Mentor Moves On

Let's begin our moment with God with a Bible knowledge question: Who are the only two people recorded in His-story who did not experience death? (Hints: One is found in our verses for this day; the other is found in Genesis 5:18–24.) Write their names here:

_____ and _____

Have you ever wondered how they got out of death as the door to eternity while Jesus, God's Son, had to go through it? (See Hebrews 10:5–10 for the reason Jesus had to die.) Of course, only Jesus experienced Resurrection! As to God's choice to bring the other two into eternity without meeting death we can only speculate. Both can be viewed as "types" for Jesus' Resurrection and point to that historical event in the New Testament.

Read 2 Kings 2:11–12. Underline the objects of Elijah's departure and Elisha's cries. What did Elisha do after the spectacle ended?

A "chariot of fire and horses" swept Elijah into eternity as Elisha cried out to his spiritual father or mentor. The elder disappeared into a "whirlwind," a physical reality in that part of the world and symbol of the God's presence.

Have you ever heard the American traditional song "Swing Low, Sweet Chariot"? An American slave wrote that song, known as a "spiritual" and based on God's taking Elijah home in a fiery chariot, to remind others of God's promise of eternal life in Christ Jesus.

Read 2 Kings 2:13–14. Highlight the name of God in verse 14. Underline Elisha's question. Was it a literal question? (He asked because he did not know the answer.) Or was it rhetorical ? (He made a statement in the form of a question although he knew the answer.) When you study the Bible, even grammatical nuances make a difference in your interpretation. His actions that followed his question give a hint to its meaning.

Elisha struck the water with his cloak. What happened? What possible conclusion to this act was similar to Elijah's actions before his departure?

God took Elijah into eternity without the experience of death. Elisha performed the same act as his spiritual father did. How do these actions expand your trust in God? How do they challenge your reasonable explanation of this episode? What do they tell you about God's purposes?

_____

_____

## 35.5 An Empowered Learner

Miracles give signs that point to God, not the spirituality of the one performing it. Any intrusion by God into the created order is designed to point the observer to God and provide a possibility to trust God for who He is.

Read 2 Kings 2:15. Underline the conclusion the 50 observers made after seeing Elisha part the waters.

The miracle of parting the waters presented evidence that "the spirit of Elijah" rested on Elisha. Their conclusion was wrong in the sense it was really the Spirit of God in Elijah's life that now dwelt with Elisha. Their actions were wrong because they bowed to worship the man, not God. Elisha remained silent to their actions. We can conclude he understood their intentions and accepted them.

Read verses 16–18. Highlight "the Spirit of the Lord" and underline the prophets' request. What answers did Elisha give them? (vv. 16–17)

The company of the prophets wanted to make sure the whirlwind had not picked Elijah up and dropped him somewhere else. Like them, we often want additional proof to the miracle of God we have just seen. We are trained skeptics. Sometimes that training works against our acceptance of what God has clearly done. Elisha told them not to go but finally said "OK." They later found him in Jericho. He bluntly replied, "Didn't I tell you not to go?" (v. 18) How does skepticism challenge your faith? How does it help you trust Jesus?

Read 1 Thessalonians 5:12–28. The Memory Verse for this chapter is verse 24. Write your paraphrase of the promise here:

_____

_____

God empowered Elisha to follow in the work of his mentor, Elijah, with the Spirit of God. Jesus empowered His disciples to follow in the mission He began on earth with the Holy Spirit (Acts 1:8; 2:1–4). Paul wrote to the followers of Jesus in Thessalonica that God would remain faithful to them because He had called them in Christ Jesus, and that they could count on that.

Apply the promise of God to your life. In what situations do you need to trust God's Word? Memorize the promise and say it as a promise to someone today.

**For further study:**
- **1 Kings 19:19–21**
- **1 Thessalonians 5:12–28**

# 36—Accepting God's Unconditional Love (Prophet Hosea)

His-story is essentially a love story. God, the Lover, constantly seeks to woo His loved ones back to Him. We are fickle lovers, however, and we often get seduced away from our One True Love by the wealth of this world and those who whisper lies in our ears.

We find it hard to accept the love of God when we can so easily embrace the cheap substitute of another's arms. God chose Israel as His covenant bearers, and God's unconditional love held the relationship together. While God remained true to His covenant love, Israel wandered away to other partners like an unfaithful spouse. The story of Hosea presents an enactment of God's unconditional love toward His people even though Israel continued to live unfaithful to God through their worship of other gods.

The Memory Verse for this chapter is Hosea 6:6. These words of God remind us God prefers our complete devotion to Him above our religious activity around Him. This message lays the foundation for an authentic relationship with God.

Our question to consider this week is: Why is it hard to accept God's unconditional love? Most of us have never experienced unconditional love in human relationships. We have suffered betrayal, abandonment, and mistreatment by those who say they love us. All of these factors can make it difficult to accept God's unconditional love.

## 36.1 God's Unusual Command

Adultery is the one reason almost anyone would accept as the basis for divorce. Even Jesus allowed "marital unfaithfulness" to be the sole reason for divorce (Matt. 5:32). So when a spouse stays with a partner who has committed adultery, we all acknowledge that person's capacity for forgiveness and love. Most of us would walk away and feel completely justified for our actions. Justice allows separation. Love refuses to give up even when grounds for parting exist.

Read Hosea 1:1. This verse sets the scene for the love story you will read. Highlight the names of the kings and countries. Use Bible study tools to identify them. Hosea acted out God's message to Israel about 760–730 B.C.

God continued to send messengers to tell His people of their unfaithfulness and about His desire to have a love relationship with them. God chose Hosea to serve as His messenger to the northern kingdom of Israel during this time in His-story.

Read Hosea 1:2–3. Highlight the characters in the story. Circle the word "because" in verse 2. This points to why God asked Hosea to do what he did. Who did Hosea marry? Write her name here: _____

Sometimes God gave His prophets a verbal message to speak to the people. God gave Hosea instructions to first act out God's message to the people. Hosea would speak later, but first God told him to find a prostitute for a wife as a picture of God's love toward Israel. Why would God have His prophet do something so out of character? The covenant God made with Abraham and his descendants was like the marriage vows exchanged at a wedding. God chose Israel as His bride and pledged His eternal love (literally) to Israel (Hos. 2:19–20). Also, as in marriage, love between the spouses keeps the relationship together. God, too, declared His continued love toward Israel.

Read Exodus 20:4–6. Underline what God told His people not to do. Highlight how God described Himself. What are two responses of God because of His jealous nature? (Hint: Both words end in "–ing.")

God did not want His people to make and worship idols because He said He was a jealous God. This protective love punished those who hate God by their actions and showed love to those who love God and keep His commandments. The word for "love" (NIV) or "loving-kindness" (NASB) in Hebrew is *checed*, which uniquely described God's covenant love for Israel (v. 6; for example, see Genesis 32:10 and Psalm 25:6–7).

Hosea pursued Gomer even though she made an unfaithful wife because of prostitution. What would this message send to Israel (and you) if you heard of the marriage? Would it help you better understand God? Would you think Hosea was crazy and go on with your life? Be honest and write some of your thoughts here:

_____

_____

_____

_____

## 36.2 A Powerful Metaphor

To reconcile with and love someone who has acted unfaithful once is heroic. To accept and love someone after multiple affairs is divine. Most marriage counselors and pastors would say, "Let him go. He's hurt you so much and it looks like he will not change. It's best for you to divorce him." If the spouse continues to accept the partner, you might call him or her weak and say that spouse has no boundaries in life. God is anything but weak and without boundaries. Hosea's love for Gomer is a picture of God's love for us. Hosea's actions are not a lesson in marital reconciliation but a metaphor of God's love toward all of us. We have all acted unfaithfully to Him.

Bible Study Note: When studying the Bible, make sure you know the intent of the first writer before you apply a passage to a contemporary situation. This historical narrative does not directly teach on marriage; it makes marriage the central metaphor.

Do you know of someone who continually welcomed back an unfaithful partner? Did the partner ever change? Why did the person keep receiving back his or her spouse? What lessons have you learned by observing that situation?

_____

_____

_____

_____

Read Hosea 3:1. Underline what Hosea must do for his wife. Circle the word "though" the two times it appears to see what Hosea must do in spite of what Gomer had done. Highlight the phrase "as the LORD loves."

God told Hosea to act out his love for his unfaithful wife "as the LORD loves the Israelites." God's covenant love for Israel served as the benchmark for Hosea's love for Gomer. (See Ephesians 5:25 where Paul tells husbands to love their wives as Christ loved the Church.)

The word for love in this verse, *ahab*, was the common Hebrew word meaning, "love for another person or things." Here, the subjects of love are Hosea, another man, and God; the objects of love are Hosea's wife, the Israelites, and "sacred raisin cakes." God's love in the Book of Hosea is most often described by this word.

Read Hosea 3:2. Underline Hosea's responses to God's directions. Circle the amounts of currency used in the verse. Use a Bible dictionary or commentary to find a relative equivalent price Hosea paid to get his wife back.

Gomer cost Hosea. He paid with currency, silver, and goods—barley. Gomer had become a slave due to her prostitution and stood on the block to be sold to another man for his use when Hosea bought her back. Hosea's purchase price freed Gomer to be his wife again.

Read 1 Corinthians 6:20 and 7:23. Paul wrote that since we were "bought at a price" we must live a certain way. What was that price? (See John 3:16 and 1 John 3:16 about the sacrifice made.) What does it say about your worth to God that He paid such a high price for your freedom? Record these thoughts in your journal.

## 36.3 Love that Knows Boundaries

As a pastor I walk alongside parents of teenagers who refuse direction and get themselves into trouble. These parents love their children, but the child refuses the guidance that goes along with their parents' love. Love has boundaries. Love gives unconditionally, but it refuses to allow the one loved to stay "just the way you are" or to do things that will harm them. Divine love has no conditions to receive it, but God has no intention of leaving the one loved to his or her destruction. For this reason, tough love is sometimes necessary.

Have you ever had to place clear boundaries around one you loved? How did that make you feel? How did the one you loved respond to those boundaries?

_____

_____

Read Hosea 3:3. Summarize the three things Hosea told Gomer in the space below.

1._____

2._____

3._____

How are Hosea's instructions to Gomer similar to God's instructions to Israel in Exodus 20:2–6? Write your comparisons here:

_____

_____

Read Hosea 3:4–5. Circle the word "For" in verse 4 and underline the words that tell what Israel will experience or do according to Hosea's prophecy. Underline what Israel would do after their judgment and the phrase "in the last days" at the end of verse 5.

We know from our place in His-story that Hosea told Israel of its destruction and exile at the hands of the Assyrians in 722 B.C. by King Sargon II. (See Isaiah 20:1–2 for a biblical reference to the king.)

Judgment is always redemptive in His-story. While Hosea said Israel would be conquered, he also told them of what that punishment would cause them to do. They would return to Yahweh, the One true God; and to David their convenant king. They would also come in repentance and find the blessing of His love.

Read Isaiah 2:2, Micah 4:1, 2 Timothy 3:1, and 2 Peter 3:3 for other examples of the phrase "In the last days." Note both the context of the immediate verses and the place of the Bible book in history as you draw a conclusion to its meaning.

Hosea would later describe Israel and Judah's love as a "morning mist, like the early dew that disappears" (Hos. 6:4). How is your love for God like a "morning mist"? Spend some time allowing God's Spirit to point out examples in your life, and then take time to affirm His covenant love for you in Christ Jesus and to ask forgiveness for your wandering love.

## 36.4 Learning to Confess

"Who drew on the wall with the permanent marker?" I asked my two pre-school daughters. Both sat silent. I knew who had done it because she still had ink on her hands, but as in every act of discipline, a confession of guilt is always better than an accusation following by fact-finding. I asked again, "Who drew on the wall with the permanent marker?" The tension grew until the oldest pointed to the youngest and said, "She did it, Daddy. She did it." The youngest broke out in tears and wiped her eyes with her ink-stained fingers. Which one do you discipline? Do you scold the big sister for outing her sister or the little sister for marking on the wall?

You make the call. What would you do? How much harder would it have been if neither confessed to the drawing? What would you say and do to both children to help mold their character?

God desired for Israel to repent from their devotion to the gods and idols of Canaan. To repent literally means, "to turn around," and it includes confessing a transgression and asking for forgiveness. God helped the people by giving them directions through Hosea on how to repent.

Chapters 1 and 3 record the narrative of Hosea's prophecy. The remaining 12 chapters give God's message to Israel through His prophet. The divine message is written in poetic form and illustrated with many images. Ancient Israel was an oral society and such picturesque speech helped the listeners to form images in their minds so they could "see" what the prophet said.

Chapter 14 tells part of God's spoken message to Israel, and can be divided into two sections: God's call for Israel to return to Him and ask for forgiveness (vv. 1–3) and God's promise to love Israel (vv. 4–9).

Read Hosea 14:1–3. Circle the imperative words (words of command) in the verses. These tell what God wanted the hearers to do. (Hint: The first words in verses 1–2 are imperative.) Summarize what Hosea told the people to say when they returned to Yahweh (vv. 2–3).

_____

_____

Read 2 Kings 15:19–20 and 17:1–3 for some of the historical background behind their confession, "Assyria cannot save us," in verse 3.

One way a parent molds the character of a child is by teaching him or her to confess wrong doing and to say, "I'm sorry," or "Please forgive me." God did the same for Israel in Hosea 14:1–3. Personalize the verses by placing your name in the place of Israel and substituting the first person pronoun for those referring to Israel. Add your own wrong doings as a confession to God. Let this prayer become your confession to God today.

## 36.5 Experiencing God's Love

God concluded His message through Hosea by confessing His love and forgiveness toward Israel. While God felt angry toward Israel's unfaithfulness, His covenant love would not allow Him to disown them. Like Hosea's love for Gomer, God continually redeemed Israel because He chose them among all the nations for His own. Love and mercy balance the anger and judgment of God. It will always remain a mystery as to when God will choose to judge or show mercy, but ultimately God's love wins over His wrath, and His Son, Jesus, came in the love story between God and people to rescue all who trust Him.

Read Hosea 14:4–9. Underline God's promise to Israel in verse 4. Circle the word "like" in verses 5–8. The word introduces picturesque metaphors of how God will respond to Israel's repentance. Underline the last three lines of verse 9 as a confession of the goodness of God.

Pick one or two of the "like" phrases and write in the space below what God revealed about His character through the metaphors.

_____

_____

_____

_____

The Memory Verse for this chapter is Hosea 6:6. The word for "mercy" in the NIV is a translation of the Hebrew word *checed*, the word most often used for God's unconditional covenant love for Israel. Paraphrase God's words in the space below. What does this tell you about what God desires from you in His covenant relationship with you through Jesus Christ? Write your answer here:

_____

_____

_____

Our question to consider this week was: Why is it hard to accept God's unconditional love? Given your observations about Israel and Gomer's wandering love, how would you answer this question now? Write your thoughts here:

_____

_____

_____

End this defining moment with God by reading aloud God's revelation in Hosea 11:1–9 as a prayer of God's love for Israel and ultimately a description of His love for you. After reading it as written, replace the nouns and pronouns for Israel with those for you to personalize it.

**For further study:**
- **Hosea 1:4–9; 2:1–5; 6:1–10; 11:1–10**
- **Psalm 136**

# 37—Surrendering to Service (Prophet Isaiah)

Biblical servant leadership begins with a call from God to take our place in the divine rescue mission to capture the hearts of all people with the love of Christ. Calling is often confused with a career choice, and because of episodes like this with Isaiah we tend to believe God's call only comes in the form of the spectacular or the miraculous accompanied by angels.

God's call comes in many forms, and it produces the confidence that what we do with our lives plays a part of the bigger Story we find ourselves in. God's revelation to Isaiah came in the context of worship and resulted from the priest's surrender to God's call to service. His life was never the same after he accepted God's invitation to join Him in His-story.

The Memory Verse for this chapter is Isaiah 6:8. God asked, and Isaiah answered. The question still forms God's invitation for us to join Him, and the answer is still our worship-filled response that launches us into the epic of God's love.

Our question to consider this week is: How does worship open us to God's majesty and prepare us for His calling? The answer to this question rests in the observation of Isaiah's encounter with Holy God. Watch and see what happens before you answer the question.

## 37.1 Experiencing the Majesty of God

I traveled to Wales once and took time to see the Edwardian Castle, Caernarfon, the site of the formal inauguration of Prince Charles of Wales in 1969. I observed the native slate disk upon which the throne sat. As I looked at pictures from the ceremony, I was impressed with all the royal fixtures such as mounted guards, banners, and ranks of dignitaries that accompanied the event. I imagined sitting in the July crowd and watching as Charles was invested as the heir to the throne of England. While I prefer the representative democracy in which I live, my experience in the castle gave me a sense of the history and dignity of the royal line of the kings and queens of England.

Have you ever stood in the presence of a dignitary? If so, who? How did you feel? What is your most prominent memory of the event?

_____

_____

Read Isaiah 6:1. Highlight the names in the verse. Underline what Isaiah saw in the Temple.

Isaiah, the main character in this episode of His-story, served as a priest during the reign of Uzziah. King Uzziah (also known as Azariah in 2 Kings 15:1) began his reign at age 16 and ruled Judah, the southern part of the divided kingdom, for 52 years. He died around 740 B.C. God afflicted him with leprosy when he sought to burn incense in the Temple in place of the priests. He lived with that disease until his death. (See 2 Chronicles 26:21;

the entire chapter 26 tells of his reign.) Isaiah marked the date of God's call on his life at the time of Uzziah's death.

Isaiah described the revelation of God's presence as best he could: the Lord sat on a throne, "high and lifted up" (KJV), and "the train of his robe filled the temple." God's revelation of Himself to Isaiah was set in a throne room before which His servant stood in awe. This revelation is known as a theophany or epiphany. (The burning bush in Exodus 3 and the creatures in Ezekiel 1 present similar manifestations of God.)

Read 1 Kings 10:18–20 for a description of King Solomon's throne and Revelation 4 for what John saw in his revelation of the heavenly throne room.

Sit quietly and imagine sitting in the presence of God. Review verse 1 of this passage or reread Revelation 4 to get a picture of God's presence enthroned in heaven.

## 37.2 In the Presence of Angels

The summer after I graduated from high school, I served on staff at a conference center located outside of Santa Fe, New Mexico. One weekend we filled our days off with a trip into the Pecos Wilderness, located not far from the center. We backpacked into the wilderness a short way the first day and set up camp. That evening a thunderstorm roared through the canyon. Lightning began to pour out of the sky with hail and rain. We huddled under our makeshift lean-tos as lightning lit up the forest and the boom of thunder made us feel like we had transported onto a battlefield on another continent. The storm passed as quickly as it arrived, and none of us got hurt other than having rain-soaked sleeping bags and clothes. I will never forget the fear and awe of being in nature's fury without the usual human structures to keep me separated from the elements. I wondered if meeting God would be anything like that?

Have you ever encountered a storm in a wilderness setting? Did you wonder if God was anywhere around in the middle of it all?

_____

_____

_____

Read Isaiah 6:2–4. Highlight the name of the creatures that circled the throne. Underline what they called out as they flew, and circle what shook the doorposts and filled the Temple.

God created angels to worship and serve Him. We met them first in His-story in the Garden of Eden (Gen. 3:24) and will see them around the eternal throne of God (Rev. 4). Angels serve as God's messengers (as in "the angel of the LORD" who came to Gideon—Judg. 6:11). They also make up the hosts or armies of God who serve Him (as in the angels who came to Jacob on a ladder—Gen. 28:12, and at Jesus' birth—Luke 2:13–14). Only this Bible passage mentions the seraph, while other biblical settings describe the cherubim (Ezek. 10:3–22).

Read Ezekiel 1:1–28. Highlight the word "creatures" or similar nouns that tell of the winged beings that came to the prophet. Note the use of *like* or *as* to describe them

and underline any actions that stand out to you. How are these similar or dissimilar to those described in Isaiah 6? Write the message of the seraph in Isaiah 6:3 here:

_____

_____

_____

Compare it to the angels' praise recorded in Revelation 5:11–12 and 7:11–12. Holy means "to separate" or "cut off." God is separate from His creation and His creatures. God is wholly other and to praise Him as holy means to confess who His is and who we are not. Smoke and shuttering doorposts give evidence to the presence of Holy God in the Bible.

One way to meditate on Scripture is to put yourself in the place of the character about whom you read. Take time now to imagine yourself in Isaiah's place as he watched and sensed the worship of God before him. Record your thoughts in your journal.

**Yahweh – Divine Encounters** in the Old Testament

## 37.3 Responding to God's Holiness

The proper response to the holiness of God is the confession that you are neither holy nor God. When you and I realize who God truly is—either by a theophany like that of Isaiah or revelation through Scripture or the Holy Spirit—our response is worship. One form of our worship involves confession of who we are as we stand in the presence of Holy God. Isaiah worshiped God as he stood in the Temple, but his first words did not offer praise (like David—Ps. 99). Rather, he confessed his uncleanness.

Read Isaiah 6:5. Underline Isaiah's initial response to sensing the presence of God and seeing the seraph. What do "unclean lips" symbolize in his confession?

_____

_____

The first words out of Isaiah's mouth were, "Woe to me . . . I am ruined!" Or "I'm in trouble here." Or "Doom! It's Doomsday. I'm as good as dead" (MSG). (See Jesus' pronouncement of "woe" on the Pharisees in Matthew 23 for another use of the concept.)

How would you say what Isaiah said? Write your paraphrase here:

_____

_____

_____

"Unclean lips" represented the immoral lifestyles of Isaiah and the people. The Law of Moses taught that a person must do whatever his or her lips uttered because it was said freely before the LORD (Deut. 23:22–24). Not to do so would be the same as breaking a vow. Israel had broken its vow to worship only Yahweh by building altars to Baal and by not living according to God's laws. This truth became very real when confronted with the presence of Yahweh! Isaiah based his confession on the fact that he had "seen the King, the LORD Almighty" (v. 5).

Read Psalm 51:3–6. Circle the word "sin" or its equivalent in these verses. What does this tell you about how David saw his actions after Nathan exposed his adultery with Bathsheba and murder of her husband, Uriah? Confronted with God's holy standards, the King responded with confession before God.

Confession of our true condition before Holy God marks the beginning of atonement, at-one-ment, with God.

Read 1 John 1:8. Summarize what that verse teaches us about our confession of who we truly are as God sees us.

_____

_____

You were asked to meditate on God's appearance in the Temple in the last session. Now, take time to repeat Isaiah's prayer as your confession to God today. Allow the Holy Spirit to guide your heart and words as you repeat the entire prayer of confession in Isaiah 6:5 several times both aloud and silently.

## 37.4 Receiving Atonement for Sin

Our proper response to God's holiness is to confess of our condition before Him. God responds to our humble confession with forgiveness because atonement has been made for what we confess. The scene in the Temple continued with one of the creatures coming toward Isaiah with a hot coal from the altar.

Read Isaiah 6:6–7. Underline the words of the seraph. Circle the words "guilt," "sin," and "atoned for." Summarize the actions in these verses and describe the significance of what happened in your own words here:

_____

_____

_____

How do we know we are atoned for, or at-one with God? I have never had an six-winged creature touch my lips with a live coal, so how do you and I know we are forgiven and have at-one-ment with God?

Read Leviticus 16:29–34. Circle the word "atonement" in the verses. You may want to read the entire chapter to see the full extent of what God commanded Aaron to do. What is the modern day equivalent of this observance that devout Jews still observe today?

God required the High Priest of Israel to offer an annual sacrifice to atone for the sin of his family, all of Israel, and himself. We know it as Yom Kippur, or the Day of Atonement. While the sacrifice is not offered today in the

Holy of Holiness in the Temple of Jerusalem, the day is observed as God commanded it for all Jews. Why do Christians not observe that day? We need to be atoned for, too.

Read Romans 3:25 and Hebrews 9:5. How did Jesus complete of the requirements for at-one-ment with God? Write in your own words why followers of Jesus do not observe Yom Kippur. What is the central celebration of Christians based on Jesus' "once for all" atoning sacrifice of His life?

_____

_____

God responded to Isaiah's humble confession by sending one of His messengers to tangibly show him that his sins were atoned for. God responds to our humble confession of our sins by having sent His Son, Jesus, to die on the cross as an atoning sacrifice for our sins. (See 1 John 2:2 and 4:10 for how Jesus is our "atoning sacrifice.")

As you end your moment with God today, Read 1 John 1:9–10 in light of the angel's actions and message to Isaiah. Accept God's forgiveness through Jesus' death, burial, and Resurrection as the way God has atoned for your sins. Maybe today will be your Yom Kippur.

## 37.5 Accepting God's Call

God's call on your life sends you on a mission that defines your decisions and actions for a lifetime. One of the saddest lives to live is one in which a person does not know why he or she got up in the morning or what to do with the day God has given him or her. God's call on your life is your defining moment with God. Everything flows out of that clear encounter with God and His invitation to us. He invites us to step out of our story into His-story to play the part He has scripted for us before the beginning of time. Servant-leaders find clarity and direction for their lives when they discern God's call and answer with Isaiah, "Here am I. Send me."

Read Isaiah 6:8. Underline God's words and Isaiah's response. Circle the word "us." What does that word teach us about the nature of God? (Compare it to Genesis 1:26.)

God's call to Isaiah was his defining moment with God. Would he say, "I'll go!" or would he return to his routine—yes, having encountered Almighty God—but remaining king of his own life? Write your answer here:

_____

_____

_____

Read Matthew 4:18–22. What was Jesus' call to the fishermen? What did He tell them He would do for them? As with Isaiah, God's call by Jesus to the guys fishing by the lake that day defined the rest of their lives.

God's call and Isaiah's response make up our Memory Verse for this chapter. Familiarize yourself with the verse by saying or writing it several times and then meditating on it in your heart. Allow time for your heart and mind to embrace or resist Isaiah's response to God. Are you ready to say "Here am I. Send me," or are you not so sure you want to do that now? Be honest and listen for the "voice of the LORD" in your heart and mind.

Our question to consider this week was: How does worship open us to God's majesty and prepare us for His calling? After having observed Isaiah's encounter with God how would you answer this question now? Write your thoughts here:

_____

_____

Note: Go back through the passage and identify the five senses—touch, smell, hear, taste, and see—in God's appearance to Isaiah. (Taste will be hard to find, if it is there.) Worship involves all five senses as well as our heat and mind. God engaged the entire being of Isaiah to reveal His heart to him. What are some implications of this observation applied to your concept of worship?

**For further study:**
• **Isaiah 6:9–13**
• **Revelation 4:1–8**

## 38—Faith Against All Odds (King Hezekiah)

Darkness covered the landscape like the sunset on a cloudy day when Hoshea, the last king of Israel, came to rule. The glory days of King David and King Solomon were only stories told around the festival fires as the Assyrian army camped outside the walls of the northern capital of Samaria. Yahweh persisted as the professed God of Israel's religion but the people also worshiped at the altars of the others gods. The end of the northern kingdom of Israel was near. The end of the Age of Kings was certain.

Before the last king of Judah surrendered to Babylon, one king, Hezekiah, held to his trust in Yahweh in the face of certain destruction. Yahweh intervened for those who sought after Him as their only hope. One last ray of light shone through the storm clouds.

The Memory Verse for this chapter is 2 Kings 18:5. How do you want people to remember you? This verse records the accolades of Hezekiah and why the LORD honored his prayer.

Our question to consider this week is: How do human actions influence God's movement on their behalf? Does prayer make a difference? Observe the events of this episode in His-story to find answers to these questions.

## 38.1 Political Problems

I have said the prayer to open the day of activities in the Texas State Senate a couple of times. Each time I stand on the floor where lawmakers work to make the laws that govern the people, I realize the importance of making deals and compromise in our political process. Legislation that goes through committee, then through both houses of congress, and then across the governor's desk before it becomes law makes a messy and wonderful process. The lobbyists hovering outside the House and Senate chambers and the voters who put the lawmakers in office both play a role in producing the laws that guide our lives. So when you and I observe a theocracy like Israel, a government where God guides the people through prophet, priest, and king, we may have difficulty understanding why deals and compromise do not fit that system so well.

Have you ever took part in the political process of your city or state? How did you feel about the process? What obvious differences exist between your experience in your government and how the Bible describes the political actions of Israel and Judah at the time of this episode in His-story?

_____

_____

_____

Read 2 Kings 17:3–4. Highlight the names in the verses. Consult Bible dictionaries or handbooks to learn more about them. Notice what Hoshea did to make Shalmaneser put Israel's king in prison.

Ahaz, Israel's king before Hoshea, had made a deal with Shalamaneser's predecessor, Tiglath-Pileser, to keep other enemies out of their back yard (2 Kings 16:7–10). When Assyria's new king found out Israel no longer paid the tribute and that Hoshea had gone behind his back to make a deal with the Egyptian king, he flexed his political and military muscle and threw Hoshea in prison.

Read 2 Kings 17:5–6. What did Shalmaneser do after he captured Israel's king? Highlight the places to where he deported the people of Israel.

Dates are important in His-story because they anchor events in time and space that all people share. Your story has significant dates as markers of significant events or seasons of your life. So does His-story. The year Shalmaneser of Assyria defeated and deported the people of Israel was 722 B.C. This date marked the end of the northern kingdom of Israel.

Read 2 Kings 17:7–8. Nothing happens in His-story without purpose or at the whim of the characters in it. What do these verses tell us about the purpose of the events in the previous verses? Was this the first time you read about why this happened? (See 1 Kings 14:14–16 for more consequences of Israel's disobedience.)

Kings Ahaz and Hoshea made deals with foreign kings and compromised their trust in Yahweh as the means to save their country. If you were king, would you have made the same deals given the same circumstances?

_____

_____

## 38.2 Comprised Trust

While Israel fell to the Assyrians in the north, Judah held on in the south. The succession of kings continued, and Hezekiah followed his father Ahaz as king. Ahaz made Judah a vassal of Assyria to keep the stronger nation from overrunning them. However, in doing so he compromised the nation's trust in Yahweh as Israel's Deliverer. Ahaz chose a more familiar practice among nations in that day. Somewhere in Hezekiah's first 25 years on earth, God captured his heart. When he became king, he trusted only in Yahweh for the survival of the nation and as the one and only God of Israel.

Reflect on your faith journey. Did you have parents who taught you about God, or were they more like Ahaz? What influence did they have on how you trust God now?

Read 2 Kings 18:1–2. Highlight the names in the verses. Who was Hezekiah's mother? What does this say about his royal lineage?

Sons followed fathers in the successions of kings, and in Judah that meant the lineage of King David continued along with God's covenant agreement with His people. (You can read a fuller account of Hezekiah's reign in 2 Chronicles 29:1–32:33.) Hezekiah came to rule about 716–715 B.C.

Read 2 Kings 18:3–4. Underline the action words in verse 4 that tell why our storyteller wrote, "He did what was right in the eyes of the LORD." (To read about the story behind the bronze snake see Numbers 21:4–9.)

Unlike the kings before him, Hezekiah destroyed places of worship to alien gods. He even broke into pieces the bronze snake that Moses raised in the wilderness to save the people from snake bites. He did this because people had begun to worship it rather than the healing God.

Draw a parallel to your religious experience. How did you feel when a pastor or church leader stopped a religious practice or habit you had shared with your church for generations? How did others respond?

_____

_____

Read 2 Kings 18:5–7. Underline the actions that describe the king's trust in Yahweh as Lord. Verse 5 is our Memory Verse this week. Write out the statement in the second half of the verse here: "There was no . . ."

_____

Hezekiah was like no other king since David in his devotion to Yahweh. Because of his fidelity to the God of Israel, our storyteller wrote that "Yahweh was with him" and that "he was successful in whatever he undertook" (v. 6). (Remember God's promise to Joshua before he entered the promised land? See Joshua 1:6–9 if you have forgotten.)

What "religious relics" or pagan practices dilute your trust in God alone? Take a moment to review Hezekiah's actions and make a list of those things. You may want to symbolically or actually remove them from your lifestyle to make God truly your only hope.

## 38.3 An Impending Threat

When we take God's Word to all people we talk about offering the message of Jesus in one's "heart language." Our deaf fellowship translates the stories of His-story into the heart language of American Sign Language. We work with a European team who settles in a village to learn the ancient dialect and ways of a people group because the missionary tells us "when they pray, they pray in their heart language [the official language of the country], not in English." If you have ever traveled in a foreign country, you know the joy hearing your native language brings to you—and the person you speak with!

Are you bilingual? If so, which language is your "heart language," the one you have known from birth and consider your own? Have you ever heard your native language in a foreign country? How did that make you feel? Write some thoughts about the the importance in sharing God's Story in a person's heart language here:

_____

_____

_____

It did not satisfy the Assyrians to conquer only the northern kingdom of Israel. They wanted Judah, too. So they invaded the country and extracted a huge amount of money from Hezekiah. He gave up all the silver in the palace treasury and stripped the Temple of its gold in order to meet the amount demanded by the invading king (2 Kings 18:16). After the king made the payment, Assyria sent envoys to threaten the people.

Read 2 Kings 18:26–28. Highlight the names in the verses, and underline the languages mentioned. Why would that be an issue for the Jewish leaders?

The Assyrian representatives harassed the Judean officials in their native language of Hebrew. Eliakim and Shebna asked that they speak in Aramaic since they understood it. Aramaic had become the international language of the day. Like English in the twentieth century, Aramaic was the common language of government and commerce. The common person on the walls of Jerusalem who overheard the message would not know what someone said if the person spoke in Aramaic. The Assyrians refused the request and continued on in Hebrew.

Read 2 Kings 18:29–36. Underline each time the sentence begins with "Do not." Highlight the names of the deities referred to in verses 32–35. How did the people respond to the threats in verse 36? What was the basic message of the Assyrian official? Write it here:

_____

_____

The Assyrians knew that Yahweh was the God of Israel and Judah. The foreign power taunted those in Jerusalem by stating that no deity had helped Israel in their fight with Assyria. The people could not depend on their king's call to trust that "Yahweh will deliver us" (v. 32).

What voices in your life tell you that God cannot deliver you from what you face today? What is the basic message and how do you respond to their call not to trust in God? Write some of your thoughts here:

_____

_____

## 38.4 Earnestly Seeking God

One of the most common questions people ask me as a pastor is, "How do I pray?" People sense the need or desire to talk with God, but they do not know how or what to say. The good news is that prayers of those who trusted God with every area of their lives take part of His-story. Psalms is a book of prayers, but the cries and petitions also get nestled in the real-life narratives of those who acted out their roles in God's Story.

What role does prayer play in your relationship with God? When do you pray? Do you feel that God hears and responds to your prayers? Write your answers here:

_____

_____

The Assyrian king sent another threat to Hezekiah between battles (2 Kings 19:8–13). Notice what the King of Judah did when he received the threat (vv. 14–15a). He went to the Temple, spread the threatening letter out before Yahweh, and prayed.

Read 2 Kings 19:15–19. Read these verses in one or two other translations. Compare paragraphs and wording.

Describe the different aspects of the prayer in the space below. For example, verse 15 records the king's praise of Yahweh and a confession of who God is. What does 16 tell us about his prayer?

Verse 15 _____

Verse 16 _____

Verse 17–18 _____

Verse 19 _____

Hezekiah praised Yahweh as God alone and the God of Israel. He then asked God to hear the threats of his enemies. In verses 17–18 he honestly confessed his current situation.

He concluded his prayer by asking God to deliver them from the Assyrian king so that "all kingdoms on earth may know that you alone, O [Yahweh], are God." Hezekiah's motive focused not on saving his life but on having all acknowledge Yahweh as the one and only God.

Read verse 20. Highlight the names. Summarize Isaiah's message to Hezekiah here:

_____

_____

Hezekiah's prayer is a model prayer recorded in His-story for all to read. While the prayer does not offer a formula for "successful" prayers, it can give you hints on how to pray. End your moment with God by reading Hezekiah's prayer several times and inserting your own situation. Write your own prayer following his model if you like.

## 38.5 Trusting God for Answered Prayer

Sometimes we wish God would answer our prayers as clearly as He did Hezekiah's plea to deliver Judah from the Assyrians (2 Kings 19:20–34). God spoke to Isaiah, the prophet, and he relayed God's message directly to the king. Our storyteller recorded God's answer to help us trust Yahweh as the one and only God.

Has God ever answered you directly? Was the answer a simple, "It will be OK" or "Trust Me, I'm in control here," or was it more? If you have not known God's answer directly, what makes you certain of His presence and purpose in your life? Write your answers here:

_____

_____

_____

Read 2 Kings 19:35–37. Highlight the names in the verses. Underline the number of troops that died (v. 35) and what Sennacherib's sons did to him (v. 37).

These verses record the historical events foretold in God's answer to Hezekiah's prayer through His spokesperson, Isaiah. Consult a Bible commentary or dictionary for the details of these events. God is the God of history, and the facts recorded in the Bible give evidence of God's involvement in the events of people in order to write His-story.

Our question to consider this week was: How do human actions influence God's movement on their behalf? Does prayer make a difference? After you have observed this episode in King Hezekiah's life, how would you answer this question?

While we will not fully grasp the mystery and the certainty of God's providence in the affairs of people on this side of eternity, those who trust God know through the witness of Scripture that our prayers—our ongoing conversation in our relationship with God—do make a difference with God and can make the difference between a life well lived for God and one lived for ourselves.

Read Matthew 21:21–22. What did Jesus promise to His disciples? In what ways have you trusted Jesus' words through your prayers and actions? Reflect on Jesus' clear words and Hezekiah's example as you end your moment with God today and allow God's Spirit to guide your thoughts and prayers as you listen.

**For further study:**
- **2 Kings 17–19**
- **2 Kings 20–21; 2 Chronicles 29–32**

# 39—Loving People You Dislike (Prophet Jonah)

Jonah played his part as a prophet toward the end of Israel's existence as a nation. His story has an important part in God's Story because in the middle of all the judging and deporting, and worshiping other gods, God gave him a message for the enemies of Yahweh. God offered the people who did not know Him the same deal He offered the people He had chosen for His own centuries before. Jonah's sermon was only one sentence long: "Forty more days and Nineveh will be overturned" (Jonah 3:4), but it had the impact of a week-long Billy Graham crusade that had come to town.

Jonah felt happy to share the Good News with his own people, but it irked him to know that those who were not God's chosen would get the same reward for their repentance as would Israel. In the end, God taught him a lesson about God's grace and mercy and concern for all people, not just those who are "His."

The Memory Verse for this chapter is Jonah 2:6. While in the great fish, Jonah composed a song to God. This verse tells of how God rescued Jonah and set his feet on solid ground.

Our question to consider this week is: How do I respond when God shows compassion to evil people who repent? Grace is a hard reality for those who have grown up in its presence. We tend to own it for ourselves and forget that God gave it to us without merit. Your response to another's acceptance of God's grace says something about your understanding of it.

## 39.1 Called to Serve the Unlikable

I traveled to Russia in 1994 to teach an introduction to the New Testament to a group of seminary students in St. Petersburg, Russia. My trip came about five years after the fall of the Berlin Wall, which was synonymous with the end of the Cold War. Growing up I remember nuclear bomb drills in school, Conalrad station alerts, and stories of the horrors of life in the Soviet Union, the "Evil Empire." As I sat on the tarmac surrounded by Russian military personnel waiting to deplane to teach the former Soviet students, I felt the fear as I trained to feel coupled with the certainty that God was up to something huge in His-story because He had opened the once-atheist nation to the free flow of commerce and His truth. I could only trust all this was of God and somehow part of the storyline to help people trust Jesus.

Have you ever found yourself in a setting where you had the chance to serve a former or present enemy? Describe the situation and your feelings toward those you were sent to serve in the space below.

_____

_____

_____

_____

Read Jonah 1:1–3. Highlight the names and places in the verses. Underline God's direction to Jonah. Use a map to find the cities named here. You will see the opposite direction in which Jonah ran.

Jonah, whose name means "dove," was a real person in His-story. The annals of the kings recorded his name, his hometown, and the king he served, Jeroboam II of Israel (2 Kings 14:25). He was a reluctant servant-leader because when God gave him his mission (v. 2) he ran instead of making himself a servant to it (v. 3).

Read Jonah 1:4–12, 17. See the episode of Jonah's life as you would a scene in a movie. Imagine the wind, waves, and sounds of the sailors screaming above the storm to hear themselves. What would such a fish look like to you?

_____

_____

When we read the story of Jonah, the discussion usually stops or at least pauses at verse 17, which tells about the fish that swallowed God's messenger. We do not need to suspend our reason or blame ancient mythology for such an intrusion into the story. We can trust that the Creator makes and/or directs any creature to swallow any other creature to accomplish His purposes for its life.

The point of this episode is that God called, Jonah ran, and even a bunch of pagan sailors were more religiously astute than our man Jonah. After the sailors threw him over the side of the boat, God provided a ride to where God told him to go in the first place.

Where are you in this story as it relates to what you know God wants you to do with your life? Are you running? Are you asleep in the storm? Do you feel like God is dragging (swimming?) you to where He told you to go in the first place?

## 39.2 A Lesson in Obedience

"I'm not going to tell you a second time to clean your room!" is a line from most any child's past. Obedient children are supposed to respond to a parent's direction as soon as the parent speaks—in a fairy tale! Children display what is true of all of us: even when we know exactly what someone expects of us, we would rather do what we want than what we are told. In our lives of faith we live too much the same way. God's Word is clear in so many places. Why do we not do what it says?

Why is obeying God's clear direction so hard to do? Is it too hard? Does it change too much of how we already live? Write your answers here:

_____

_____

Read Jonah 3:1–2. Underline the phrase "the word of the Lord" and God's message to Jonah. Circle the phrase "a second time."

The fish vomited Jonah onto the beach and he headed to Nineveh (Jonah 2:10). Now that God had Jonah where He wanted him, God told him again what he must do and say. Much of our spiritual life involves getting to where God wants us so He can use us. Wonder what our lives would be like if we obeyed the first time God told us to do something?

Read Jonah 3:3–4. Circle the words "obeyed" and "went." Underline Jonah's one-sentence sermon to the people of Nineveh.

Jonah obeyed God this time and he went to Nineveh. It was a major city in Assyria on the banks of the Tigris River north of Babylon. It was so large our storyteller wrote that "a visit required three days," and that it had a population of over 120,000 (Jonah 4:11). The only words Jonah spoke to the people who heard him the first day were: ""Forty more days and Nineveh will be overturned." But that was enough.

Read Jonah 3:5. Underline the response of the people to Jonah's message.

All God has called us to do is tell people what He has revealed to us in His Word. We are not responsible for their reactions, and we never know what God's work has done in their hearts to prepare them. When the people of Nineveh heard Jonah's message, they "believed God" and "declared a fast." Whether by fear or by true repentance, they humbled themselves before God.

Consider this pattern for how God may work from these verses: a call of God (vv. 1–2); obedience by the one called (v. 3); God's message told (v. 4); trust in God by those

who heard (v. 5). If you were to teach this model of how God worked in Jonah's life, how would your lesson look and how would you apply it to your life and the lives of those who follow Jesus with you? Write your "lesson."

_____

_____

_____

## 39.3 Seeing Spiritual Change in Others

A revival is a spiritual movement among people as they respond to the presence of God. It can last a day or for years. People change as they follow God's leadership, and this leads to change in communities and sometimes entire nations. Throughout His-story God has revealed Himself to a people group and they have responded with repentance and a new way of life. The change did not happen by the force of an invading army or by the legislation of lawmakers. Revival came when everyday people trusted God with their lives. Sometimes their leaders join them.

What historic or personal revival experiences have you took part in? What did the "movement" look like? How did the work of God affect your life? Record some of your experiences here:

_____

_____

Read Jonah 3:6–9. Notice how the king of Nineveh responded to Jonah's message and the proclamation he gave for the entire nation.

The king responded like his people: he put on sackcloth and sat in the dirt as a sign of repentance, grief, and humility (v. 6). He declared a national fast where no animal or person would eat, the people would wear sackcloth, pray, and repent of (or "give up") their evil ways (vv. 7–8). He hoped God would then show them "compassion" rather than "his fierce anger."

A fast is a spiritual practice in which a person refuses food for a period of time in which he or she seeks to deepen his or her relationship with God. Spiritual food replaces physical food in order to feed the soul rather than the stomach. Israel used fasts to know the ways of God. Jesus fasted and taught His disciples to fast (Matt. 4:1–2; 6:16–18). Fasting marks personal and corporate revival. A word of caution: You should never use fasting as a weight loss program. Its purpose is spiritual, not physical.

Have you ever fasted in order to seek God? If so, what experience did you have? If not, ask a mature follower of Christ who has and seek counsel on how to practice this spiritual discipline.

Read Jonah 3:10. Underline the verse and circle the word "compassion" in both this verse and verse 9.

When God saw the genuine repentance of the king and his people, our storyteller wrote He had compassion on them and did not destroy them. They trusted God's message from Jonah and they repented and humbled themselves before God. This was revival.

Reflect on the king and people's response to God's truth as you end your moment with God today. Is God calling you to change things in your life? Should you consider a season of prayer and fasting as you continue this study? In what tangible ways can you demonstrate your own confession and repentance from sin?

## 39.4 Dealing with Anger

Jesus told a story about an owner of a field who hired workers to help him harvest. He went out early in the day and hired some men to work for a day's wage. As the day progressed he hired more men, agreeing to pay them a full day's wage for their work. At the end of the day he paid all of them what he said he would, but this meant those who worked an hour got the same amount as those who worked from the early morning. Guess how this made the all-day workers feel? You guessed it. They got mad because the owner did not pay them more. Jesus said the owner asked those who griped, "Don't I have the right to do what I want with my own money? Or are you envious because I am generous?" (Matt. 20:15) Jesus finished His story by saying, "So the last will be first, and the first will be last" (Matt. 20:16).

Have you ever felt like God has treated you unfairly? Have you ever gotten jealous of the grace someone else received when you have served God your entire life? Have you ever thought, "They had all the fun while I went to church, and they will end up in heaven just like me"? Or have you said out loud of someone else's conversion, "That's not fair." Grace-envy is part of every religious score keeper's experience.

Read Jonah 4:1–4. Underline the words that characterized Jonah (v. 1) and then do the same for those words that describe God (v. 2). Underline God's question to Jonah in verse 4.

Jonah was not happy with how either the people or God responded to his one-sentence message. The Assyrians would be the ones to destroy Israel and haul off all of its riches and people into exile. "How could God love them?" Jonah wondered. He pouted over their salvation.

Compare Jonah's reaction to the characteristics of God described in verse 2. Read the following passages to see how Scripture consistently reveals these aspects of God's character: Exodus 34:5–7; Nehemiah 9:16–18; Psalm 86:15.

Read Jonah 4:5–8. Summarize what happened in these verses in the space below. Circle the things of nature, such as vine, worm, and wind, in the verses.

_____

_____

_____

God had already used a storm and a large fish to teach Jonah a lesson or two. In this incident the God of creation used other created things to seek to change His prophet's heart. How would you describe the prophet's attitude? Was it justified? Did he not act a bit dramatic? Can you put yourself in his place?

## 39.5 The Problem of Self-Centeredness

I like stories that end well. The changed heart, the united friends, and they lived happily ever after kinds of endings are my favorites. The oddity of Jonah's story is that while the city of Nineveh turned its heart toward Yahweh, we never hear if Jonah changed his heart toward his enemies. The last we hear from him is his answer to God's question if he had a right to be angry about the withered vine. He said, "I do . . . I am angry enough to die" (Jonah 4:9).

Read Jonah 4:10–11. What answer did Yahweh give His pouting prophet?

_____

Jonah's perspective shrunk to his own wants and needs such as whether or not a vine provided him shade from the sun. He focused on the vine and what it did or did not do for him. God focused on a city of people who would perish without His compassion.

Take a moment to reflect on your perspective of God's compassion and care for you compared to your sensitivity to the sin and need of others. Do not miss how we act like Jonah and how only God's love sends us to others. Your answer to this will also answer our question to consider this week: How do I respond when God shows compassion to evil people who repent?

The Old Testament always points its readers to the new covenant in Jesus, and Jesus used the stories from the days of the old covenant to help people trust Him. His-story is not a collection of random acts by random people. It is a storyline that connects the past with the present and vice versa. This makes up part of the mystery and miracle of the Bible.

Read Matthew 12:38–41. Underline the Pharisees' question to Jesus. How did Jesus interpret Jonah's three days in the fish? How was it a "miraculous sign" to the people who wondered about who Jesus was or what he had come to do? Who was the one "greater than Jonah"?

_____

_____

_____

Jesus pointed to Jonah's three days in the fish as a "sign" that pointed to His three days in the tomb. That would offer enough proof for those who would trust Jesus. Even the "men of Nineveh" would stand in judgment over those who refused to trust Jesus (v. 41).

God used parts of His creation to guide His reluctant prophet to proclaim a message of hope to a sinful people. Jonah's heart never changed toward his enemies, but God's did when He saw their genuine repentance and worship of Him. Do not get hung up on the fish in the story. The story tells about God's love and our selfishness. Learn those lessons before you argue with anyone about the existence or size of such a fish.

**For further study:**
- **Jonah 1**
- **Jonah 2:1–10**

# 40—Renovation of the Soul (King Josiah)

God continued to write prophets, priests, and kings into the storyline of His rescue mission for all people. Each kind of leader played a role in the destruction and restoration of Israel's covenant relationship with God. In this episode of His-story we will see how all three kinds of leaders acted boldly to rid Judah of idol worship and restore God's Word as the centerpiece of their society.

The main character of this episode is Josiah, who became king of Judah at the age of eight after his father's assassination. (See 2 Chronicles 33:24–25; this happened about 640 B.C.) His father and grandfather encouraged the worship of other gods during their rule, but Josiah began to seek God at age 16, and by age 20 he began proactively reforming the religion of Judah in the ways of the covenant found in the "Book of the Law."

Although the king fell in battle against Egypt's Pharaoh, God protected him from seeing the final destruction and deportation of Jerusalem and God's people.

The Memory Verse for this chapter is 2 Chronicles 34:2. This verse describes the godly character of the king. It reminds us that some leaders do devote themselves to God first and live out God's call on their lives.

Our question to consider this week is: Why do you think some people are indifferent to God's Word? You may first want to explore sociological and psychological reasons to answer this question, but spiritual realities play a big part in your answer, too. First, observe the events of this chapter in order to answer the question.

# 40.1 Godly Influence

Growing up I was fortunate to have Christian parents and leaders in my life. I learned from them by example and by teaching me the things of God. They spent time either taking me to a teacher or teaching me themselves the stories of God and how to apply them to my life. Mr. Colvin put up with a bunch of us rowdy boys crowded into a Sunday school room. He taught us the Bible and molded our thinking into a God-centered worldview. He took us on outings and would gladly let our parents know how we behaved out of their presence. He was a friend, coach, teacher, and leader to me. I am grateful for Mr. Colvin and others who invested in my life early on to teach me the story, ways, and things of God.

Who made a positive influence early in your life? Write each person's name and how each influenced you in the space below.

_____

_____

_____

Read 2 Chronicles 34:1–3. Highlight the names and places and circle the three ages of Josiah in the verses. Underline what Josiah began to purge from the land.

Our storyteller described Josiah as a godly leader (v. 2—our Memory Verse). He broke the cycle of idolatry that his father and grandfather had started. After the assassination of his father, he was made king. Someone clearly influenced him in the things of God as an eight-year-old because we are told at age 16 he began to "seek the God of his father David" (v. 3). Josiah modeled his kingship after King David, his ancestor, rather than his own father. By age 20 he set out to "purge" Judah of everything used in the worship of other gods.

A pattern of spiritual maturity emerges from these three short verses: godly influence in childhood led to the pursuit of godly examples in the teen years that resulted in true reform of a nation toward the things of God. How would you describe Josiah's spiritual development?

_____

_____

Read Luke 2:41–52. Underline verse 52 as it describes the development of Jesus into a mature man. What role did Mary and Joseph have in His development? How does Josiah's description compare to Jesus'? How are those descriptions goals for the moral development of children and teenagers? Write your answers here:

_____

Review your moral development from age eight to age 20. How did your view of God change? What did you do differently in your teen years because of the influence of godly people in your life? Allow God's Spirit to join you and guide your thoughts as you see His handwriting in your story.

_____

_____

## 40.2 Purifying Your Life

At different times over the past couple of decades church youth groups have placed their albums, cassette tapes, or CDs in a pile and destroyed them. Their actions sometimes caught the eye of the local news. Other times their purges went unnoticed except to those who knew the students. I have personally been with men who have carried a box of pornography from the attic and dumped it in a local landfill. I know of others who have destroyed old letters from previous girlfriends or changed email addresses, or who have even placed blockers on their Web browsers in order to keep them off sites inappropriate for their moral purity.

All of these actions have one thing in common: they were done to remove the influence and temptation of those things that seduced them away from God.

What is your attitude about what these groups of people did? Were their actions too radical? Are such acts only for weak people who cannot control their desires? Have you ever done anything like that to remove a negative influence from your life?

_____

_____

Read 2 Chronicles 34:4–7. Underline each object Josiah destroyed and highlight the different towns mentioned in the passage. Consult a Bible dictionary or handbook to locate the cities and objects.

Josiah set out to "purge," or "purify" (NLT), Jerusalem and Judah of any and all worship items dedicated to other gods (v. 3). He symbolically desecrated the priests of these places and idols by pouring pieces of crushed objects over their graves (v. 4). He went so far as to burn the bones of priests on the altars where they offered sacrifices to their gods (v. 5). He personally oversaw this cultic cleansing throughout the kingdom (v. 6), and when he felt satisfied, he returned to Jerusalem (v. 7).

Josiah not only tore down the places of worship to false gods but he ordered the High Priest, Hilkiah, to restore the Temple of Yahweh (2 Chron. 34:8–13). How old was Josiah when he made this order? (See verse 8.) Write your answer here: _____

Josiah proactively moved to bring the nation he led back to the worship and ways of the covenant God of Israel. His actions went against popular opinion and practice, but he felt convinced that both the destruction of other places of worship and the restoration of the Temple would lead the people back to the God of King David.

Do you have any physical items in your life that represent ways of life that do not line up with your worship of the God of His-story? Take some time to listen to God's Spirit as you take inventory of your things to see what God would have you do about them so that you would devote yourself solely to Him.

_____

_____

_____

## 40.3 Spiritual Brokenness

I remember when I finished reading Philip Yancey's book, *What's So Amazing About Grace*. I started it a couple of days before and could not put it down. Yancey encouraged me to accept a full concept of grace I had not known in my own experience. He then ignited a fuse I could not put out as he applied that grace to real people in real life. I knew my grasp of grace would never be the same again. Yancey drug my classroom-informed knowledge about grace into the streets and left me there to fend for myself. I felt afraid and enthused at the same time. I still consider it the most dangerous book I have read in years because it so radically changed how I show the same grace God has shown me to anyone . . . yes, anyone. I go back to Yancey's invitation often to remind myself of how I am to live because God's life-giving grace has overwhelmed me.

What book has radically changed how you know things and also how you actually live? Is it a book of the Bible or another book? Write the author, title, and reason it changed you in the space below.

_____

_____

Read 2 Kings 22:8–10. Highlight the names and underline what these people found and read to the king.

During the renovation of the Temple workers found the "Book of the Law." At the end of Moses' life he instructed the Levites to keep the scrolls that contained the laws God gave Moses (Deut. 31:24–26). The the ark

of the covenant was kept in the Tabernacle and ultimately in
the Temple. This "book" was a collection of scrolls that contained the Torah, or first five books of the Bible. Previous kings had neglected them as they turned to other gods. Hilkiah gave it to his secretary who brought and read it to the king.

Read 2 Kings 22:11–13. Underline Josiah's response to the reading of the Law (v. 11). What did the king conclude about God's attitude toward the people? (v. 13)

Josiah responded in grief and repented when he heard the truth of God's commandments and realized how far Judah had turned from it. God revealed to Josiah the gravity of His anger toward the people for neglecting His ways.

When we read the Bible we read the revealed Word of God for all generations. Some of us have grown so familiar with it that it no longer moves us to action or emotion. Others are hungry to know God through

His-story and cannot wait to read the next episode. Have you been caught off guard as you read the Bible? Has this walk through biblical history created for you any defining moments with God? Ask God to reveal Himself to you in a new way as He did to Josiah when he heard the "Book of the Law" for the first time.

## 40.4 Applying God's Word to Life

Individual Bible study like this one is beneficial for becoming like Jesus and teaching others (2 Tim. 3:16). A foundational doctrine (tenet or belief) of evangelical faith is that God can and does reveal Himself as believers honestly read or hear His Word in Scripture.

However, individual study of the Bible alone can result in a subjective, narrow interpretation of God's Word. For this reason, a more mature follower of Christ can help as you learn the ways and words of God. A mentor or more mature teacher can help you interpret a passage in light of the entire Bible and other aspects surrounding the verses such as history, meanings of words, and theology. Wise learners depend on mentors and teachers to help them know God's Word fully.

Do you have a mentor or more mature follower of Christ you can go to for help with passages you find too difficult or obscure to understand? Who helps you apply the clear teachings of Jesus to your personal life? Write the name of a teacher or leader who has helped you in this way.

_____

Read 2 Kings 22:14. Highlight the names and underline

where the prophetess lived.

Josiah understood clearly what the "Book of the Law" said, but he wanted to know how it applied to his life and the lives of his people. So he sent an entourage of advisors to Huldah, the prophetess. Only two other women are recognized as a prophetess in the Old Testament: Miriam, Moses' sister (Ex. 15:20), and Deborah, a "judge" of Israel (Judg. 4:4). The king desired a fuller explanation of the consequences that might come because of the people's rebellion against Yahweh, so he sent his most trusted advisors to a respected, mature spokesperson for God.

Read 2 Kings 22:15–17. Summarize the prophetess' message to the king and why this would happen. Highlight the names of God in the entire message.

Huldah revealed God's plan to destroy Judah like He had Israel because of the people's worship of idols. Yahweh would keep consistent with the words they had just read recorded in the Torah.

Huldah's message came in two parts. Read verses 18–20 and summarize the message to Josiah in the space below. Underline the reasons why this would be true for him according to the prophetess.

_____

While God would destroy Judah, Josiah would not see its destruction. He would die before that happened. God told the king through His spokesperson that this would happen because the king had responded to the words of God. The king humbled himself before the truth of God's revealed Word and repented. God honored his genuine acts of repentance by allowing him to "be buried in peace" rather than witness the fall of his country. If you do not have someone who can guide you in the study and application of God's Word, begin to ask God for a mentor or teacher. If God has provided that person in your life, contact and thank that person for his or her help in knowing the ways and words of God.

## 40.5 Leading Others to Renewal

Servant-leaders call others to join them on mission. Biblical servant-leaders call people to join them on mission for God. Throughout His-story whenever God revealed His storyline to a servant-leader, the leader turned to tell others what he or she heard. The leader then called people to adjust their lives to join God. We have seen this happen in the lives of servant-leaders from Moses to King David. King Josiah was a servant-leader who went beyond a personal renewal with God to lead the entire nation to renew their covenant relationship with Yahweh. Servant-leaders lead by example and lead others to join in what God has called them to do.

Read 2 Kings 23:3. Underline the verbs that tell what Josiah did and what the people did in response to his leadership.

Josiah renewed his covenant with God to follow the commandments recorded in the "Book of the Covenant" found in the Temple. The people followed their leader by pledging themselves to the same covenant commitment.

Read 2 Kings 23:21–25. Underline verses 22 and 25 as summary statements of Josiah's actions.

Josiah re-established the Passover as a festival to the LORD and removed all rival spokespeople and idols from the land. Our storyteller described the Passover as the best ever. Josiah did what he did "with all his heart and with all his soul and with all his strength," just as the Torah says to love God (Deut. 6:5).

Our question to consider this week was: Why do you think some people are indifferent to God's Word? You have seen Josiah's response to the reading of the Torah, and you have observed the population's previous indifference to the commandments of God. When Josiah led them to renew their covenant with Yahweh, they followed. As you answer the question draw some parallels to your own life and the community in which you live.

Look back over Josiah's relationship with God and how he led Judah in a revival toward full devotion to Yahweh. If you were asked to present what you had learned from Josiah's life to a group of friends, what would you tell them and how would you present what you said? Write a sketch of your thoughts in the space below. Who knows, that request may come sooner than later.

_____

_____

**For further study:**
- **Deuteronomy 6:4–9; 2 Kings 22–23**
- **2 Chronicles 34–35; Jeremiah 1:1–2; 3:6–10**

# 41—Serving God with Authenticity (Prophet Jeremiah)

Some people believe that to live in the "will of God" brings peace and prosperity. We believe that if we play our part in the bigger Story of God our lives will be filled with adventure and excitement.

Jeremiah's story gives us an example of someone who stood in the dead center of God's plan for his life, but he experienced nothing other than pain and humiliation. He served in Judah under its last three kings, and he witnessed the fall of Jerusalem. He got deported with others and found himself without a country. He ended up with only the mission and message God gave him. Jeremiah faithfully lived out God's call on his life. He never backed down from those who tried to intimidate him and he suffered much for the message God gave him.

The prophet Jeremiah is an example of authentic faith, honest confession, and absolute trust in God no matter the response of others.

The Memory Verse for this chapter is Jeremiah 1:5. God's words to Jeremiah confirmed that God set his life's purpose even before his birth. This verse has implications for understanding the significance of every life.

Our question to consider this week is: How compelled am I to share truth with others—even when they do not want to hear it? Truth telling is a hard job. Most people only want to hear good things about them. The truth sometimes hurts, and those who tell it can get injured by relaying the message. Observe Jeremiah's example as an answer to this question.

## 41.1 The Value of a Life

Every life has a role to play in God's Story. I do not write that because some sociology or psychology professor told me that people need to hear this piece of wisdom to help them have a good self-image. No, I believe this truth because it is a core idea we learn about ourselves from God's Story. To know one's purpose is to know one's worth. And how do we know the worth or value of our lives? Several sources speak into our lives. Our parents or guardians let us know early on in life how much they value us. Our peers and social networks tell us our value to the group, organization, or business. Grades, income, earned degrees, and the amount and size of our possessions all represent measurements of value. We take our lead from each of these sources and build a portfolio of value that guides our thoughts and actions.

What or who is the most influential voice of value in your life? What did that voice say about who you were and the value you hold to them and others? How do you keep score of your worth?

_____

_____

God came to Jeremiah when he was 18 years old and explained He had a purpose for his life—one that God had set in place long before Jeremiah was conceived.

Read Jeremiah 1:4–5. Highlight the phrase, "the word of the LORD," and underline God's message to Jeremiah. Circle God's purpose for Jeremiah in verse 5, which is our Memory Verse for this chapter.

Another source for how we come to know our worth is God's message to us. Yahweh came to Jeremiah and described the purpose of his life. He was to serve as "a prophet to the nations." God had set apart and chosen him for this purpose even before his birth. Jeremiah had an important role to play in His-story. God's call on his life marked the beginning of Jeremiah's servant leadership to Judah. That same call would sustain him on his mission when others refused to listen to him and even persecuted him for what sounded like such a negative message.

God gave Jeremiah a specific call, which teaches us every life has worth. Read the following passages and then record what they teach you about the worth and purpose of your life.

Psalm 139:13–16 _____

_____

Genesis 1:27 _____

_____

Ephesians 2:10 _____

_____

After observing God's words to Jeremiah and reading the other verses about how God sees your worth, use your journal to write in your own words the worth God sees in your life. Ask God to allow His words to serve as the mirror you look into to see your worth to Him.

## 41.2 Transparent Inadequacy

God's call to join Him in His-story is not always what we would pick for our career choice or for our favorite vacation spot. We would rather choose more conventional paths like finding a job, getting married, having children, and retiring to Hot Springs, Arizona. Our initial response to God's invitation usually sounds more like Moses' answer, "Are you kidding? You want me?" rather than Isaiah's answer, "Here I am. Send me." (Both followed a direct encounter with God.) To say yes to God is dangerous and uncomfortable at times, and we can come up with many reasons why it feels safer to stay at home instead of following God into the adventure.

Read Jeremiah 1:6. Highlight the name of God and underline Jeremiah's excuse. (Read Exodus 4:10 for a similar excuse by Moses.)

What excuses did Jeremiah give for resisting God's call? What excuses have you given for not answering yes to God's clear call?

_____

Jeremiah used the excuses of his youth and his inexperience in speaking to fend off God's clear call on his life.

Read Jeremiah 1:7–10. Highlight the name of God in each verse and underline what Yahweh said to Jeremiah. Circle the word "appoint" in verse 10. Summarize God's answer to Jeremiah's excuse here:

_____

Read the corresponding New Testament passages that echo God's words to His chosen one.

"Do not say . . ." (Read 1 Timothy 4:12.)

"Go to everyone . . ." (Read Matthew 28:19–20.)

"Do not be afraid . . ." (Read John 14:27.)

"I have put my words in your mouth . . ." (Read Luke 12:11–12. Remember a similar action by God in Isaiah's call in Isaiah 6:6.)

"I appoint you over nations . . ." (Read Ephesians 1:18–23; 2:6–7.)

Compare the corresponding New Testament promises

(on the previous page) to those God gave Jeremiah. Then write your interpretation of God's promises to you as He calls you to live out your part in the Story of God in the space below.

_____

_____

_____

## 41.3 Telling the Hard Truth

God's news is not always good news. Truth is truth, and sin is sin. We believe that God approves of our good religious habits or civil lifestyle. So when someone reads something from God's message that challenges our status quo or way of life, we either ignore it or do something to quiet the one speaking. We think ignorant bliss seems better than wrestling with the truth when it comes to how we live. Jeremiah 1–19 gives a compilation of Jeremiah's negative news to Judah and his conversations with God about the difficulty of his mission and message. God graciously answered his prophet's questions but never released him from the mission God created him to do. Jeremiah had become a nuisance by chapter 20 of this saga, and both people and leaders stood ready to respond to him when he came to their town.

Read Jeremiah 20:1–2. Highlight the names and places in this passage and underline what the Temple officer did to Jeremiah.

When Jeremiah preached the bad news in the Temple courts, the Temple Chief of Police, Pashhur, had him beaten and put in stocks in the public square where everyone could see what happens when someone speaks against the religious authorities of the day. Compare Pashhur's actions to those of the defenders of religion toward Jesus (Mark 14:53–65) and Paul (Acts 21:27–36). See a pattern? What may you conclude could happen if you speak for God before religious authorities?

Read Jeremiah 20:3–6. Highlight the name Jeremiah gave Pashhur. Compare different translations for the meaning of the name. Underline the action verbs that tell what Jeremiah said would happen to the priest and the nation.

Jeremiah would not let the religious leader off so easy— no matter his motives for letting him go. He named the priest, Magor-Missabib, which meant "terror on every side" (v. 3). The priest would become "a terror" on every side to his fellow priests and friends as well as to himself (v. 4). He then proceeded to explain what would happen to the country, to the priest, and to his family and friends (vv. 5–6). Jeremiah pinpointed the country of Babylon as God's instrument to judge His people.

God's revelation teaches us to respect those in authority over us; for example, Romans 13:1–7 and Hebrews 13:17. Jeremiah spoke against both the civil and religious authorities of his day with a message from God. When is it right to speak against the ruling authorities? If you decide to do so, based on the examples given by Jeremiah, Jesus, and Paul, should you resist the punishment the authorities give to you? Record these thoughts in your journal.

## 41.4 Honest with God

One of the most difficult messages I ever delivered to the church where I served as Senior Pastor for over 20 years was, "We have to change." Those four words caused more struggle and pain for all of us than any other message I had spoken. On the other hand, it also provided us opportunities to experience God's love and power in ways we would not have otherwise. That short message came from what I knew as a clear call from God to remove the religious habits and inward focus we had accumulated over generations of religion in order to reach and serve our mission field. Any servant-leader who has spoken for God has brought that message at one time or another. At some point in the journey of change he or she felt like Jeremiah did when he complained to God about his assignment and message.

Read Jeremiah 20:7–10. Circle the word "like" in verse 9 to describe how God's message felt in Jeremiah's heart when he said he would not speak anymore because of his trouble. Read Jeremiah's prayer to God from one or two other translations and then write your own paraphrase of it in the space below.

_____

_____

_____

Jeremiah walked away from a beating and a night in the stocks to a time of prayer with God. His prayer is not like King David's prayer of confession (Ps. 51) or Hezekiah's prayer of deliverance (2 Kings 19:14–19). He started with, "O Lord, you misled me, and I allowed myself

to be misled" (NLT). Not the most enduring way to start a conversation with the God who "formed" you and "appointed" you to work for Him, but Jeremiah knew God well enough through his on-going conversations with Him that he could be honest.

Do you need or want to write a prayer to God about your honest feelings? Remember, Jeremiah did not complain simply because times were tough. What happened resulted from his obedience. If you choose to complain, make sure you are justified in doing so like Jeremiah. Otherwise, pray to obey God first.

Read Jeremiah 20:11–13. Circle the word "like" in verse 11 to describe how Jeremiah saw God in his time of trouble. Underline the words of praise in verse 13 and the reason for Jeremiah's praise.

Jeremiah's prayer started with justified complaining about people's response to his message, but he ended in a few short paragraphs with a praise to Yahweh as his "mighty warrior" and rescuer. Jeremiah spoke honestly about his feelings—he was human after all—but remained submitted to the mission and message God assigned to him.

Read your paraphrased prayer of Jeremiah aloud to God three different times. Pause between readings to listen for the Spirit's nudging as to the part or parts that ring truest in your heart. When you have finished, say the prayer that rests on your lips as it relates to what you have just prayed to God.

## 41.5 The Weeping Prophet

Jeremiah was nicknamed the "Weeping Prophet" because of the sad news he had to deliver to his people and the burden he had to bear. You may want to call him the "Whining Prophet" after you read the verses for today. But, do not call him that just yet. Remember the fuller context in which he cried out to God and the hard message he had to give his friends—even to the godly king he loved, Josiah (Jer. 3:6–10). The chosen man of God faithfully proclaimed Yahweh's message to the people and accepted their negative responses and persecution until one day he broke down and told God he wished he had never been born.

Read Jeremiah 20:14–18. Underline the objects of his curses and his question in verse 18.

Jeremiah became so frustrated he cursed the day of his birth (v. 14) and even the man who announced his birth (vv. 15–17). He wondered why he was born if he would only "see trouble and sorrow" and "end [his] days in shame" (v. 18). You may say he was depressed, but unlike some with that clinical illness, he continued to get out of bed and do what God had called him to do.

Have you ever prayed what Jeremiah prayed that day? What circumstances surrounded your feelings? Did you feel OK with being that authentic with God? With your family and friends?

_____

_____

Our question to consider this week was: How compelled

am I to share truth with others—even when they do not want to hear it? The bottom line of obedience is doing what you know God has called you to do no matter the response of those you tell or serve. Obedience overcomes the need to have others like and accept you, and even the feelings of failure and shame.

After observing Jeremiah's ministry, what can you apply to your relationship with God and how can you answer the question posed to you? (Read Ephesians 4:14–16 for a New Testament teaching that may apply to your answer.)

**For further study:**
- **Jeremiah 2:1–19**
- **Jeremiah 8:21–9:1; 32:6–25**

## 42— When God Seems Unfair (Prophet Habakkuk)

We find it easier to trust God as the Author of His-story when everyone appears to be following the storyline; when and God and His people are victorious and in control. It seems much harder to trust God as the Writer and Editor of life when evil wins over good and pagans overrun those who worship God. How can God have control when those who worship other gods massacre those who supposedly belong to Him?

Habakkuk was God's spokesperson to Judah before the Babylonians invaded and destroyed Jerusalem (about 605 B.C.). He served during the days of Jeremiah, Nahum, and Zephaniah, and he brought the same truth his contemporaries delivered: God would soon judge their disobedience by allowing the nation's enemies to defeat and deport them.

While Jeremiah opened his hurting heart to God, Habakkuk asked hard questions about why God allowed evil to walk over His people and purposes.

The Memory Verse for this chapter is Habakkuk 2:4. "The righteous will live by his faith" is the hallmark of this verse, and its truth echoes through the pages of Scripture as the foundation for our relationship with God.

Our question to consider this week is: Is life ever out of God's control? Observe Habakkuk's conversation with God, and then answer this question.

## 42.1 Tough Questions

I ride bikes with a friend who cannot get past the fact that God allows evil to prevail and the innocent to suffer unjustly. We train for and ride 30-mile to 150-mile rides, which means we have plenty of time to talk about these things. He trusts God is real. However, he does not understand how a loving God not only allows evil to prey on the innocent, but how the victims spend eternity separated from Him because they did not know Jesus. Sometimes we ride in silence after we have presented all the arguments. The only option is to trust that God has control and works out His purposes even though we cannot fully explain it all. I pray we will ride many more miles together and someday his trust in God alone will satisfy what his "inquiring mind" cannot conceive.

Do you have a friend who asks the same questions? Do you ask those questions too? How have you wrestled with the presence of evil in your faith?

_____

_____

_____

Read Habakkuk 1:1–3. Highlight the name of the prophet and the name of God. Circle the question marks to identify the prophet's requests of God. Summarize Habakkuk's core issue with God here:

_____

_____

The Book of Habakkuk is one of the Minor Prophets preserved in the Bible. We refer to it as minor simply because it has less content than that of the Major Prophets, like Jeremiah. Habakkuk does not have a minor message in the sense of a minor league baseball player who does not have enough skill for the majors. God's words to a minor prophet are as significant as His words to those who spoke of Jesus' coming. God gave his spokesperson an "oracle" (NASB) or "burden" (NKJV). But first, Habakkuk had some questions. He asked why God kept silent as he cried out about the violence and injustice he saw (vv. 2–3). His core question to God was, "Why do you tolerate wrong?"

Read verse 4. Circle the word "Therefore" and underline the words "law," "justice," and "righteous."

"Therefore" marks a conclusion based on what was said or written before. The prophet concluded that because God did nothing about the violence and injustice that plagued the nation, "the law is paralyzed, and justice never prevails." The apparent absence of God wreaked havoc with the legal system of the day. (See 1 Kings 21:1–16 for another picture of the corrupt courts.)

Enter Habakkuk's questions of God by restating his prayer or writing your own prayer to God. Pray for those you know who wrestle to find reasonable answers to these difficult questions of faith.

## 42.2 Look for What God is Doing

If God is in control and God allows nations to exist can God use *any* nation for His purposes? What about Hitler's Nazi Germany, Stalin's Soviet Union, Pol Pot's Cambodia, or Saddam Hussein's Iraq? We cannot fathom how God could allow evil men to rule much less exercise their authority and strength to bring such destruction on the lives of others. Our minds will not allow "loving God" and "death of innocent people" to belong in the same sentence. Therefore, since we know evil people kill innocent children some people eliminate a loving God from the equation. But God offers an answer that may surprise you. As a matter of fact, He said His answer will do just that.

How do you reconcile the existence of God with evil regimes that so willingly destroy life? What leaders that seem to flourish in your world cause you to wonder with Habakkuk, "Why do you tolerate wrong?"

Read Habakkuk 1:5. Underline the last two phrases of the verse. Paraphrase them in your own words.

_____

_____

_____

After the prophet asked his questions, God answered by saying, "Watch the nations around you. I'm about to do something you would not believe even when I tell you." God basically told Habakkuk, "You think injustice in your legal system is bad, check out what's about to happen!"

Read Habakkuk 1:6–11. Highlight the name of the country God would use to destroy Judah and circle the word "like" for images of their strength. Underline the last phrase in verse 11, which tells the god they serve.

The Babylonians, or Chaldeans (NASB), signified an ethnic group who succeeded in dominating Babylonia, now known as southern Iraq. King Nebuchadnezzar (2 Kings 24:1–15) was a brilliant military leader who laid siege to Jerusalem and deported the upper class of Israelites to Babylon in 586 B.C. God described the power, swiftness, and numbers of the Babylonian army that He would use to destroy Judah. (See Deuteronomy 28:49 for the reason God allowed this to happen.)

Read Romans 13:1. Underline what it teaches about the "authorities" that exist. Who establishes them?

God is the Author of His-story. Paul explained to Christians in Rome who would die at the hands of that government that no authority exists except by God and they were to respect that authority even if it sent their families off to death. God revealed to Habakkuk that He pens the movements of nations—even the wicked Babylonians "whose own strength is their god."

Apply God's message to Habakkuk to the world situation in which you live. What countries that live far from God's purpose seem to be gaining power? Can you believe God "established" them? Can you accept that God can accomplish His purposes through their behavior?

_____

_____

_____

_____

## 42.3 Understanding God's Character

His-story is recorded in many kinds of literature. We have spent most of our time in narrative, historical stories about God and people, but in these verses we read an allegory—an extended metaphor where the meaning of the people, objects, and actions lie outside the story. Habakkuk used vivid language to state his second case before God. He envisioned the people of Judah as fish and their enemies as fishermen who netted them and pulled them from the sea. Jeremiah 24 gives another example of an allegory with an interpretation, and Jesus' Parable of the Sower is a story or parable with allegorical meaning (Matt. 13:1–23). To interpret a passage properly you must know the literature and intent of the author.

Do have a favorite allegory from Scripture? What about literature from other areas of life? If so, describe the story and why it appeals to you in the space below. Two of mine are John Bunyan's Pilgrim's Progress and C. S. Lewis' version, The Pilgrim's Regress.

_____

_____

_____

Read Habakkuk 1:12–13. Highlight the names of God and circle the question marks of the questions the prophet asked God. Underline the word "My" in verse 12 to signify the personal relationship Habakkuk sensed with God. What does the first sentence in verse 13 tell you about the holiness of God?

Habakkuk acknowledged God's holy character as he began his second set of questions to God. In the space below, write a description of the character of God revealed in these two verses. (See Psalms 18:2, 31 for another description of God.)

_____

_____

Read Habakkuk 1:14–17. Underline "men" in verse 14 and "wicked foe" in verse 15 to recognize the subjects of these verses. Underline "Therefore" in verse 16 to see the conclusion he drew from his previous observations. Consider the imagery the prophet used to portray his feelings. For example, the people were like fish and their foe was like a fisherman who catches them in his nets and is happy with his catch. The god of the fisherman was his net (v. 16), which interpreted meant that Babylon worshiped its military strength as its god. (See also Habakkuk 1:11.) Habakkuk wanted to know if Yahweh would continue to let Babylon keep on "emptying his net and destroying nations without mercy?"

Habakkuk continued to contend with God about the apparent injustice brought on Judah by the Babylonians. He was creative in his approach, but his questions stayed the same: would God allow the wicked overpower the righteous? God answered yes.

## 42.4 Seeking God through Prayer

Jesus taught His followers to anticipate an answer from God when they prayed. In His inaugural teaching to His disciples He told them to ask, seek, and knock and God would respond.

Read Matthew 7:7–1. Summarize what Jesus taught about prayer and what to expect from God.

_____

Describe how you have experienced God's response to you in prayer. Has He answered you in tangible ways or have you simply felt more of His presence? How has God responded like Jesus said He would?

_____

_____

Jesus said God would answer, help us find a way, and open doors for us if we would consistently pursue Him in prayer. He said if an earthly father would not think of giving a child a snake if he or she asked for bread, "how much more will your Father in heaven give good gifts to those who ask him!" (Matt. 7:11)

Read Habakkuk 2:1. Underline the verbs that tell what the prophet will do. What metaphor did he use to describe how he would wait on God's answer?

The prophet wrote he would stand like a soldier on his watch waiting on the ramparts of the city to "see" what God would say to him. He wanted to know how God would answer his complaint so he could tell others.

Read Habakkuk 2:2–3. Underline the first sentence of verse 2 for it marks God's reply to the prophet. Circle the word "revelation" in both verses and summarize what God said about it. Consult other translations to get a fuller meaning of God's reply.

God answered Habakkuk. God told his messenger to write down the "revelation," or "vision" (NASB) on tablets to make it clear enough to read on the run. God also said the answer He would give was for a later "appointed time," a time in the future. God told of Babylon's destruction that would not come until after it had subdued Judah (vv. 4–20). God told him to "wait for it," because it would surely come to pass (v. 3).

Waiting is part of prayer. Read Psalm 27:14, 33:20, and 37:7, 34. What do these words from the Book of Psalms teach you about waiting upon the LORD? Summarize what you observe in the space below. Practice "waiting on the LORD" this week as you worship Him.

_____

_____

_____

## 42.5 The Righteous Live by Faith

When the visible nation of Israel and the priestly sacrificial system were near their ends God revealed to Habakkuk a bedrock truth upon which all people build their relationship with God: trust in God rather than trust in one's own efforts is the only hope for salvation. Trusting God rather than trusting ourselves is the basic principle for right living.

Read Habakkuk 2:4. Underline the words that describe "he" in the verse and highlight the last phrase of the verse. This revelation was a defining moment with God. The verse is our Memory Verse for this chapter.

God revealed to the prophet that there are two kinds of people: those "puffed up" by their own efforts who do not have "upright" desires and those "righteous" who live by "faith." God revealed the eternal truth that those in right standing with God would live their lives by actively trusting God for salvation, not their own efforts.

Which kind of person are you more like? Take a moment to assess how your actions reveal what you truly believe.

Remember the context of this revelation. Kings made treaties and sent out their armies to fend off the enemy that Yahweh allowed to crush His own people. The people put their trust in the walls of their cities, the size of their armies, and the religious activity they practiced each day for protection and safety. Yet, Assyria had already defeated and hauled off Israel in the north, and Babylon moved closer to the walls of Jerusalem as the prophet spoke. God taught Habakkuk, who in turn spoke to the people, that their only hope was to trust in God alone for their salvation. The "right ones" would live their lives by faith in God, not by building bigger armies and practicing more religion.

Read Romans 1:17, Galatians 3:11, and Hebrews 10:35–39. Highlight the truth God revealed to Habakkuk in each passage. Note the context of each verse and why the author used the prophetic truth in his argument.

The Holy Spirit inspired those who wrote to help people trust Jesus to remember God's revelation to Habakkuk. The new covenant writers trusted Jesus' death, burial, and Resurrection as sufficient to satisfy all of the requirements of holiness set by God, the Father. Trust in Jesus' actions, not in our own efforts to be right, is the basis for standing right before Holy God and how we live our lives each day.

After reading these verses, write your interpretation of the biblical teaching of faith alone as the basis for righteous living. Review Habakkuk's conversation with God and answer our question to consider this week: Is life ever out of God's control?

_____

_____

_____

**For further study:**
- **Habakkuk 2:5–3:19**
- **Isaiah 54**

## 43—Warning Others (Prophet Ezekiel)

God chose Ezekiel to speak for Him as one era of His-story ended and another began. Ezekiel lived through the pain of Jerusalem's final destruction in which his wife died, and he finished his life estranged and exiled in Babylon. His peers and the rest of the people thought he was eccentric in his words and actions, but he appeared that way to those who no longer respected the "word of the LORD." They chose for themselves other gods as their sources of strength and objects of worship. The words from Yahweh seemed out of place in their pluralistic society. Ezekiel faithfully acted the part God called him to play in God's Story about 600 years before Jesus was born. Ezekiel serves as an example of an humble servant of God who warned people of a coming storm, but they continued to play outside until it was too late.

The Memory Verse for this chapter is Ezekiel 33:9. God wants us to tell others of His love and to warn them of the consequences of their sins. Our part is to speak God's truth to others whether they accept it or not.

Our question to consider this week is: How do you respond to people who are in danger because of sin? Some people are naturally more straightforward than others. Personality tendencies, however, cannot offer an excuse for refusing to help a drowning friend. Observe God's call to Ezekiel for answers to this question.

# 43.1 A Prophet Among People

I love stories about a teacher or coach sent into a tough situation who through patience and tough love reaches the students' hearts and causes them to change for the better. From Sydney Poitier's role in *To Sir, with Love* (1967) to Matthew McConaughey's part in *We Are Marshall* (2006), the storytellers featured a lone messenger who entered a chaotic situation and was able to lead others to a better way of life. Patient persistence won over rebellious hearts or fear of the future.

What are some of your favorite films that tell a similar story? Who are the actors or actresses and the characters they played? What scene did you find the most powerful?

_____

_____

Read Ezekiel 2:3–4. Highlight the name God called Ezekiel. Underline the words that described the Israelites; for example, "rebellious," "rebelled," "revolt," and others.

"Son of man" is God's favorite name for Ezekiel, which He uses in His-story more than any other in the Old Testament. The only other prophet called by this name is Daniel (Dan. 8:17). The phrase was also Jesus' favorite term for Himself. For example, He equated Himself with the "Son of Man" when He asked His disciples who did people say that He was (Matt. 16:13–16).

God's assignment to Ezekiel was a tough one. God told him to warn Jerusalem before its fall in 587 B.C. and then to speak to them while they were in exile. Yahweh sent the "son of man" to a people who were "obstinate" (literally, "stiff of face") and "stubborn" (literally, "hard of heart"). The Israelites were not always receptive to the message of God. But they were exactly to whom God sent His messenger with a warning that hopefully would turn their hearts back to Him.

Read Ezekiel 2:5. Underline the last phrase of the verse. Whether the people listened or not they would at least know "a prophet has been among them."

God gave His chosen people one more chance to change their ways before their destruction, but if they did not, they could not say, "You didn't warn us." God would point to Ezekiel as evidence of His persistent efforts to draw them back to Him.

Have you ever had to go to an "obstinate and stubborn" friend or loved one to warn them if they continued in their lifestyle they would come to ruin? How long did it take you to tell them that message? What finally caused you to speak the hard truth to them? Write some of your experience in the space below. Take time to pray for that person as you remember that time with them.

_____

_____

_____

_____

## 43.2 The Hindrance of Comfort

Human nature tends to seek comfort over pain and ease over struggle. Those tendencies have brought us innovations that make our lives more comfortable and easy.

However, those same values can make us stay in or even cling to what we have found comfortable, and we refuse to change in order to grow. For example, my couch in my centrally heated home feels more comfortable than a 10-mile training run on a cloudy, 40-degree day, but unless I get up and run, I will never reach my goal of finishing the next marathon.

The truth that God loves me and accepts me for who I am is more comfortable than His command to go and make disciples of those who do not know Him. So I would rather go to some place in the church building than to go to my neighbor next door who is angry with me because my friends park in front of his house when they come over for small group.

What physical or spiritual comforts do you have that can also serve as a hindrance to your continued growth as a person and/or follower of Christ? List them in the space below and explain both the positive and negative impact they have on your life.

_____

_____

Read Ezekiel 2:6–7. Underline the phrase "do not be afraid" in the verses. What absolute command did God give Ezekiel no matter the people's response?

Three times in one verse God told Ezekiel to not be afraid of the people. He must not fear what they said, even if he felt he lived "among scorpions" (v. 6). People's looks may seem like "briers and thorns," and their words like scorpion stings, but he must continue on with the message God would give him.

God does not always give easy assignments, but He never sends one of His own without a promise of His presence. For example, God told Abram and Joshua to not be afraid of the assignments He gave them (Gen. 15:1; Josh. 8:1). Jesus also told His disciples to not fear those who would oppose them for that was the nature of the work He sent them to do (Matt. 10:26–28). God's message of obedience sounds disruptive to those who hear it for most people have built a life around their values and priorities, not God's. To speak a message like that is to invite resistance, especially if the person or people act "rebellious."

**Yahweh—Divine Encounters** in the Old Testament

God told Ezekiel to tell the people what God told him to tell them "whether they listen or fail to listen" (v. 7). His job simply involved delivering the message, not convincing them to listen. The same message holds true for you and me in our witness to others. Our job involves telling people about Jesus whether they listen or not.

Who do you need to tell about God's message for them today? Pray for them and for God to give you the courage to speak to them.

## 43.3 Consuming God's Word

I can eat most anything. The Korean dish kimchi is about the only Asian food I do not like. I will go for sushi any day, and I will try most any local delicacy—although I have not traveled to the continent of Africa yet. I hear some of the native foods in the villages take the cake. Most people eat out of necessity. Others love food for its taste, and they love to cook and eat combinations of flavors they can create. I have a friend who loves to cook and even has taken chef classes. I am fascinated by the many ways he can prepare the most common food like fish or vegetables.

What are your favorite foods? Do you cook or prefer to have someone else prepare your food for you?

_____

Read Ezekiel 2:8–10. Underline God's warning and instructions to the prophet in verse 8. Circle what God gave Ezekiel to eat in verse 9, and underline what was written on the scroll God gave him to eat in verse 10.

God warned Ezekiel to not act rebellious like the people. In order to show his obedience, God told Ezekiel to "eat" what He would give to him. The line between a literal and figurative interpretation is fuzzy here, but either way leaves you with the fact Ezekiel had to choose whether or not he would do what God called him to do. God told His prophet to eat a scroll in His hand. (See Revelation 5:1 for similar instructions to the Apostle John.) Written on both sides of the parchment were "words of lament and mourning and woe" (v. 10). The dish was not a delightful one: both sides of the scroll comprised a message of sorrow, crying, and anguish.

Read Ezekiel 3:1–3. Underline God's repeated instructions to Ezekiel. How did the scroll taste to Ezekiel (v. 3)?

To eat the scroll meant to accept the message God gave the prophet to give to the people. He must eat and digest its meaning and "then go and speak to the house of Israel" (v. 1). Prayerful study and meditation on God's Word precedes our proclamation of it. We must know God's Word before we teach and instruct others in it. God wanted His message to be part of Ezekiel's life before he spoke to the people. When he finally took the scroll with its message of sorrow it tasted "as sweet as honey" in his mouth (v. 3; see also Psalm 19:10 and 119:103 for similar descriptions of God's words.)

How do you interpret God's instructions for Ezekiel to eat the scroll? What was the significance of the act of eating for the prophet? How would you apply this passage to understanding God's Word?

_____

## 43.4 Be a Watchman

Every outpost has a sentry. This person is responsible for sounding an alarm or reporting anything that may threaten the outpost. In ancient Israel sentries or "watchmen" stood stationed on city walls, watchtowers, or hilltops and had to alert others about hostile action in times of danger.

Read 2 Samuel 18:24–28 for the example of a watchman when David reigned as king of the united kingdom of Israel. Describe the watchman's actions in that event. Write your own description of the role of a watchman in the space below. Have you ever served as a sentry or known someone who stood post for an army?

_____

_____

Read Ezekiel 33:7–9. Circle what God said He had made Ezekiel in verse 7. Underline the word "accountable" in verse 8. Consider the prophet's responsibilities. What would God hold him responsible for? How would he know if he did his job?

Babylon had destroyed and deported the people of Judah by this time in the story. Ezekiel and his countrymen were in exile in Babylon (Ezek. 33:21). But God used a metaphor from the days when the walls stood around Jerusalem and watchmen stood on those walls to show what Ezekiel would do. He would warn the people about the dangers of not following God's words. The condition of his responsibility was that he tell the message. The responsibility for action rested on the part of the people.

Ezekiel stood accountable to warn. If he did not warn the people and they died as a result of their sin, he would be held accountable for their death. On the other hand, if he did his job as a watchman and warned of the coming danger, and the people died because of their own disobedience, Ezekiel would have "saved" himself from destruction. Verse 9 is our Memory Verse for this chapter. How can you apply it to your life of witnessing to others?

God holds us accountable to warn others what sin and disobedience can do to their lives. We should not to act as a moral police and ticket their actions or penalize them for their miss-takes. We warn with the motive of a watchman who sees coming danger and gives others an opportunity to change in order to avoid what the danger may bring.

Read 1 Peter 3:15. How does this verse tell us to prepare to share with others the hope that we have? How is this different or the same as God's instructions to Ezekiel?

_____

_____

## 43.5 Caring Enough to Confront

Our question to consider this week was: How do you respond to people who are in danger because of sin? Some of us confront people more easily than others. I tend to naturally lean on the side of non-confrontation, but like Ezekiel, I do it when I sense God leading me to act with boldness or if I truly believe someone's behavior is endangering them. On a scale of one to 10 (with one as the least confrontational and 10 as the most) how would you rate your natural tendency to confront others about their sin? Write the number here: _____

Who do you know that may be in danger because of his or her actions? List some reasons why you should talk to that person even if it means risking your relationship with him or her. List reasons you have accumulated that keep you from confronting him or her. Pause to ask God for the boldness to caution that person about the danger he or she may face if his or her actions do not change.

_____

_____

Read Ezekiel 33:10–12. Highlight the names in the verses. Underline the word "turn" in the verses. Contrast God's message to the "righteous" and the "wicked." What is the bottom-line action God desired from both? What did God say about "former righteousness" in verse 12?

_____

_____

God does not take pleasure in the death of the wicked but desires all turn from their own ways and live! The concept of the word "turn" means the same as repent. God's bottom-line act for both the wicked and the righteous is that they turn to Him and make Him their God alone. Disobedience cancels any "former righteousness" the people of Israel may have done, and only doing God's words that He speaks now will lead to salvation.

Summarize what these verses teach you first about God and secondly about your relationship with Him. Write your confession in the space below. Pray that God will give you the courage to speak to both the "wicked" and the "righteous" and that you will obey God's words to you.

_____

_____

_____

**For further study:**
- **Ezekiel 2:1–3:15**
- **Ezekiel 33:1–20**

## 44—Refusing to Compromise (Prophet Daniel, Part 1 of 3)

You may have heard the story of "Daniel in the Lions' Den" growing up. It is one of the most famous stories in God's Story because it teaches a lesson of no compromise in the face certain death. It is more than a story of courage, however, it presents the truth about absolute trust in God and one man's refusal to change that trust no matter the challenges.

This episode of Daniel's story takes place in the ancient city of Babylon, which was ruled by the Medo-Persians at the time about 539–537 B.C. Daniel, whose name means "God is my judge," had served his foreign kings well. The king of the Medes and Persians, Darius, planned to make him head over his officials. At the same time, Daniel's rivals plotted to remove him from power. Daniel refused to compromise his dedication to Yahweh although he knew the consequence meant death by hungry lions.

The Memory Verse for this chapter is Daniel 6:10. Daniel continued his daily habit of prayer even after the death penalty was put in place for those who worshiped any god other than the king. To know this verse means that you have an example of uncompromising faith in your heart.

Our question to consider this week is: How important is it to live a life of integrity? The adage goes something like, "I can't hear what you say because your actions speak so loudly." Observe Daniel's consistent lifestyle and witness, and then let's talk at the end of the chapter.

## 44.1 A Person of Character

Integrity in the workplace matters. Ask any manager or vice president and he or she will tell you the importance of integrity in employees whom he or she can trust with company assets. The word integrity comes from the same Latin word for integer. It means, "to be complete or undivided" like an integer (a number that is not a fraction). Integrity means consistency in what one does when observed by others and when alone. Give me someone with integrity, and I will choose him or her over the most talented person whose actions I question when I am not around.

Write the name of a person you would describe as someone with integrity here: _____
What qualities does that person exhibit that makes you trust him or her? Is that person's faith a reason for his or her undivided lifestyle?

Read Daniel 6:1–3. Highlight the name of the king and "Daniel" in these verses. Underline the words "satraps" and "administrators." What did the king plan to do with Daniel? (v. 3)

Darius, the Mede, followed Belshazzar, son of Nebuchadnezzar, as king of Babylon (Dan. 5:30–31). Nebuchadnezzar was the king who invaded and over- threw Judah and its capital, Jerusalem. Daniel had been among those deported to Babylon. In exile he found favor with the king. Through God's protection and empower- ment Daniel rose in the ranks of the foreign government. Darius wanted to place Daniel over all of his officials because of his "exceptional qualities" in order to ensure the king lost no revenue from taxes (v. 3).

Read Daniel 6:4–5. Where did Daniel's rival satraps first look to discredit him? Circle the words that described Daniel's character in verse 4. Underline the officials' conclusion in verse 5.

Political rivalry has existed since people formed themselves in groups. Human nature drives those in power to be the more powerful. The Babylonian officials did not want the Israelite, Daniel, as their boss, so they sought ways to bring charges against him in order to remove him from his position. They looked first in how he did his job (v. 4), but found nothing "because he was trustworthy and neither corrupt nor negligent." They realized they could only get him charged and convicted if it had "something to do with the law of his God" (v. 5).

What reputation do you have at work or among your peers? If someone wanted to remove you from your position, could they do so through your behavior at work? Would a challenge to your lifestyle based on your faith make a vulnerable place to start? Pray for God to reveal the weak areas of your life and for His protection. Pray also for integrity in your faith and habits.

## 44.2 Vocational Dilemmas

I sat with a church member once who faced a dilemma. His job as a salesman involved getting people to use his company's trucks to haul their materials. The competi- tion for business was tough, and those with the materials more or less set the rules of engagement for the trucking companies. Taking clients to "gentlemen's clubs"—which is a misnomer because no true gentleman would go within 100 yards of such a place—had become an acceptable place to do business. The situation had gotten so bad for this man that he had to choose between entertaining clients at the clubs or losing their business, which meant ultimately losing his job. We talked and prayed a long time, and he eventually changed jobs—to one where entertaining clients at professional sporting events was the accepted place of doing business.

What practices in your business or community are acceptable but run counter to your core values and beliefs? Have you ever said no to those practices by changing jobs or moving? In what areas have you felt justified to compromise in order to gain a hearing with your peers or to serve them in the name of Jesus?

_____

_____

Read Daniel 6:6–9. Highlight the proper names in the verses and underline the titles listed in the verses. Circle the word "decree" in the verses and underline the content of the edict. Use a Bible dictionary or handbook to discover the historical background behind the written laws of the "Medes and the Persians."

If you cannot bring down a rival by his or her actions, then appeal to the boss' ego to create a rule that you know your rival cannot keep. Those who wanted Daniel out of office knew of his deep devotion to the God of Israel. From his first days in captivity to the present he had always lived by the ways of his God; for example, in his choice of foods at the king's table (Dan. 1:8). "The administrators and the satraps" went as a group to the king and suggested he write an irrevocable decree that everyone must pray only to the king for 30 days. This would ensure political and religious loyalty to the new king and would allow him to weed out any who acted disloyal. It made sense politically, and the king signed it into law.

Have you ever been the object of a scheme by your peers or boss to remove you from your job? How did you feel? What did you do? Have you ever joined in a plot to remove a rival from his or her position? What motives did you have for doing so? Did your plan work?

_____

_____

Take time to allow the Spirit of God to examine your heart when put in either situation. Pray for integrity no matter the temptation to compromise your trust in Him.

## 44.3 Spiritual Strength Training

Spiritual disciplines are to our souls what physical exercises are to our bodies. Both keep you healthy and make it possible to experience that part of your life more fully than if you lived a sedentary lifestyle. Trust in the middle of trials, for example, produces perseverance, character, and a hope that will not fail (Rom. 5:3–4) just like lifting weights produces muscle endurance and strength when you need it.

Many of us resist spiritual exercises just like we do physical ones. We make excuses about not having enough time or feeling too tired to add those things to our cluttered schedules. But as we will observe, those daily practices produce the courage and consistency that when tested sustain our trust in God.

What are some of your daily habits of spiritual or physical exercises? Completing this study of the Old Testament is one. What differences do these daily exercises make in your life? What excuses do you give for not having them in your life?

_____

_____

_____

Read Daniel 6:10, the Memory Verse for this chapter. Underline the second sentence in the verse. What does this verse teach you about Daniel's habit of prayer?

Prayer was a spiritual discipline for Daniel. He had no reason to change his ways although the current laws had changed. He knelt before the same window that faced Jerusalem three times a day, and he did it "just as he had done before" even after the king wrote the law. Spiritual habits order our lives toward God. Changing laws and cultural climate changes do not alter those practices that help us encounter the Living God.

Read Daniel 6:11–15. Write a synopsis of what happened in these verses. Describe the scene like you would one from a television drama where spies seek to bring down a rival and force a lead to stand by his word although he knows it will result in his trusted aide's demise.

Describe the frantic efforts of the leader to get around the law to save the accused.

_____

_____

_____

Read Daniel 6:16. Underline the king's last words to Daniel as they threw him into the pit of lions. Use a Bible commentary or handbook for a description of how the Persians used lion pits for executions.

Darius respected Daniel and learned through that respect to show some honor to Daniel's God. So as the king's favored servant entered the pit filled with hungry lions, he cried out his own confession to trust in Yahweh. He asked that the God whom Daniel served save him (v. 16).

Does your faith at work or school cause others to consider trusting Jesus? Write the names of those who "watch" you either out of curiosity or because of their position in your life. Ask God to allow your witness through your lifestyle to help your friend or coworker trust Jesus.

_____

_____

_____

## 44.4 Making It Through

One of the hardest things I do as a pastor is wait to learn whether or not a person makes it through the night. As I write this sentence two families connected to our church will wait through the night for a loved one to wake in the morning to battle cancer or Multiple Sclerosis another day, or they will grieve because their loved one went home to be with the Lord. The only thing that helps me through those times with others is the hope we share in the Resurrection of Jesus and the promise of eternal life to those who trust Him. I always wonder how those who do not share that trust make it through those same nights.

Have you ever waited through the night with a loved one near death? What or who helped you have hope regardless of the outcome? Write your experience in the space below.

_____

Read Daniel 6:17–18. Underline the actions the king took to ensure his orders were carried out. Underline the last sentence of verse 18.

Daniel was not King Darius' loved one, but he was a respected official whom the king knew had been treated unjustly. Although he followed protocol to seal the death pit so no one could accuse him of not being true to his word, he could not sleep nor did he desire any entertainment that night. His actions betrayed his conscience about what was right and just.

Read Daniel 6:19–22. Highlight Daniel's name and the title the king called him in verse 20. What was Daniel's confession to the king, and why do you think he mentioned to the king he had done no wrong?

_____

First thing in the morning, the king ran to the execution chamber and called out to Daniel. The king of the Medes cried out to hear Daniel, "servant of the living God" whom Daniel had served his whole life. Daniel confessed his survival was because of God alone. God had found him "innocent in his sight" (v. 22). He also wanted the king to know he still remained loyal to him although the king followed the law and ordered his execution (v. 21).

God rescued Daniel so the king would see the God of Israel as a powerful and just God. Daniel's unwavering trust in God combined with God's intervention into His creation acted as a strong witness to the king who knew that others had manipulated him into executing one of his best officials.

Replay the events of that night and morning in your mind again. Place yourself in the king's shoes and then in the bare feet of Daniel. Imagine the helplessness of one and the faith of the other. Invite God's Spirit into the scene with you. Thank Him for His power to rescue and His witness to those far from Him.

## 44.5 Exiting the Lion's Den

In the world of high stake politics kings must prove their strength. King Darius made a good king from a purely pragmatic perspective because he did not bend from the written law he made and he followed through with the execution of his favored official. He also showed his power when he did not allow the treachery that sentenced Daniel to death to go unpunished.

Who do you respect as a strong leader in a highly political environment? What characteristics of that person impress you? How do their actions cause others to respect them? Darius showed strength one way. Daniel exhibited strength in another way. How would you compare the two? Write your answer here:

_____

_____

Read Daniel 6:23–24. Contrast the emotions in verses 23–24. Underline the evidence of God's complete deliverance of Daniel (v. 23) and the cruelty of the punishment to those who maneuvered his sentence (v. 24). When they uncovered the pit and lifted Daniel out of it he had no evidence of wounds from the lions.

How could that happen? Our storyteller answers for us "because he had trusted in his God" (v. 23). The king felt overjoyed at Daniel's health, but he quickly turned to deal with those who had bamboozled him. They and their families suffered the same sentence as Daniel, but this time, the lions had their fill. We can only imagine the horror and brutality of such a death. This is one way the ancient Persians gained their reputation among the nations.

Our question to consider this week was: How important is it to live a life of integrity? Now that you have observed Daniel's experience, record your answer here:

_____

_____

_____

You can say Daniel's no-compromise trust in God got him into trouble with his peers, but God's deliverance made an even greater witness than that of God's servant. Faith risks immediate consequences for a trust in God to accomplish His purposes no matter the outcome. Trusting God is a greater value than surviving the day for those who know their lives only make sense when they live out their parts in God's Story. Compromise is not an option for those who know who they are and the part they play in His-story.

**For further study:**

• **1 Corinthians 15:58; 16:13**
• **Hebrews 11:33–34**

## 45—Refusing to Compromise (Shadrach, Meshach, and Abednego, Part 2 of 3)

The Babylonians, like other conquering nations, carried their captives back to their country and integrated the brightest and best into their culture. When Nebuchadnezzar conquered Jerusalem in 587 B.C. he did the same. Among those carried to Babylon were four young men.

We studied Daniel in the last chapter. This story focuses on the other three. Ironically, we know them by their Babylonian given names not their Jewish names. The willingness of Shadrach, Meshach, and Abednego to be martyred for their refusal to bow before the king's image inspires us to stand firm against any challenge to our devotion to God.

Christ-followers in many countries today face the same death sentence for their faith in Christ alone. This episode in His-story is not a dusty bedtime story. It tells how God's people live in societies where they make up the minority and their way of life runs counter to the prevailing culture in which they live.

The Memory Verses for this chapter are Daniel 3:17–18. These verses mark the confession of the three Israelites before the king. Their acceptance of death if Yahweh does not rescue them shows the depth of their devotion to God.

Our question to consider this week is: Is it ever OK to give glory to someone other than God? This question is harder to answer when the consequence for not giving honor to someone other than God results in the death penalty. However, the three Israelites and many Christians today face that consequence and refuse to compromise. What would you do? Let's talk at the end of this chapter.

## 45.1 A Giant Idol

I remember standing with my family on the observation level of the World Trade Center in the summer of 2000. We went there on vacation before my oldest daughter's senior year in high school. We peered over the enclosed deck to look down 110 stories to Battery Park and the southern tip of Manhattan Island. Little did we know it would no longer stand the next year. Those twin towers and Pentagon buildings the terrorists attacked on September 11, 2001, represented the United States power in commerce and military might. That is most likely why the terrorists targeted them that day. Structures stand as symbols of cultural values and ways of life.

What are some structures or buildings in which you have stood? Why did you choose to seek them out? What did they mean to the country where they were built? Who built them and what reputation did the builder have? Write some of your impressions here:

_____

_____

_____

Read Daniel 3:1–3. Highlight the proper names in the verses and underline the titles of the officials in verse 3. Circle the size of the image built by the king in verse 1.

Nebuchadnezzar ruled in Babylon from 605–562 B.C. and was the foreign king who defeated Judah. He constructed a 90-by-nine foot image on a plain outside the city of Babylon in Dura. Giant statues were common

in the ancient world; for example, the Great Sphinx in Egypt stood at this time (built about 2500 B.C.). As king of the most powerful country in the world at the time he had access to enough materials and craftsmen to complete such a colossal image.

The king gathered the country's officials, seven ranks plus "all the other provincial officials," for the dedication of the image. The king "summoned" (v. 2), the officials "assembled" (v. 3a), and together they "stood before" the object (v. 3b). Our storyteller does not say it was an image of the king. It may have resembled the figure he saw in his dream that Daniel interpreted. (See Daniel 2 for that story.) Whatever it looked like, this "image of gold" (v. 1) must have sparkled in the bright sunlight of the Middle East.

The culture in which you live erects objects that people are expected to honor. Civilized cultures insist that people honor churches, synagogues, and mosques. Courthouses, government buildings, and schools are places of respect in American culture.

What do these buildings represent? What values lie behind the respect we offer them? Do any of those values present a challenge to your faith in God? Process some of your thoughts here:

_____

_____

_____

## 45.2 Experiencing the Rage of Others

Nebuchadnezzar used worship of the golden image as a way to unite the different religions and ethnic groups in his kingdom. Politically, it made a savvy move, and bowing to one more image probably made little difference to any pluralist or politician. "The end justifies the means," as they say. This strategy, however, does not sit well with those who have devoted themselves to God's plan for their lives. Survivalists would say, "Do whatever it takes to stay alive." Faithful followers of Christ agree with Paul in saying, "To live is Christ and to die is gain" (Phil. 1:21).

On a continuum from "Do whatever it takes to survive" to "No compromise," where would you place yourself? Explain your answer in the space below.

_____

_____

Read Daniel 3:4–7. Circle the quotation marks that indicate the king's order and underline the word "Therefore" at the beginning of verse 7 and how the people responded when the music sounded.

The king ordered through his "herald" that at the sound of stringed and wind instruments the people must fall down and worship the image. When that happened the first time after the order, "all the peoples, nations and men of every language" worshiped the image. The king had gained the unity he desired through the worship of the image he created.

Read Daniel 3:8–12. Highlight the names for the two ethnic groups mentioned in verse 8. Summarize the complaint in the space below. Underline the names of the three Jews in verse 12.

_____

_____

A group of "astrologers" or "Chaldeans" (NASB) complained that high-ranked Jewish officials in the king's court refused to honor his decree to worship the image he erected. Those who wanted to impress the king with their loyalty by exposing traitors named Daniel's three friends as the disloyal ones. Read Daniel 1:1–20 for the details of their Jewish and Babylonian names, their association with Daniel, and how they entered the king's service.

Read Daniel 3:13–15. Circle the king's emotional response to the news of treachery at the beginning of verse 13, and underline what the king promised to do

if they did not comply with his orders (v. 15). What challenge did the king present to them?

_____

_____

The king responded in rage. He could not allow anyone to go against his law for fear of showing weakness and losing his grip on the people. He summoned the three Jewish officials, and he restated to them the law and the consequences of breaking it (v. 15).

Has an authority figure ever summoned you to explain behavior that did not sync with those expected by the leader but ran contrary to your own beliefs? If so, what was the experience like, how did you feel, and what did you do about it? If not, put yourself in the three young men's shoes as they stood before the king. Ask God to reveal what you would really do if put in that situation.

## 45.3 Unswerving Commitment

Moses refused to change his commitment to God's call on his life although Pharaoh refused to let God's people go. Jeremiah did not compromise his message from God to Israel when the religious leaders put him in stocks (Jer. 20:1–2). Esther risked her life for her people when she entered the king's chamber without permission (Esth. 5:1–8). The religious leaders imprisoned and beat James and John because they witnessed about Jesus (Acts 4:18–20). Stephen, the first martyr of the church, suffered death because he boldly held to the certainty of Jesus' Resurrection (Acts 7:54–60). All of these give lesser examples of Jesus, who suffered death at the hands of both

the religious and political leaders of His day because He would not waver from the Father's will for His life (Mark 15). Uncompromising people are the heroes of His-story.

Which of these "heroes" impress you the most? Are there other figures in His-story who inspire you because of their no-compromise trust in God? Write what their examples mean for your faith in the space below.

_____

_____

Read Daniel 3:16–18. Outline Shadrach, Meshach, and Abednego's reply to the king in the space below. Underline the phrase "But even if he does not" in verse 17. See Exodus 20:1–5 for the core belief behind their refusal to bow to the king's image. Daniel 3:17–18 are our Memory Verses for this chapter.

_____

_____

The three Jewish men belonged to the covenant people of Yahweh. They accepted not only the goodness of God but devoted themselves to the ways of God. Yahweh had commanded His people not to worship any deity but Him. The Jewish people were in Babylon because they did not keep that commandment. On the other hand, a "remnant" or core group had remained faithful to God and refused to compromise that way of life for any reason. These three lived among that group. (Remember Isaiah's prophecy to King Hezekiah in 2 Kings 19:30–31?) Their message to the king was:

1. We do not need to defend ourselves to you in this matter. You know who we are and the God we serve.
2. We trust our God is able to deliver us from the furnace if you put us there.
3. Even if God does not rescue us, we will not bow down to that image or serve any of your so-called gods. We put our trust in Yahweh alone.

Along with their confession of trust in Yahweh, the three men did not resist the consequences of the law. They did not trust God in order to escape danger and death. They trusted Him in spite of them.

Make a list of things that challenge your absolute trust in God no matter what the consequences. Offer that list to God as a confession of your weakness of faith. Invite God to strengthen you if you ever have to face those situations. If you know of some group or person who faces persecution because of his or her faith, pray for that group or person today.

## 45.4 Feeling the Heat

Rulers with absolute power think they can do whatever they like to keep their power. Dictators throughout history have made examples of those who defied them or refused to carry out their orders. We have seen too many images on news channels of the cruelty humans can devise in order to keep their perceived power. The king of Babylon became enraged at the Jewish men's refusal to follow his orders. His response is possible of a man who has no boundaries in his life but his ego.

Read Daniel 3:19–23. Underline the descriptive words

for the king's emotional response, the heat of the fire, the soldiers, and how the three were dressed as evidence of the extremes in the situation. Circle the words tied in the verses to show the certain fate of the men.

Many ancient cultures practiced capital punishment, or the death penalty, to execute those who violated state laws. We have record of burning as a means of execution in Babylon both in this passage and in Jeremiah 29:22. The "blazing furnace" described here most likely referred to a Mesopotamian smelting furnace. They took the shape of an old-fashioned glass milk bottle, and could reach temperatures as high as 1800 degrees Fahrenheit in order to refine the ore placed in them. The king stoked the fire to its hottest and ended up sacrificing some of his strongest soldiers to get the three men into the fire.

Read Daniel 3:24–25. Underline what the king saw in the furnace. Circle the word "like" to denote what the fourth man looked like. Check various translations for how the king described the fourth person.

Nebuchadnezzar's rage turned to amazement when he saw a fourth person standing in the fire with Shadrach, Meshach, and Abednego. The NIV and NASB translated that the person looked like "a son of the gods," a confession consistent with the king's pagan background. The KJV and NKJV interpreted the phrase to mean that he looked like "the Son of God," causing some to believe this is a pre-incarnation appearance of Jesus. Both translations are possible and reliable. The bottom line is that the king threw three guys in the furnace and four ended up walking around inside. God sent a helper to encourage His servants in their most desperate time of need. Jesus promised another "Comforter" or "Counselor" to

His followers (John 14:15–21). He did not promise to take us out of the furnace but to walk with us through it. Allow the furnace to serve as a metaphor for persecution or hard circumstances in your life. Let the "fourth person" be God's presence with you in the middle of it all. Take time to meditate on what that picture means to you. Write a prayer of thanksgiving to God for the promised Holy Spirit through His Son, Jesus.

## 45.5 The Impact of Uncompromised Living

Saul of Tarsus was on his way to Damascus when he encountered Jesus. He told of his experience before a crowd in Jerusalem (Acts 22:1–20). He witnessed that Jesus told him He was the one whom Saul had persecuted and that Saul must go into the city where someone would tell him what Jesus wanted him to know. After he lay blind in bed for three days, a follower of Jesus came to his house and told him God had chosen him to tell the non-Jewish people about Jesus. That event was the defining moment with God for the Jewish Pharisee, and it redirected his life in every way.

What event or experience convinced you God exists or that He truly got involved in your life? What changes did you make in your life and in the lives of others after your encounter with God?

_____

_____

_____

Read Daniel 3:26–27. Highlight what the king called

Shadrach, Meshach, and Abednego when he told them to come out of the furnace. Underline the evidence our storyteller recorded that proves the three had not gotten burned in any way.

The Babylonian king called the three in the fire "servants of the Most High God" (v. 26). (See Genesis 14:19, Numbers 24:16, and Isaiah 14:14 for other examples of pagan leaders calling the God of Israel this name.) The fire had not touched them, and they did not even smell as they had went near a fire.

Read Daniel 3:28–30. What did the king confess about their God? Underline the decree he made in response to his confession and underline the word "promoted" in verse 30.

Whether or not the king's confession was authentic—the evidence made clear that the God of the Jews protected His servants and that the king had to appear to take the side of the winning deity—is not the point of the story. Our storyteller wanted his readers to know that even the one who had tried to execute Yahweh's servants could not deny the power of God with those who trusted Him. The king even "promoted" or "caused [them] to prosper" (NASB) to show his support of their God.

You have observed the uncompromising witness of Shadrach, Meshach, and Abednego. How will you answer our question to consider this week: Is it ever OK to give glory to someone other than God?

**For further study:**

• **Exodus 20:1–5**

• **Acts 4:1–22; 22:1–20**

Daniel refused to compromise his relationship with God when offered a fast track to upper management (Dan. 1:8–10) or when his peers tried to remove him from office by treachery (Dan. 6). He continually gave God credit for his gift to interpret dreams (Dan. 2:27–28), and God used his gifts to guide the affairs of Babylon (Dan. 5). So how do you think Daniel acted when God was supposed to accomplish His promise? Would he insist God "pay up" for his faithfulness? Would he remind God of what God said and play his "Get out of Jail" card? His response may surprise you. When you read the script of Daniel's words to God in this episode of His-story, you will see Daniel had a gentle and repentant heart in submission to God's purposes no matter what he thought should happen.

The Memory Verse for this chapter is Daniel 9:19. Repentance is not about saving our skin but about honoring God as the One who is just to judge. Our desire to stand right with God is for His honor, not to save us from trouble.

Our question to consider this week is: What is the proper response toward the consequences of sin? Write your initial responses to the question in your journal and then observe Daniel's prayer for an additional perspective.

## 46.1 Prayer, Daniel-Style

Study of the Scriptures and prayer are time-honored ways those who trust they play a role in God's Story can know their parts and live within the plot of God's storyline. You have often heard that the basic practices of prayer and Bible study lay the foundation for a joy-filled relationship with God. These disciplines are like learning the alphabet in order to read a novel or practicing scales in order to play a symphony. Study is growing familiar with the novel, and prayer is having a conversation with the Author. These basic habits in faith are essential to knowing the One in whom you have placed your trust. No exotic or trendy routine can replace these two primary ways of knowing and trusting God.

What part do prayer and Bible study play in your relationship with God? Are they habits in your life? Do you long for something "more" than those ways of knowing God? Write your confession of what these spiritual practices mean to your relationship with God.

_____

_____

Read Daniel 9:1–2. Highlight the names in the verses. Underline the word "Scriptures" and circle the words "seventy years."

Darius the Mede, son of Ahasuerus (Xerxes), ruled Babylon beginning in 536 B.C. By this time Daniel was over 80 years old. One day while he studied the "Scriptures" or "books" (ESV) of Jeremiah, he remembered that the prophet said Judah's deportation would last 70

years. That much time had passed since the prophecy, and Daniel wanted to know from God when the Israelites would get to go home. Daniel trusted God's words through Jeremiah and trusted the time would soon come to return to Jerusalem.

Read Daniel 9:3. Underline the ways in which the prophet "turned to the LORD God."

To know Jeremiah had the right timing, Daniel turned to the LORD God. Daniel prayed intensely "in prayer and petition, in fasting, and in sackcloth and ashes" (v. 3). Prayer and petition represented how Daniel asked Yahweh about the future. "Fasting" indicated an extended time of prayer in which he denied himself food. (See Hezekiah's example in 2 Kings 18:5–7 and Jesus' teaching on fasting in Matthew 6:16–18.) "Sackcloth and ashes" expressed humble mourning (Esth. 4:1–3; Ps. 35:13–14).

Daniel gives us a model of practices that creates an atmosphere of prayers. Read the New Testament examples below of the practices of prayer and then write out ways you can incorporate them into your prayer life.

Acts 13:2–3 _____

_____

Philippians 4:6 _____

_____

1 Peter 5:6 _____

_____

## 46.2 The Power of Confession

"I was wrong" are three of the hardest words I ever say. I would prefer to explain why I did what I did or offer how circumstances or other people were the real cause of the wrong I did. To take responsibility for a miss-take marks the beginning of an authentic relationship with another person or a group of people. Until we confess without excuses that the offense was our fault we can never know the full extent of another's forgiveness or love for us. The same holds true in our relationship with God. We can know only how much God truly loves and forgives us when we are honest about how we have wronged Him. In the vulnerable position of confession we experience the safety of God's love.

How hard do you find it to admit you were wrong? To whom do you find it hardest to admit your mistakes? Do you make confession a regular part of your conversation with God? Record your thoughts here:

_____

_____

Read Daniel 9:4. Highlight the names for God and underline the characteristics of God.

Daniel addressed God with His covenant name, Yahweh, and acknowledged Him as "my God." Yahweh, the covenant name for God, appears eight times in this chapter (Dan. 9:2, 4, 8, 10, 13, twice in 14, and 20). Daniel addressed God as the One who made His covenant with Israel and who spoke the prophecy of 70 years through Jeremiah. Daniel praised God for being

"great and awesome," and he added that God kept His "covenant of love with all who love him and obey his commands" (v. 4). "Covenant love" is the term most often used when speaking of God's love for Israel. Chesed is a loyal love of God by which He faithfully keeps His covenant promises to his people.

Read Daniel 9:5–6. Underline the words that describe Daniel's confession for what the people did.

Daniel did not turn immediately to ask God for anything. He first confessed his people's sin and rebellion. They had neither done what God commanded them to do nor listened to those God sent to bring them back to Him. Jeremiah was one of God's "servants the prophets" who warned the people (v. 5). Daniel praised who God was and then he confessed who he was. God was "great and awesome" (v. 4); he and his people had "sinned and done wrong" (v. 5).

Daniel's praise and confession presents a pattern in which we can follow as we approach God with our needs and desires. Read the following passages to prompt your praise of God and confession of your sin. Write how each passage helps you follow this pattern of prayer.

Psalm 103 _____

_____

Psalm 51 _____

_____

## 46.3 Discipline Received

Punishment as part of discipline is not the fun factor in parenting. As a father I would rather do anything than punish my daughters. However, unless they experienced consequences to their behavior (both good and bad) they would not know my character nor would I help form theirs into a consistent or godly one. Trustworthy character behaves consistently in every situation. While it is impossible for you and me to act completely consistent with our character, the God of His-story always acts true to who He has revealed Himself to be.

In what ways do you try to mold your child's character? If you do not have children, did the discipline you received growing up stay consistent with a set of rules or the character of your parents? What has this study of His-story taught you about the character of God?

_____

_____

Read Daniel 9:7–14. Highlight the names of God and circle the words that describe His character.

Daniel confessed the character of God upon which His actions were justified. God is "righteous" (vv. 7, 14), "merciful and forgiving" (v. 9), and shows "favor" (v. 13). Based on God's righteous character, the "curses and sworn judgments written in the Law of Moses" were justified (v. 11). God's righteous character does not allow disobedience to go unpunished. God simply "fulfilled the words spoken against" Israel. (v. 12; see also Deuteronomy 28:15–68.)

Although God showed favor to those who seek forgiveness, Israel did not seek it out (v. 13). God acted consistently according to His Word. (See this also in Titus 1:2.)

Read the passage again and underline the words that tell how Daniel described Israel's spiritual condition.

Daniel continued to confess his people's sin before God. They were "covered with shame" since they had experienced the judgment of God for their actions (v. 7). He confessed they had "unfaithfullness" (v. 7), and they had "sinned" (v. 8), "rebelled" (v. 9), "not obeyed" (vv. 10, 14), "turned away" (v. 11), and "not sought the favor of the LORD" (v. 13). Their unfaithfulness led God to act consistently with His character. Daniel never complained about his situation but took responsibility for the actions of the people. He accepted God's response to their disobedience. We often forget that the circumstances in which we find ourselves may partly result from our own actions.

God remained true to His character and Word in both His warnings and judgment. Israel did not turn to Him and so did not experience His mercy and forgiveness. Conclude this moment with God by meditating on the character of God. Focus on who God is and His consistency to His Word rather than on the circumstances around you. Use Daniel's language to articulate your confession to God.

## 46.4 A Request for Mercy

One side of discipline is justice. The other side is love. When I disciplined my girls to mold their character by demonstrating justice, they learned that their actions have consequences. When I forgave them for what they had done and sometimes did not punish them, they learned that my love was greater than justice. They knew my love for them outweighed my desire for justice so they could count on fairness from me—but more than that, they could depend on my love.

Was justice and love balanced in the discipline you received growing up? How did that balance or imbalance affect your understanding of God's love? What have you learned of God's justice and love since you have begun this study of His-story? Write some of your impressions here:

_____

_____

_____

Read Daniel 9:15–16. Highlight the names for God and the places. Underline Daniel's request in verse 16.

Daniel recalled Israel's defining moment with God, the exodus. He recognized God's mighty act of rescue for his people and the name He made for Himself that "endures to this day" (v. 15). He asked that God turn His wrath away from Jerusalem, His "holy hill," so Israel would no longer be "an object of scorn to all those around" him (v. 16). Daniel called upon God's work instead of his goodness as the reason for God to act.

Read verses 17–19. Underline Daniel's requests to God. Underline the last sentence of verse 18 for the basis of his prayer.

Daniel asked that God "look with favor" (v. 17), which literally means, "make your face shine," on the ruined Temple in Jerusalem. (See Numbers 6:25 and Psalms 80:19 for a similar expression.) He petitioned God to "give ear," "hear," "open your eyes," and "see" (v. 18). His multiple pleas to God reflect the intensity of his requests. Daniel called upon God's mercy to act not because he was righteous. The people's sins caused God's righteousness to bring judgment and wrath. Only God's mercy offered hope. Daniel asked God to "listen" and "forgive" (v. 19).

God's character stays consistent across the old and new covenants. God is righteous and judges. God is also merciful and forgives those who love Him.

Read Titus 3:4–7 and Romans 3:23–24. Underline in each passage the basis for our right standing before God in Christ Jesus.

God forgives us not because of our good works but

because of His mercy and goodness. Our sin brings God's judgment, which grows out of His righteousness. God's mercy, not our efforts, allows us to have right standing with Him. End this moment with God by thanking Him for His mercy and love.

## 46.5 God Sends an Angel

Prayer is to our relationship with God what conversation is to a friendship or marriage. Without it both will soon end. We must talk and listen with God in order to have a relationship with Him and to know our part in God's Story while sharing our needs, our joys, and praises of Him. "God answers prayer" does not mean He answers every request any more than a loving parent gives a four-year-old everything he or she asks for. The truth about prayer revealed in God's words and actions toward His people is that God hears and responds to those who love Him and bring their hopes and hurts to him. Daniel had a special relationship with God, and God answered his prayers on behalf of his people.

Read Daniel 9:20–23. Highlight the name of the messenger sent by God to Daniel. Underline his message to Daniel.

God answered Daniel's prayer. Daniel tells us in his own words that as he was "speaking and praying, confessing my sin and the sin of my people Israel and making my request to the LORD my God," the angel "Gabriel, the man I had seen in the earlier vision" appeared (vv. 20–21). (See Daniel 8:15–16 for Gabriel's first visit to Daniel.) The messenger came "in swift flight" (v. 21) to Daniel because Yahweh saw Daniel as "highly esteemed" (v. 23). God honored Daniel for his faithful-

ness and He sent His closest messenger swiftly to answer His servant's prayer. Gabriel was a special angel to God. He would reveal God's purposes later in His-story related to

Jesus' coming.

Read Luke 1:19; 26–27. What role did Gabriel play in the story of Jesus' birth?

God answered his prayer by sending an angel directly to him. Gabriel gave Daniel a "message" and a "vision" (v. 23). Gabriel's message told about the coming eras of His-story and the promise of a Messiah and the restoration of Israel (Dan. 9:24–27). Daniel pleaded with God and God answered with a vision of His-story to come.

Our question to consider this week was: What is the proper response toward the consequences of sin? After observing Daniel's prayer to God for his people, how would you answer this question? Write your answer here:

_____

_____

_____

End this chapter by writing out your own prayer to God. Daniel has given you a model to follow. Use it if you like. Otherwise, like Daniel, open your heart to God and listen for His reply. He may not send Gabriel, but God will hear you and respond in love and mercy.

**For further study:**
- **Daniel 1:1–6**
- **Jeremiah 25:11–12; James 5:16**

# 47—Divine Appointments (Esther)

To trust His-story means to trust God as the Author of the Story. God alone guides the events and characters in His-Story for His purposes. This facet of God is known as the sovereignty of God. The mystery of this reality is that God allows us free choice while working to complete His ultimate purposes.

God allowed both King Xerxes to choose Esther as the queen of Persia and Haman, Xerxes' prime minister, to convince the king to make an edict to destroy all the Israelites. We see from our vantage point that God allowed both choices in order to put Esther in a unique place at a unique time to protect Israel while in exile. The queen boldly entered the king's court to intercede for her people, and they were saved. The Jewish girl who became queen to a foreign king truly was a divine appointment in God's Story.

The Memory Verse for this chapter is Esther 4:14. This verse serves as a confession of confidence that our lives at the present time in His-story in the present circumstances matter to completing God's Story. Mordecai's words to Esther are God's assuring words to you and me to pay attention to where God has placed us to accomplish His purposes.

Our question to consider for the week is: How can I be useful to God in times of difficulty? Write some of your first impressions in your journal and then observe the episode in Esther's life to add to your answers.

## 47.1 Being in the Minority

Legally and by experience, I am not a minority. However, I have served on a diversity advocacy committee for my city's school district. As we work to gain information related to diversity issues to recommend to the school board, I have learned much about the issues related to being a minority in our schools. One issue concerns the feeling that the rules favor the majority, and minority students find it difficult at times to maneuver through those rules to find equal opportunity with other students. While we wrestle with the facts and feelings around the different issues, I have grown more sensitive to the perceptions and needs of our minority students.

What status do you hold in your community? If you are a minority, what issues do you wrestle with? If you are in the majority of ethnic groups, how sensitive would you consider yourself toward the needs and feelings of minorities? Write your thoughts here:

_____

_____

_____

The Israelites in Persia were not only a minority ethnic group but also a captured people. Their customs, religion, and habits seemed foreign to those among whom they lived. Since a faithful Jew would not bow down to anyone or anything but Yahweh, when Mordecai refused to bow to the king's prime minister, Haman, the noble convinced the king to sign an edict that would eliminate "a certain people" who lived in his country by promising to pay a large sum of money into the king's treasury (Esth. 3:8–9). The king agreed and the date was set for the extinction of the Jews in Persia.

Read Esther 4:1–5. Highlight the name of the main characters in these verses. Underline the phrases that describe Mordecai and Esther's responses to the edict. Read Esther 1–3 for the background events that led to this situation.

We can only imagine the horror of realizing someone had set a date for our execution simply because of race. This has happened too many times in history for it to be novel, and Israel has experienced the pain throughout history. Mordecai's response was not unexpected. The habits of mourning—wearing sackcloth, fasting, weeping, and wailing—signified the deep pain of knowing their execution was set and that they could do nothing in their power to change it. Esther used her royal influence to try to help her cousin, but he refused her help. She then set an envoy, "Hathach, one of the king's eunuchs assigned to attend her," to find out why he felt so distressed (v. 5).

Have you ever been a minority population? Use your experiences to empathize with the fate and emotions of Mordecai and his people. Write some of your feelings in the space below. Also, do you think this situation may have added to their sense of "Where is God in all of this?" since they were deported to Persia?

_____

_____

_____

## 47.2 Friends in Right Places

You may have heard the adage, "He has friends in high places." It means a person knows people with influence who can use that influence to make things happen for the benefit of others. We often associate political or business positions with influence and see people in such positions as influential. For example, if I want a law created to protect my fellow cyclists from cars that pass too closely, I call someone in my state government who can begin the process of making laws related to that issue. If my hotel room does not satisfy my expectations and the person at the front desk will not help, I contact the hotel manager. You know the process. In His-story influential people who used their positional power to serve others have made a difference in the course of God's Story.

Who do you know of influence? This person does not need to be a Senator or CEO to have influence. Have you ever requested his or her help? How did he or she respond?

_____

Read Esther 4:6–8. Highlight the names in the verses and circle the words that establish the setting of the conversation. Underline the details of Mordecai's message to Hathach. Write Mordecai's request to Esther in your own words in the space below.

_____

_____

The queen's attendant sought Mordecai out in the "open square of the city" (v. 6) where he mourned the potential genocide of his people. When the royal servant inquired about his actions, Mordecai gave him the details of the law that the king had made in regard to the Jews. He even told Hathach the amount Haman offered to pay the king although the king refused it. He handed all of the evidence over to the eunuch and asked that the queen plead for mercy before the king (v. 8). Mordecai could only inform Esther. He left the response up to her.

Although God allowed Haman to bring about the edict just as He had allowed Babylon to defeat Judah, God had put in place the people who could use their God-given influence to allow the purposes of God to continue. A defining moment with God for some people is when they realize they stand in a position of influence for a higher purpose than to make money or widgets. That realization does not always come at once but through a series of events that God uses to reveal the bigger reason they are where they are.

How do you view your place in work, school, or the

**Yahweh – Divine Encounters** in the Old Testament

community? Who may see you as a person of influence although you may not see yourself that way yet? Are you a parent, teacher, Bible study leader, or manager in a corporation? Use your journal to record the names of those who may depend on your influence to help serve God's Story.

## 47.3 Fear or Faith

We all have good reasons for not helping others. Sometimes we excuse ourselves because our schedules seem too tight or the person's request does not seem worthy of our efforts. The hardest requests for me as a pastor are those who drop in the church office or call for assistance. Like seasoned police officers that see the bad side of people more than the good, pastors sometimes get calloused to the needs of others because they deal with them all the time. The motives of a person also play a role in a decision to use your influence to help that person or not. People also have legitimate reasons for not helping others. Danger and expense may offer real reasons for not fulfilling a request. And sometimes we are simply too lazy to get outside our comfort zone to help.

What excuses or reasons have you used for not helping someone? Pick an incident and explain the request and why you chose not to help.

_____

_____

_____

Read Esther 4:9–11. Write Esther's three-part response to Mordecai in your own words in the space below. Do you believe she had a good reason to resist his suggestion?

_____

_____

Esther sent word back to her cousin that the rules of the court did not allow anyone to enter the king's court uninvited. The king's bodyguards would execute a person on the spot for such a breach of protocol. The only exception to the rule was if the king extended his scepter to the person and spared his or her life. Thirty days had passed since the king had invited her to his inner court and going now would most surely result in her death.

Take a moment to evaluate Esther's response to Mordecai. Motive was not an issue. She trusted Mordecai and knew the gravity of the situation. Did she simply state the reality of her situation, or did she try to excuse herself from the danger of going to the king?

_____

_____

Esther did not jump at the chance to risk her life for her people. God's chosen most often do not. Remember Moses, Gideon, or Jeremiah's response to God's call to serve His purposes for His people. Those God chose to join the storyline of His-story are not automatic hero material. They were real people like you and me who would rather live the life they have rather than jeopardize it for others.

Spend some time reflecting on Esther's situation and her

response. What would you have done? How would you have answered Mordecai?

_____

_____

## 47.4 For Such a Time as This

People explain their success in different ways. Some take credit through hard work and ingenuity for why they are where they are. Some credit luck or "who you know is more important than what you know" as the reasons for their success. A biblical worldview—one in which God is the maker and mover of all things—gives those with influence a perspective. It allows them to confess they stand in their position by God's goodwill rather than their efforts alone. A healthy and biblical perspective on success in life includes the confession God has put us where we are ultimately for His purposes not our happiness.

How does your worldview explain your success or accomplishments? You may not consider yourself successful, but the fact you bought this book and can read these words and write your responses on the page make you a success in many cultures around the world. Write out your worldview related to your station in life the space below.

_____

_____

Read Esther 4:12–14. Write out Mordecai's three state-ments to Esther in the space below. Underline the last sentence in verse 14, the Memory Verse for this chapter.

_____

_____

Mordecai did not let her excuse about entering the king's court prevent him from speaking the hard truth to Esther. He reminded her she too was a Jew and even though she was the queen she would suffer the same fate as her people (v. 13). The death sentence applied to her as well. He then confessed that if she did not step up, "relief and deliverance for the Jews" would come from somewhere else (v. 14). He trusted God to protect the existence of His covenant people. God ultimately did not need Esther. Finally, he told her, "Who knows but that you have come to royal position for such a time as this?" (v. 14) She needed to look beyond her personal well-being to God's Story to know why she was queen of a foreign people at this time.

Mordecai's word to Esther was her defining moment with God. From that moment on, she had to decide whom she would trust for her safety and the safety of her people. Mordecai spoke from a worldview that saw God's purposes at work even in a Jewish girl winning a contest to become queen of the country in which her people remained in exile.

Write or repeat the final words of Mordecai to Esther. Apply them to your setting in life. Allow them to serve as God's words for you today. What would be different in your decisions and perspective if you trusted that you are where you are "for such a time as this"? What "time" or circumstances surround you now? How can you serve God's higher purposes by exerting your influence in your situation? Pause and ask God to reveal to you answers to these questions.

## 47.5 Risking Everything for Others

Every act of faith involves some risk. God seldom invites us into His-story without cost. God's purposes and ways require bold acts of trusting Him because many times His ways run contrary to the ways of the world in which we live and counter to the enemy who seeks to stop them. The heroes of God's Story are not extraordinary people, just people with extraordinary faith. For this reason, the eleventh chapter of the Letter to the Hebrews is sometimes called the "Hall of Faith" for those who risked living for God. God does not call us to live a safe life. He calls us to trust Him and to live out of that trust so that others will come to trust him.

Have you ever come to the point to trust God although it involved great risk? Maybe you refused to comply with a culture or company because you trusted God more than your place in that setting.

Read Esther 4:15–17. Underline Esther's instructions to Mordecai and circle her final confession in verse 16.

Esther resolved to use her position as queen and as a member of God's covenant people to influence the king. She, however, did not do this by her efforts alone. She asked that Mordecai and all the Jewish people join her in a three-day fast to pray for God's help as she entered the king's court uninvited. She put her full trust in God

and confessed, "If I perish, I perish"(v. 16). She had more at stake than to keep her life and place as queen.

Read Esther 5:1–3. Reflect the response of the king to Esther's bold act to enter his court uninvited.

Read the rest of the Book of Esther to see the result of her bold act of faith. It reads like a suspense novel filled with intrigue and political maneuvering. Esther's act of trust in God alone resulted in the salvation of the Jews. Justice was served Haman, and to this day the Israelites celebrate Mordecai and Esther's actions that prevented a holocaust in Persia with the Feast of Purim (Esth. 9:18–28).

Our question to consider for the week was: How can I be useful to God in times of difficulty? Now that you have observed Esther's actions in her time of difficulty, how would you answer this question? One answer is simply to remain faithful to God in those situations. He put you where you are, in relationship with the people you know, and in those circumstances. If you have faith, He will do the rest—even if you cannot see the direct result of your faithfulness.

This chapter can create a defining moment with God for you if you begin to accept God's purposes for your life are part of God's Story and more than ways to "bless you" and "make you happy." Prosperity is overrated. Purpose is all that matters to those who trust God.

**For further study:**
- **Esther 2:15–17; 3:8–11**
- **Romans 5:1–8**

## 48—Be a Difference-Maker (Nehemiah)

Nehemiah, God's servant-leader who rebuilt the walls of Jerusalem, stars in the final episode in our survey of His-story. Nehemiah, whose name means, "The Lord encourages," served as cupbearer to the king of Persia, King Artaxerxes (Neh. 1:11). He received word of the city's demise and asked the king for permission to go to his home country and repair the wall. The king granted his wish, and he made his historic trip about 445 B.C. He was a contemporary of Ezra, who led Jerusalem to return to the ways of God, and Malachi, the name on the last book of the Old Testament.

Upon his return to rebuild the walls, he faced opposition by enemies and discouragement among his people. Nehemiah presents an ideal example of a servant-leader chosen by God to accomplish a grand mission to help complete the Story of God.

The Memory Verse for this chapter is 2 Timothy 3:12. This verse reminds us that following your part in the Story of God will bring tough times, especially if God calls you to lead His people on mission for Him. Paul forewarned his apprentice Timothy that he would face opposition like every other servant-leader.

Our question to consider this week is: What will it cost for me to be on mission with God? Answer this question now from your own experiences of leading others on mission. Then observe what Nehemiah faced in this chapter of his leadership, and you can add to the lessons you have learned.

## 48.1 The Making of a Difference-Maker

Leaders by nature bring change and, in turn, bring conflict. Leaders always challenge the status quo in order to offer a new future. Biblical servant-leaders do the same thing, but they always seek to lead people to change in order to join God in His-story. Change and conflict are realities for God's leaders. Any leader of a church or ministry knows this. When you bring a plan that you are convinced came from God to a group someone will always resist it; those who perceive their power or control especially feel challenged by the plan. This resistance can be internal or external to the group you lead, but as a leader of God's purposes you will face opposition in many forms. God's clear mission requires servant leadership, and that leadership brings change and opposition to that change. Being a servant-leader is not an easy calling but a fulfilling one, because you know you act as God's servant to write part of the bigger Story of His rescue of all people.

Write about a situation in which you have led through opposition or in which you are trying to lead now. Who opposes your plan? What reasons do they give for opposing you? Have you sought counsel? Do other leaders concur this is what you should do?

_____

_____

_____

Read Nehemiah 4:1–3. Highlight the names in these verses. Consult a Bible handbook or commentary to discover the historical setting of this incident and the identification of the people. Circle the question marks and exclamation point to identify the content of the enemy's harassment.

Nehemiah came to Jerusalem with King Artaxerxes' support. (See Nehemiah 2 for details.) Therefore, the local Persian officials could not attack Nehemiah's efforts directly; so they turned to the next best tool of opposition: harassment. Sanballat, the local official, knew that if Nehemiah succeeded he would lose his power and rule over the city. He knew he could not change Nehemiah's heart. Nehemiah was the leader, and true leaders seldom get distracted from their mission. But Sanballat thought he could badger the people into not completing the project. Like bullies on the playground, Sanballat and Tobiah shouted insults at the people who worked on the walls. (By the way, excavations on the Jerusalem walls have shown they were nine feet wide— plenty of foot space for a fox!)

What insults or reasons do others give that your plan will not work? Make a list of them in the in your journal. Do not allow your frustration over the ideas keep you from seeing the heart of the person or people opposing you. Ask God to allow you to see them the way He does. Ask God to teach you to trust Him more as you seek to lead others on His mission with you.

## 48.2 A Difference-Maker Moves Forward

Biblical servant-leaders' first move in the face of opposition is to turn to God, the One who called them on the mission and who provides their strength and direction. Take King David, for example, who called out to Yahweh as he fled the opposition of his son, Absalom (Ps. 3). His prayer was filled with emotion, but he trusted God to protect him. Paul, whom God sent on mission to those outside the Jewish community, invited others to pray for him as he waited in prison to continue his quest to win the world for Christ (Eph. 6:19–20). Even Jesus turned to the Father in the face of opposition in order to know the heart of the One who sent Him (Luke 22:40–42). Prayer is a conversation with the One who called and sent you. Overcoming opposition as a servant-leader begins with prayer to the One whose mission call you lead others to complete.

Describe the role prayer plays in your servant leadership. Is it your first move or last resort as you lead? Have you brought the insults you listed in the previous lesson to God? Take some time now to do that by writing your thoughts in your journal.

Read Nehemiah 4:4–6. Paraphrase Nehemiah's prayer in verses 4–5. Underline the phrases "half its height" and "with all their heart" in verse 6.

Nehemiah responded to his enemy's insults with prayer. He acknowledged the reality that others despised the Jews for doing what God called them to do. He prayed an honest prayer. He did not pull any punches about how he felt toward his tormentors. He wished them no ill will and asked that God not "cover up their guilt" in His eyes (v. 5). Biblical servant-leaders are honest with God about how they feel in their situation, knowing God can and will work through it to accomplish His purposes. Nehemiah noted that the wall "reached half its height" and the people worked "with all their heart" (v. 6).

A leader cannot ask for more from those he or she leads than that they work from their hearts. Great things occur when people get inspired by a God-sized vision and join together to make it happen.

Nehemiah prayed and the people worked with all their hearts. This combination of prayer and inspired effort accelerated the work on the wall.

How have you been inspired by a leader to work with all your heart? Or as a leader, when have you seen people grasp the vision God gave and worked to make it happen? Write some of your experience(s) here:

_____

_____

_____

## 48.3 Difference Making and Opposition

Opposition to God's mission call on your life and those you lead does not only come from external enemies. Sometimes the hardest struggles come from those you try to lead. Fear and discouragement among those you lead cause as major hindrances to progress as direct assaults by your enemies. Biblical servant-leaders must help those they lead to overcome their fears and the sense that God has given them too big of a job. Jesus was honest with His disciples about whom they should fear (Luke 12:4–5), but He also reminded them they had nothing to fear ultimately because He would empower them in their time of need (Acts 1:8). Jesus also helped them see that "What is impossible with men is possible with God" (Luke 18:27). Helping those he or she leads overcome their fear and discouragement is one way a servant-leader leads by serving those on mission with him or her.

Read Nehemiah 4:7–9. Highlight the names of those who opposed the people building the wall. Underline Nehemiah's response to their threat in verse 9.

Sanballat formed an alliance with others to harass the people as they worked. They "were very angry" at the progress of the wall rebuilding, because with every new height in the wall their influence dropped in the region. Most conflict comes from those who perceive they will loose their power when a new plan comes into play. Nehemiah prayed to God and posted guards in response to the renewed threats. He used prayer and action as his strategies to continue the work.

Read Nehemiah 4:10–12. Underline in each verse the different sources of concern that came to Nehemiah. For example, in verse 10 "the people in Judah" spoke to Nehemiah.

The "people of Judah" grew discouraged at the size of the project (v. 10). Their "enemies" promised to infiltrate the ranks of the workers and kill them (v. 11). The Jews who lived near their enemies came to Nehemiah and exaggerated their claims "ten times over" (v. 12). Nehemiah faced discouragement from those he led, his enemies, and those who loved to exaggerate danger.

If you have ever led a group of people, you have faced these kinds of opposition. Do you face any now? If so, put names with the sources and write out their complaints

or threats. Offer them to God in prayer and ask for how He would have you address each of them. Continue to thank God for allowing you to do something with eternal impact in His-story.

_____

_____

_____

## 48.4 Servanthood and Planning

Biblical leaders understood their role was to accomplish the mission call of God, not to have their needs met. Actually, their job required meeting the needs of those they led rather than the other way around. Too many leaders fail because they loose sight of this truth. Jesus modeled servant leadership with a towel when He washed

His apprentices' feet the night of His betrayal (John 13:1–17). While He dressed like a servant and acted like a slave He still led by helping His followers understand fully the Father's mission of the Suffering Servant Messiah for His life and theirs. Nehemiah was a servant-leader like Jesus. His sign of servant leadership came in a trowel, not a towel, but it signaled the same thing to those he led.

What symbol would you choose to represent your style of leadership? Be honest. No church answers here. How are you like or unlike Jesus' model of leadership? Write your answers here:

_____

_____

_____

Read Nehemiah 4:13–15. Underline Nehemiah's message to the people in verse 14. Notice how the people responded (v. 15).

Nehemiah organized the people by families, the strongest social unit among any people, and positioned them on the most vulnerable sections of the wall (v. 13). He then stood and addressed their fears and discouragement. He reminded them they served Yahweh who would not fail them. He encouraged them to fight for their family members. He took their eyes off their enemies and placed them on God, and he took their fears and directed that energy toward those whom they loved.

Read Nehemiah 4:16–18. Underline the different kinds of people mentioned in these verses and what they did. For example, "half of my men did the work" and "the other half were equipped" for battle (v. 16).

Nehemiah then took his leaders and organized them to serve the people as they worked. Servant-leaders know their job involves serving those on the front lines, and in this case, that meant protecting and working alongside them. Some call this the "inverted pyramid" of leadership. Rather than the people serving the needs of the leaders, the leaders serve those of the people in order to accomplish greater things for God. The leaders worked with a trowel in one hand and a weapon in the other. The only one who did not work on the project was the trumpeter who would sound the alarm if enemies attacked (v. 18).

Review what Nehemiah did to address the fears of the people in this passage. Devise your own response plan to a similar situation you face now or may face in the future. Ask God to guide your thinking as you prepare this plan to accomplish His purposes, not your wishes.

## 48.5 Demonstrating Commitment

A privilege of leadership is often favored accommodations and a lesser workload. The leader has the right to a nicer place so he or she can be fresh when duties call. We all get that. As a conference speaker I sometimes get offered a nicer place to stay than the participants to whom I speak. I must admit that at times I accept those nicer places to stay between sessions. However, if it is about work, I stay with the workers. From teaching in a foreign country to "gutting" houses in Mississippi after Hurricane Katrina to counseling at children's camp, I stay with those who do the work. Presence and participation are the hallmarks of servant-leaders who have made themselves servants to the mission and to those on mission with them. Those whom you lead know very well your commitment to the mission by your choices to join them or separate yourself from them.

Where do you stay or what do you require when you lead a service project outside your community? What have you seen leaders do that make you want to follow them, or what have they done to let you know they were not as committed as you were to what they had asked you to do? Write some of your examples here:

_____

_____

Read Nehemiah 4:19–20. What did Nehemiah have planned to do if they got attacked? In whom or what did he place his ultimate confidence? (v. 20)

_____

_____

Nehemiah continued to plan for the worst and work with all of his heart. He told his leaders and the people to gather at the trumpet sound for there would be the height of the enemy's attack (v. 19). While he planned for attacks, he put his confidence for success in God alone. He reminded them, "Our God will fight for us!" (v. 20)

Read Nehemiah 4:21–23. What instructions did Nehemiah give to the people?

_____

_____

Underline what Nehemiah and his leaders did to demonstrate their commitment to the project in verse 23.

Nehemiah instructed the workers to stay within the walls of the city to protect them from their enemies and to keep their focus on their work. As an example of his commitment to what he asked them to do, neither Nehemiah nor his officers changed their clothes and carried weapons to protect the people. Nehemiah modeled his commitment and brought a calming presence among the people as they worked. Sometimes the best thing a leader can do is stay with the people and work alongside them to demonstrate his or her desire to complete God's mission call on their lives.

God sent Nehemiah to rebuild the wall around Jerusalem, the City of David. While God called him, Nehemiah had to lead the people to accomplish that calling. This marked the beginning of servant leadership and an opportunity to join God's Story to make an eternal impact.

**For further study:**
• **Nehemiah 2:17–18; 6:15–7:4**
• **Nehemiah 8–9**

# CONCLUSION

Congratulations! You have completed a study of 48 key moments in the Old Testament. It is my hope that God has worked greatly in your life during your study of *Divine Encounters in the Old Testament*.

Although you have completed this book, the journey is still just beginning. All of us who have encountered God know we have a long way to go. We are like Isaiah. When he encountered God, he saw his own imperfection more clearly (Isa. 6). However, as Christ-followers we are called to personal transformation (Rom. 12:1–2). This is good news. There is even more good news for us when we remember that God does not change. The God of Abraham, Isaac, and Jacob is the same as He was when He parted the Red Sea, brought down the walls of Jericho, and provided a chariot of fire to give Elijah the ride of his life. This God— Yahweh—desires that you and I seek Him every day.

I encourage you to study God's Word each day. I pray that you will continue to use some of the Bible study methods that you have learned. Something powerful happens when you interact with the Scripture. The Holy Spirit takes the Word and moves in your life. As the writer of Hebrews puts it, "The word of God is living and active. Sharper than any double-edged sword, it penetrates even to dividing soul and spirit, joints and marrow; it judges the thoughts and attitudes of the heart" (Heb. 4:12).

God is at work. Join in the story and never stop encountering Him.

*Divine Encounters in the Old Testament* is part of a three-year Bible study curriculum designed to lead adult Sunday school and small groups through the story of Scripture. Student Life, which publishes Student Life Bible Study for students, introduced Life Bible Study for adults in June 2007. Visit www.lifebiblestudy.com to see how your church can take a walk through the entire Bible using our interactive online resource. Each volume has an optional book to further individual study.

Volume 1, *Yahweh*, provides a chronological overview of the Old Testament in 48 snapshots of God's divine encounters with people. *Yahweh* covers the same biblical stories and examples found in *Divine Encounters in the Old Testament*.

Volume 2, *Christos*, focuses on God's transforming touch through the life of Christ. *God's Transforming Touch* gives adults the opportunity to deepen their understanding of the life of Christ in their individual reading and study time.

Volume 3, *Ekklesia*, deals with the unstoppable movement of God through the New Testament Church and Christian community. *The Unstoppable Movement of God* allows adults to individually read and study about the importance of functioning in connection with others as the unified Church.

Volume 4, Kaleo: Called to Be Holy, is a 48-week topical study that traces the theme of consecration throughout the Bible by examining those who were consecrated in holiness.

Volume 5, Mathetes: The Making of a Disciple, was written for believers who want to spend the year focused on what it means to be a disciple of Christ. Within the study, weekly lessons support eight areas of discipleship.

So when can you start using Life Bible Study? Anytime you want! The online system works around your schedule. Each volume contains 48 lessons, which leaves your group four weeks of flexibility to accommodate holidays, special occasions, or other events. The curriculum also includes four holiday lessons.

For more information, you can also call 877.265.1605, visit www.lifebiblestudy.com, or write to:

Life Bible Study
5184 Caldwell Mill Road, Suite 204-221
Hoover, Alabama 35244

## ABOUT LIFE BIBLE STUDY

Life Bible Study, is a Christian Publisher serving churches and Christian communities in order to advance the Gospel of Jesus Christ, making disciples as we go. At Life Bible Study, we have identified 8 truths vital for every Christian to know and understand. These 8 Essential Truths are the basis for all of our publishing work.